Ethical Consumerism and Comparative Studies Across Different Cultures:

Emerging Research and Opportunities

Ebtihaj Ahmad Al-A'ali
University of Bahrain, Bahrain

Meryem Masmoudi
University of Bahrain, Bahrain

A volume in the Advances in Business Strategy and Competitive Advantage (ABSCA) Book Series

IGI Global
DISSEMINATOR OF KNOWLEDGE

Published in the United States of America by
IGI Global
Business Science Reference (an imprint of IGI Global)
701 E. Chocolate Avenue
Hershey PA, USA 17033
Tel: 717-533-8845
Fax: 717-533-8661
E-mail: cust@igi-global.com
Web site: http://www.igi-global.com

Library of Congress Cataloging-in-Publication Data

Names: Masmoudi, Meryem, 1979- editor. | Al-A'Ali, Ebtihaj Ahmad, 1957- editor.
Title: Ethical consumerism and comparative studies across different cultures : emerging research and opportunities / Meryem Masmoudi, Ebtihaj Al-A'Ali.
Description: Hershey, PA : Business Science Reference, [2019]
Identifiers: LCCN 2019019469| ISBN 9781799802723 (hardcover) | ISBN 9781799802730 (paperback) | ISBN 9781799802747 (ebook)
Subjects: LCSH: Consumption (Economics) | Social responsibility of business. | Customer relations.
Classification: LCC HB801 .E84 2019 | DDC 174/.4--dc23 LC record available at https://lccn.loc.gov/2019019469

This book is published in the IGI Global book series Advances in Business Strategy and Competitive Advantage (ABSCA) (ISSN: 2327-3429; eISSN: 2327-3437)

British Cataloguing in Publication Data
A Cataloguing in Publication record for this book is available from the British Library.

Advances in Business Strategy and Competitive Advantage (ABSCA) Book Series

ISSN:2327-3429
EISSN:2327-3437

Editor-in-Chief: Patricia Ordóñez de Pablos, Universidad de Oviedo, Spain

MISSION

Business entities are constantly seeking new ways through which to gain advantage over their competitors and strengthen their position within the business environment. With competition at an all-time high due to technological advancements allowing for competition on a global scale, firms continue to seek new ways through which to improve and strengthen their business processes, procedures, and profitability.

The **Advances in Business Strategy and Competitive Advantage (ABSCA) Book Series** is a timely series responding to the high demand for state-of-the-art research on how business strategies are created, implemented and re-designed to meet the demands of globalized competitive markets. With a focus on local and global challenges, business opportunities and the needs of society, the **ABSCA** encourages scientific discourse on doing business and managing information technologies for the creation of sustainable competitive advantage.

COVERAGE

- Co-operative Strategies
- Value Chain
- Competitive Strategy
- Globalization
- International Business Strategy
- Foreign Investment Decision Process
- Business Models
- Joint Ventures
- Small and Medium Enterprises
- Core Competencies

IGI Global is currently accepting manuscripts for publication within this series. To submit a proposal for a volume in this series, please contact our Acquisition Editors at Acquisitions@igi-global.com or visit: http://www.igi-global.com/publish/.

The Advances in Business Strategy and Competitive Advantage (ABSCA) Book Series (ISSN 2327-3429) is published by IGI Global, 701 E. Chocolate Avenue, Hershey, PA 17033-1240, USA, www.igi-global.com. This series is composed of titles available for purchase individually; each title is edited to be contextually exclusive from any other title within the series. For pricing and ordering information please visit http://www.igi-global.com/book-series/advances-business-strategy-competitive-advantage/73672. Postmaster: Send all address changes to above address.

Titles in this Series

For a list of additional titles in this series, please visit:
https://www.igi-global.com/book-series/advances-business-strategy-competitive-advantage/73672

Entrepreneurial Innovation and Economic Development in Dubai and Comparisons to Its Sister Cities
Heather C. Webb (Dubai Men's College, UAE) and Hussain A. Al Numairy (Dubai Men's College, UAE)
Business Science Reference • ©2020 • 364pp • H/C (ISBN: 9781522593775) • US $210.00

Theoretical and Applied Mathematics in International Business
Bryan Christiansen (Global Research Society, USA) and Fatima Shuwaikh (Université Paris Saclay, France)
Business Science Reference • ©2020 • 358pp • H/C (ISBN: 9781522584582) • US $225.00

Strategic Marketing for Social Enterprises in Developing Nations
Nigel Chiweshe (University of KwaZulu-Natal, South Africa) and Debbie Ellis (University of KwaZulu-Natal, South Africa)
Business Science Reference • ©2019 • 373pp • H/C (ISBN: 9781522578598) • US $195.00

Handbook of Research on Entrepreneurship, Innovation, and Internationalization
Nuno Miguel Teixeira (Polytechnic Institute of Setúbal, Portugal) Teresa Gomes da Costa (Polytechnic Institute of Setúbal, Portugal) and Inês Margarida Lisboa (Instituto Politécnico de Leiria, Portugal)
Business Science Reference • ©2019 • 761pp • H/C (ISBN: 9781522584797) • US $395.00

Handbook of Research on Corporate Restructuring and Globalization
Antonio Carrizo Moreira (University of Aveiro, Portugal) and Pedro Silva (University of Aveiro, Portugal)
Business Science Reference • ©2019 • 408pp • H/C (ISBN: 9781522589068) • US $295.00

Responsible, Sustainable, and Globally Aware Management in the Fourth Industrial Revolution
Ziska Fields (University of KwaZulu-Natal, South Africa) and Stefan Huesig (Chemnitz University of Technology, Germany)
Business Science Reference • ©2019 • 396pp • H/C (ISBN: 9781522576389) • US $225.00

For an entire list of titles in this series, please visit:
https://www.igi-global.com/book-series/advances-business-strategy-competitive-advantage/73672

IGI Global
DISSEMINATOR OF KNOWLEDGE

701 East Chocolate Avenue, Hershey, PA 17033, USA
Tel: 717-533-8845 x100 • Fax: 717-533-8661
E-Mail: cust@igi-global.com • www.igi-global.com

Editorial Advisory Board

Table of Contents

Foreword

I am delighted to write the foreword for the first edition of the edited book entitled *Ethical Consumerism and Comparative Studies Across Different Cultures: Emerging Research and Opportunities* and published by IGI Global.

This book investigates the issue of ethical consumerism in relation to different disciplines. Ethical consumerism practices in financial sector is examined in two chapters. Roles of auditing firms in promoting ethical consumerism is discussed as well. Health services develop their own programs to instigate ethical practices. E-commerce, on-line shopping and fair trade are all discussed by chapters presented in this book. Participants and sample units representing different businesses and contributing to chapters in this book are diversified in term of specialty, nationality and hierarchical positions. Businesses are different in term of their geographical focus (domestic, regional and international).

I hope that this volume will provide readers and researchers with a valuable information on Ethical Consumerism and pave the way for other research developments on this important field of research.

Hatem Masri
University of Bahrain, Bahrain

Preface

Nowadays, ethical consumerism is a major concern for all governmental bodies, businesses and Non-Governmental organizations. It refers to different terms among them environmental sustainability, fair trade and ecological focus. The different issues manifesting ethical consumerism have been studied since the second half of the last century. Ethical consumption, ethical purchasing and ethical sourcing state that consumers have a say along every step of product and/or service value chain.

This book contains 9 selected chapters from proposals that were submitted by researchers. We tried to produce a book that offers students, academics, and practitioners a refreshed and enhanced view of the importance of Ethical consumerism in Business, Science, Engineering and Technology. The book includes theoretical and real case studies with a short, precise, and concise up-to-date information. The topics included are the following:

1. Organizations an environmental sustainability
2. Marketing, ethical consumption and branding
3. Organizational attempts to enhance ethical consumerism
4. Corporate social responsibility and ethical consumerism
5. Fairs trade and ethical consumerism
6. Ethical dilemmas such as human rights, environment, animal welfare and politics:
7. Green products and ethical consumerism
8. Decision making processes and ethical consumerism
9. Islamic, western and eastern cultures and ethical consumerism

In the first chapter, the author presents fundamentals of ethical consumerism and its importance in achieving the sustainability target for any organization. It also studies the impact of the government laws and policies on ethical consumerism.

The second chapter discusses ethical practices that influence customers decision to choose a product or a service through a case study of a Bahraini bank that shows the importance of implementing an anti-money laundry on ethical consumerism.

The third chapter continues the discussion on ethical consumerism faced by banks and how to enhance the understanding of ethical consumerism in financial institutions.

In the fourth chapter, the author provides guidelines for auditing firms to develop ethical programs and to promote ethical consumerism.

The fifth chapter discusses ethical consumerism for the health care sector and how the 2030 vision of the kingdom of Bahrain guided the development of ethical resolutions, procedures, policies and programs.

The sixth chapter addresses the concept of ethical green consumerism and its role in stemming global warming through a case study on energy consumption behavior and emissions in the Kingdom of Bahrain.

The seventh chapter discusses how fair trade could uphold ethical consumerism and proposes policy recommendations on gender issues.

In the eighth chapter, authors investigate the effect of demographic factors in ethical consumerism through a study on university students and staff in using online shopping.

The last chapter is behavioral study of consumers and sellers of e-commerce in Bahrain that explains the ethical challenges and problems confronted by the buyers and the sellers of e-commerce.

We hope that these studies across different cultures will be useful for the readers and researchers who aim to study aspects of ethical consumerism.

Ebtihaj Al-A'Ali
University of Bahrain, Bahrain

Meryem Masmoudi
University of Bahrain, Bahrain

Acknowledgment

Editing a book about a new topic is a surreal process. We are forever indebted to Hatem Masri for his editorial help, ongoing support and encouragement. Thanks to everyone who helped us so much in finalizing this book.

Chapter 1
Ethical Consumerism in Kingdom of Bahrain

Asma Ayari
University of Bahrain, Bahrain

ABSTRACT

Today, with the growing number of consumers caring about where products come from, companies need to be at the forefront of this upward trend if they want to maintain their profit. In this chapter the authors presented an overview of ethical consumerism in the kingdom of Bahrain. They also highlighted how societal and cultural shifts have influenced Bahraini consumerism over time. The chapter begins by discussing the debatable origins of ethical consumerism since longtime. Throughout the chapter, there is an emphasis on the importance of the ethical consumerism to achieve sustainability target, with particular attention to how ethical consumerism gives a competitive advantage to the organization. The chapter shows also how organizational transparency is a strategic key to build trust and influence costumers' behavior. The chapter also argues that government support is important to influence ethical consumerism by creating laws and policies.

INTRODUCTION

The technical progress, innovation and changing lifestyles, including the use of the social media, lead to a change in consumer preferences. Consumers' concern for sustainable development and fair trade has increased. They become more and more aware to the impact of their daily consumption, on the planet, economy, society and health. Media, consumers and businesses are increasingly talking about "responsible consumption", "Green product" and "ethical consumerism". As a result, ethics become

DOI: 10.4018/978-1-7998-0272-3.ch001

important in today's consumer society confronted with the notions of sustainable development, fair trade and ethical commerce.

Consuming ethics is choosing to consume according to social and environmental criteria. Concretely, the ethical purchase is to buy and produce fair products, by companies, without harming or exploiting people, animals or the environment (Bechwati, Nasr & Baalbaki, 2016). An ethical and responsible consumer become a consumer who tries to avoid as much as possible food waste or overconsumption, which favors a more ecological consumption of his food, by choosing less polluting and polluted foods, which favors good products for the planet, but also short circuits and local products (Perryer & Ladd, 2014).

While previously, consumer responses to these issues were "I can't do anything about it". Today, they start to think of another way to consume in order to change the situation (Albert & Horowitize, 2009). More and more consumers are sorting their waste, reducing their consumption of water and energy, and some are beginning to favor public transport.

The term "ethical consumer" carries various meanings and covers a multitude of virtues, because this reflects the diversity in the market. Consumers are more interested about one or more ethic characteristic rather than other one (Willis and Schor 2012). There is no consensus among consumers on what constitutes a responsible company. For some people, the innovative approach of a company such as Virgin, based primarily on customer service and fair prices is considered ethical towards the customer. For others, they judge the company on the basis of good human rights policy rather than quality and customer service. However, ethical consumerism remains new and linked to a wealthy social class especially in the Arab country. Little researches (Al'Ali & Al Sarraf, 2016) have been done to evaluate the adoption of ethical behavior; the influence of government as well as the commercial opportunity and threat on producers.

This chapter presents an overview of ethical consumerism in the kingdom of Bahrain, highlighting how societal and cultural shifts have influenced Bahraini consumerism over time. The chapter begins by discussing the debatable origins of ethical consumerism. Throughout the chapter, there is an emphasis on the importance of the ethical consumerism to achieve sustainability target, with particular attention to how ethical consumerism give a competitive advantage to the organization. The chapter shows also, how organizational transparency is a strategic key to build trust and influence costumers' behavior. The chapter also argues that, government support is important to influence ethical consumerism through creating laws and policies.

ETHICAL CONSUMERISM

Consumerism has focused traditionally, on customer rights, product quality and safety, rather than ethical issues. The rise of the ethical consumer was an important phenomenon of the 1990s, motivated by problems such as child labor and genetically modified products (Sebastiani, Montagnini & Dalli, 2013). Environmentalism, on the other hand, has helped to raise public awareness of ethical issues that had not been addressed before. Ethical and responsible consumerism became a mode of consumption that takes into account the criteria of sustainable development.

By analogy with sustainable development, we find various terminologies such as sustainable consumption, responsible consumerism, ethical consumption, green consumption and Fair Trade movement (Lang & Gabriel 2005; Willis & Schor 2012).

Philosophers define ethics as the theory of the action that man must have to lead his life and achieve happiness. Many are the researchers whom tried to define ethics; if it's a science or a concept (Vesilind, 1988; Vitell & Hidalgo, 2006). However, "there is no one single definition for ethics. However, there is general consensus among various definitions presented by researchers. Ethics for most of these researchers represent a set of right and wrong conducts related to individual moral philosophy" (Al'Ali & Al Sarraf, 2016, p 136).

Thereby, ethical consumer is a mindful consumer who is "in all stages of consumer behavior, aware of himself, his community and society as at large and behave in ways that contribute to the well-being of all these entities" (Bechwati, Nasr & Baalbaki, 2016, p 100). Ethical consumerism is also called ethical consumption and green consumption, appeared in 1989 to differentiate companies which preserve the environment or those that create environmental problems (Al'Ali & Al Sarraf, 2016).

Ethical consumerism involves an internal facet called also individual influences and external facet or situational influences. The internal facet represents the personal characteristics of the individual, such as his health, financial viability and level of satisfaction and happiness (Albert & Horowitize, 2009, Seshadri & Broekemier, 2009, Khalizani, Omar & Khalisanni, 2011, Perryer & Ladd, 2014). The external facet is related to the environment and society in general. As a result, the various problems related to nutrition, exercise, medical treatment and budgeting are all examples of internal problems. Consuming in a responsible way, going green and giving for noble causes are examples of external problems. The internal and external facets are related. For example, an ethical expense for may allow consumer to have the opportunity to donate money to help those in need.

The consumer can be ethical at all stages of consumption. The stages of consumer behavior include acquisition, consumption including possession and maintenance, and disposal of goods and services (Hoyer & MacInnis, 2008). At the acquisition stage, consumers can be ethical while making product and brand choices and choose healthy food, environmentally and friendly goods and be cautious about the way they invest their time and money. At the consumption stage, ethical consumers consume moderately, share, and take care of their possessions. Finally, consumers can recycle, donate and pass possessions to others at the disposal stage (Bechwati, Nasr & Baalbaki, 2016).

Researchers have examined different aspects of ethical consumer behavior but not the construct in totality. Some researchers examined health-related issues such as fitness, nutrition and processing of medical information (Bolton et al., 2008; Hong & Lee, 2008). Other Researchers have investigated spending wisely and materialism (Burroughs & Rindfleisch, 2002). In addition, a growing body of research has focused on consumers' care for the environment and their social responsibility (Booker, 1976; D'Astous & Legendre, 2009). Lee and Sirgy (2004) tied consumer well-being to different stages of consumer behavior. Recently, research in macro-marketing has examined how the field of marketing can contribute to quality of life. The focus, however, has been on what marketers can do to improve consumers' quality of life such as which products to offer and which markets to target (Lee & Sirgy, 2004; Bechwati, Nasr & Baalbaki, 2016).

ETHICAL CONSUMERISM IN THE KINGDOM OF BAHRAIN

Kingdom of Bahrain is among the smaller economies in the GCC with an Area of 765 km2. However it is also one of the more diversified, with well-developed financial services and manufacturing sectors. The estimated 2019 population of Bahrain is 1.501 million people was made up of 677,506 Bahrainis (45%) and 823,610 non-nationals (55%)1. The state religion of Bahrain is Islam. Economic conditions have fluctuated with the changing price of oil since 1985. The IMF estimated GDP per capita at BD9146 ($24,200) in 2017, up from BD8511 ($22,600) the previous year. In purchasing power parity terms, GDP per capita stood at $47,500, according to the World Bank.

The Bahraini population is young (average age is 30), urban (up to 90%), has a high level of income (real GDP/capita is around USD 22,570) and is composed of a large number of expats (more than half of the population). The foreign population in Bahrain is divided within the large number of high-earning Western expats and low-income workers from South Asia.

Bahraini consumers give great importance to the quality of products and are sensitive to Halal products. The Halal utility is a legal Islamic principle. So, as Muslims, the ethics have an excellent standing among Bahraini consumers. They consider that ethical consumerism involves a number of good attributes and moral values such as: honesty, decency, fairness and goodness. These values are supported and stimulated by the Islamic Shariah to generate positive wisdom within the human being.

Also, the presence of many multinational chains in the country, as well as a large expat community, encourages the adoption of Western consumer habits. Bahraini consumers are becoming more sophisticated and spending more, their purchases focusing especially on high quality and expensive products. Online shopping is also growing, driven mainly by the younger segment of the population and the use of social networks influences consumers' habits. Bahraini consumers become aware to the ingredients of the products, to watch their diet and becoming healthy. Ethical consumerism is considered as a solution to protect body from all the chemical and harmful ingredients present in the food, cosmetics and also in the household products (Albert & Horowitz, 2009).

However, the global economic crisis has brought in many changes to consumer behavior (Vesilind, 1988). In general, ethical, green and responsible products are more expensive than the ordinary products. Bahraini consumers reduced their purchases of expensive goods in favor of basic goods and have been focusing on cheaper and sustainable products. Thus, they start to consume locally products manufactured by Bahraini startups. Consuming locally is cheaper than buying imported products. Moreover, Bahraini products are generally products manufactured by young Bahraini entrepreneurs and the productive families whom know better than other producers the Bahraini culture, values and needs. Therefore, consuming ethical becomes a trend and even an identity especially for the youngest consumers.

Ethical consumerism ends up dividing consumers, especially those in the middle class. Therefore, those who buy "ethics" are more moral than those who do not; whatever means they have. This is wrong. Whether or not they have the means to buy "ethical" products is an entirely different question. Here comes the role of the government to put pressure on producers and organizations to produce "ethical" products with an "ethical" profit.

BAHRAINI GOVERNMENT AND ETHICAL CONSUMERISM

Consumers are able to influence the behavior of companies through their decisions. Generally, they are confronted to the lack of information as a reason for not taking their ethical consumption. However, there are many places to get the information such suppliers, distributers governmental and producers' websites. Consumers keep having a mistrust of the transparency of corporate behavior. Therefore, government can play a key role in industry relations.

The Bahraini Government acts on different levels. First, through the development of policies and initiatives about the quality of information aimed to influence positively consumer behaviour. However, consumer awareness is often seen ineffective to understand the choice of commercial pricing policies. Second, Bahraini Government is stimulating also the creation of green goods by putting pressures on producers. Consumers would purchase more ethical products if they were available.

Bahraini Government is paying close attention compare to other countries in the region regarding ethical consumerism and sustainability management. Various are the initiatives taken by the government concerning the protection of the environment, the respect of the human rights in the work. As an example, the relevant Bahraini authorities are currently working on the implementation phase for the remaining plastic products by the end of July 2019. Guidelines were issued for manufacturers and suppliers on reducing plastic waste to ensure a smooth transition. Bahrain has joined a number of leading countries in banning the import of plastic waste, following the United Nations' call to mitigate ocean pollution and climate change.

The Bahraini government takes into consideration the labors' work during summer and implements a law. The decision by the labor ministry for the 5th year in a row prevents any work under direct sunlight between 12.30pm and 3pm for three months. The minister declared the order is based on general health and safety procedures that the kingdom adopts according to international standards and aimed at preventing work-related injuries. The ministry has urged employers to provide all necessary means to protect workers against injuries and illnesses during their working hours and to educate them on keeping safe at the workplace.

Certainly, when we speak about ethical consumption, we have to mention the ethical production and the responsibility of producers on this filed. However, has producers and organizations behavior evolved? Have companies become more sensitive and aware of the issue of ethical consumption?

ORGANIZATIONAL TRANSPARENCY AND ETHICAL CONSUMERISM

Bahraini Consumers become more demanding, about quality, safety, product manufacturing processes, health, well-being and the environment. Companies in Bahrain show high awareness for ethical consumption instead of the cost of the ethical product and services. Companies moving in the right direction and supporting the right causes to survive and to have a good reputation.

Becoming ethical consumers requires to be informed, to compare, and to orient customers' choices according to quality and price criteria as well. Therefore, the pressure is strong for organizations to be concerned with ethics. The reputation of the producer becomes an important factor of competitiveness. Reputation means trust, without it most companies can hardly fulfill their missions and goals. To survive and to achieve goals, every organization needs a certain level of trust not only with its customers but also its partners and society at large. Building trust with consumers is a priority, if companies want to claim social and ethic. Companies have to start being honest and transparent about theirs consumers, prices, production methods and the business practices they adopt. Companies have, also to incorporate their sustainable initiatives and ethical values into their marketing strategies.

Telecommunication companies namely Zain, Batelco and Viva compete to convey an ethical image of the company at the level of consumers. Therefore, several strategies have been implemented. Zain support the local startups and businesses by offering space in the company headquarters to showcase their products and services every Thursday. The company also has many social marketing campaigns about autism, health and breast cancer. Last Ramadan viva install "donation screens" in to collect donations for Royal Charity. Batelco also engages in an ethical program "Nasna" which focuses on giving back to the community through volunteer work.

McDonalds Bahrain is also committed to offering customers 100% halal and pure meat without additives. The company communicates also its strategy in terms of ethical recruitment of human resources by employing special needs staff.

However, ethics requires time and hard work. Organizations should work on their mission, sense and meaning of business. Certainly, this will take time and time is money. So, in this context of cost reduction and shortage of resources, ethics would not be a luxury that we believe we can do without it.

CONCLUSION

In this chapter we presented the ethical consumerism as concepts brought by sustainable development and fair trade to overcome all problems by ensuring the preservation of the planet, respecting the work of small producers, creating sustainable products (Albert & Horowitz, 2009; Al'Ali, E. & Al Sarraf, 2016; Bechwati, Nasr & Baalbaki, 2016). Ethical consumerism involves the change of purchasing habits to promote a certain set of moral values. Generally, this involves providing green products and boycotting others considered unethical, which can minimize the risk to harm humans, animals and the environment.

The current study contributes to the literature in many different aspects. Firstly, the study contributes to the literature on consumer ethics in Bahrain which is in its nascent stages. Secondly, the study shows how the religion is a significant factor influencing this responsible choice same other factors such as the standard of living, the educational attainment, and the age of consumers.

Then, the study shows how despite the positive beliefs of Bahraini consumers in favor of ethical consumption, they are not prepared to finance additional costs over conventional products. Finally, the chapter mentioned how Bahraini government is taking action for ethical consumerism and sustainable development. Certainly it's slow but compared to neighboring countries; Bahrain is ahead in adopting the green, responsible and ethical consumerism. The Bahraini government has the responsibility to develop policies and regulations about the ethical production and to ensure the information aimed to influence positively consumer behaviour.

REFERENCES

Al'Ali, E., & Al Sarraf, A-R. (2016). Ethical Consumerism: Contextual Issues of Ethical Decision-Making Processes: An Exploratory Study. *Ethical and Social Perspectives on Global Business Interaction in Emerging Markets*, 133-149. DOI: . doi:10.4018/978-1-4666-9864-2

Albert, L. S., & Horowitz, L. M. (2009). Attachment styles and ethical behavior: Their relationship and significance in the marketplace. *Journal of Business Ethics, 87*(3), 299–316. doi:10.100710551-008-9918-6

Bechwati, Nasr, N., Mounkkaddem Baalbaki, A., Nasr, N. I., & Baalbaki, I. B. (2016). Mindful consumer behavior: A cross-cultural comparison. *Journal of International & Interdisciplinary Business Research, 3*(10, 100–113.

Bolton, L. E., Reed, A. II, Volpp, K. G., & Armstrong, K. (2008). How does drug and supplement marketing affect a healthy lifestyle? *The Journal of Consumer Research, 34*(5), 713–726. doi:10.1086/521906

Brooker, G. (1976). The self-actualizing socially conscious consumer. *The Journal of Consumer Research, 3*(2), 107–112. doi:10.1086/208658

Burroughs, J. E., & Rindfleisch, A. (2002). Materialism and well-being: A conflicting values perspective. *The Journal of Consumer Research, 29*(3), 348–370. doi:10.1086/344429

D'Astous, A., & Legendre, A. (2009). Understanding consumers' ethical justifications: A scale for appraising consumers' reasons for not behaving ethically. *Journal of Business Ethics, 87*(2), 255–268. doi:10.100710551-008-9883-0

Hong, J., & Lee, A. Y. (2008). Be fit and be strong: Mastering self-regulation through regulatory fit. *The Journal of Consumer Research, 34*(5), 682–695. doi:10.1086/521902

Lang, T., & Gabriel, Y. (2005). *A brief history of consumer activism*. The Ethical Consumer.

Sebastiani, R., Montagnini, F., & Dalli, D. (2013). Ethical consumption and new business models in the food industry. Evidence from the Eataly case. *Journal of Business Ethics*, *114*(3), 473–488. doi:10.100710551-012-1343-1

Seshadri, S., & Broekemier, G. M. (2009). Ethical decision making: Panama–United States differences in consumer and marketing contexts. *Journal of Global Marketing*, *22*(4), 299–311. doi:10.1080/08911760903022515

Sirgy, M. J., & Lee, D. J. (2006). Macro measures of consumer well-being (CWB): A critical analysis and a research agenda. *Journal of Macromarketing*, *26*(1), 27–44. doi:10.1177/0276146705285669

Vesilind, P. (1988). Rules, Ethics and Morals. *English Education*, *2*(1), 289–293.

Vitell, S. J., & Hidalgo, E. R. (2006). The impact of corporate ethical values and enforcement of ethical codes on the perceived importance of ethics in business: A comparison of US and Spanish managers. *Journal of Business Ethics*, *64*(1), 31–43. doi:10.100710551-005-4664-5

Willis, M. M., & Schor, J. B. (2012). Does changing a light bulb lead to changing the world? Political action and the conscious consumer. *The Annals of the American Academy of Political and Social Science*, *644*(1), 160–190. doi:10.1177/0002716212454831

ENDNOTE

1 Bahrain.bh/eGovernment

Chapter 2
Anti-Money Laundering Practices and Ethical Consumerism:
A Case of a Bahraini Bank

Ralla Mohammed Alazali
University of Bahrain, Bahrain

ABSTRACT

There is no doubt that ethics is important to businesses. Managers can enhance their business reputation and increase customer satisfaction by acting ethically. Interestingly, the concern of ethics goes beyond businesses' practices to customers role in making an ethical purchasing decision. This phenomenon is known as ethical consumerism that show the way consumers view products and organizations based on their ethical concerns. The importance of studying ethics in the financial sector is emphasized in previous studies. The purpose of this chapter is to highlight the importance of implementing ethical practices by businesses that positively influence customers decision to choose their products or/and services. A case study of one of the leading Bahraini banks demonstrates the importance of implementing anti-money laundry (AML) on ethical consumerism.

INTRODUCTION

There is no doubt that ethics is important to businesses. The concern of ethics goes beyond businesses' practices to customers role in making an ethical purchasing decision. Nowadays customers are more aware of their contribution for an ethical

DOI: 10.4018/978-1-7998-0272-3.ch002

society. The purpose of this chapter is to highlight the importance of implementing ethical practices by businesses that positively influence customers decision to choose their products or/and services. A case study of one of the Bahraini banks demonstrates this relationship.

Ethical Consumerism

Ethics is a vague concept as people understand it differently. However, ethics is vital to businesses regardless of its type and size. Jalil, et al. (2010) advocate that business managers are guided to the right direction following business ethics that will enhance their businesses reputation and customer satisfaction. Globally, businesses are involved in unethical practices that cause harm to business stakeholders (Jalil, et al., 2010). In the case study highlighted in this chapter, the bank under study follow one of the most important laws forced by the Kingdom of Bahrain government, namely, anti-money laundary. Recently, changes in the markets lead to change in competition, players power, directions, and priorities of these markers (Ali & Wisniesk, 2010). Consumers are crucial actors in the marketplace as their power influence businesses' decisions contrary to the nineteenth century (Ali & Wisniesk, 2010). Further, Parihar (2014, p. 1) state that "[c]orporations must accept responsibility about the way the business gets initiated to meet the ethical sustainability norms of the consumers." Clearly, the bank studied in this chapter recognizes the importance of following the law on customers perception that motivate their purchasing decision. Thus, businesses now realize that a key for competitive advantage is to meet customers' demands (Yeow, et al., 2014). In contrary, Parihar (2014) claim that ethical practices have no value to consumers, thus, are not important to company competitive advantage. Ethics strategies of businesses need to be changed to accommodate the shift in consumers' norms and values (Govind, et al. 2019). The case study in this chapter describe the importance of an appropriate ethical strategy to apply anti-money laundry law to business existence and development. Jalil, et al. (2010, p. 146) confirm that "[p]roper implementation of business ethics in organizations can ensure maximization of lawful profits and effectively protect the interests of all stakeholders of business organizations including corporate social responsibility". Again, this will lead to a competitive business environment that is essential to businesses and the capital market alike (Jalil, et al., 2010).

Accordingly, Cho and Krasser (2009) believes that ethical consumerism is a complex phenomenon that consists of different factors. Ethical consumerism started to grow in popularity in the academic field (Yeow, et al., 2014; Bray, et al., 2010), despite the fact that it is a phenomenon that was existed for centuries (Low & Davenport 2007). Accordingly, Govind, et al. (2019) notice that ethical products have increased in consumption in the recent years. Although in a global scale, the authors observe that the demand for ethical products considered as a "niche market". Ali and Wisniesk (2010, p. 39) define consumerism as "a form of political and social protest against certain goods or firms based on ethical deliberation and considerations, the behavior of customers." Several authors define ethical consumer, for instance, Cooper-Martin and Holbrook (1993) state that consumers' ethical concerns influence ethical consumer behavior related to decision-making, purchase, and consumption experience. More specifically, Cho and Krasser (2009) describe ethical consumerism to show the way consumers view products and organizations based on their ethical concerns. It is noticed from the description of ethical consumerism that it is more focused on products rather than services. Although, Barnett et al. (2005) argue that ethical consumerism can be related to practices such as banking. Hence, it is vital to highlight ethical consumerism in the service sector specifically the banking industry. A group of ethical failures is individual moral in which they behave in an inappropriate manner that lead to the financial crisis (Callejas-Albinana et al., 2017). Consequently, Callejas-Albinana et al. (2017) recommend an investment philosophy that emphasis on ethical values. They claim that ethics in finance study increase in popularity. The scope of this study is the Kingdom of Bahrain financial sector represented by one of leading banks in the Kingdom.

According to Micheletti and Stolle (2008) there are three forms of ethical consumerism:

1. **Boycotts**: Reject unethical products;
2. **Buycotts**: Choose ethical products; and
3. **Discursive**: Choose products based on "vulnerable points" such as brand name and logo.

Carrigan and Attalla (2001) claim that there is no simple and straightforward relationship between customers boycott and ethical/unethical behavior of companies. However, they find that negative information only affects customer attitudes. Interestingly, people do not always act based on their positive attitude of being ethical consumers (Yeow, et al., 2014). However, Carrigan and Attalla (2001) state that consumer ethical awareness increased as many people bought products or recommend a company based on its ethical reputation. A study by d'Astous and Legendre (2009) find that the reasons behind consumer reluctance to behave ethically can be justified to three types, they are:

1. **Economic Rationalism:** Behaving ethically is costly;
2. **Economic Development Reality:** Acting ethically will hider economic growth and acceptable standard of living; and

3. **Government Dependency:** Government do not enforce consumers to act ethically.

Bray et al. (2010) highlighted several factors that may influence consumer behavior that is shown in Table 1 below. In 2011, Bray et al. conducted a study that identified seven barriers to behaving ethically, namely: price sensitivity, personal experience, ethical obligation, lack of information, quality of goods, inertia and cynicism.

The focus of this chapter is to explain how the implementation of ethical policies represented by AML law may affect ethical consumerism. This is related to one of the three forms of ethical consumerism discussed earlier in this section, that is buycotting. Buycotting is also known as 'girlcott', 'procott', 'reverse boycott', 'antiboycott' or 'positive political consumerism' (Peretti, 2004). The objective of boycotting is "to reward selected companies or governments whose policies are considered ethically, socially or politically correct." (Komninou, 2014, p. 45). Therefore, it can be argued that the proper application of AML law will positively influence customers to choose the bank under study. This is supported by Komninou (2014, p. 45) that boycott is a "positive form of political consumerism ………. that guide consumer choices". According to Harisson et al (2005), "screening" is one type of ethical consumerism practices. This practice – screening – can be related to boycott as it guides consumers decision to select a specific company (Komninou, 2014).

Recently, both ethical conduct and sociopolitical issues are forces of the consumerism trend, while, in the past consumerism movement focus on consumer rights and environment protection (Ali & Wisniesk, 2010). The main concern of this chapter is to study the importance of implementing ethical practices – namely anti-money laundry (AML). As mentioned earlier, this the new trend of ethical consumerism that sociopolitical issues that involve laws and regulations. MoneyGram (2008, p. 2) defined money laundering as "the attempt to conceal or disguise the nature, location, source, ownership or control of illegally obtained money." The three stages of money laundering are: (a) placement, (b) layering, and (c) integration

Table 1. Factors effect consumer behavior

Author	Year	Theory	Factors
Fishbein and Ajzen	1980	Theory of Reasoned Action	Individual attitudes and social norms
Ajzen	1988	Theory of Planned Behaviour	One's attitudes, one's perceptions of societal pressure and the control one feels one has over the purchasing action
Shaw and Clarke	1999	Consumers' belief structures	Information, and normative social factors

(Schott, 2006; MoneyGram, 2008). As been shown in the above literature, ethical practices have positive impact on consumers' behavior. Businesses reputation is an important factor that motivate consumer decision. Callejas-Albinana et al. (2017) argue that many banking consumers based their decision on morality, transparency, fairness, and sustainability of their bank. They add that new regulatory standards are necessary to accommodate the development of ethical culture in the financial industry. This chapter highlight the need to implement AML to attract more customers to choose the bank under study. As it is described in this section, many authors examine the effect of businesses' ethical practices on consumerism. In this chapter, a well-known Bahraini bank is studied to underline the importance of AML and how it can be implemented properly.

METHODOLOGY

A case study of one of the first commercial bank in the Kingdom of Bahrain was conducted to examine the relationship between anti-money laundering law on ethical consumerism. As one of the first types of qualitative methodology, case studies are applied in many research – for instance management (Starman, 2013). Baxter and Jack (2008, p. 544) describe qualitative case study as "an approach to research that facilitates exploration of a phenomenon within its context using a variety of data sources." Moreover, Starman (2013, p. 31) define case study as "a comprehensive description of an individual case and its analysis; i.e., the characterization of the case and the events". Regardless of the limitation of case studies – lack consistency and objectivity – they offer better insights and considered a useful tool for the initial exploratory stage of research (Rowley, 2002). Rowley (2002) add that case studies are useful for exploratory, descriptive or explanatory research. Thus, this chapter study one of Bahrain well-known bank and show how this bank implement anti-money laundering (AML). An interview with the bank Head of AML & MLRO was conducted. The case under study can be classified as theory formation (Atheoretical/configurative idiographic case) case study that has no direct relation to the theory (George &Bennett, 2005). George and Bennett identified four advantages of case studies:

1. **Conceptual Validity:** Identify and measure of the theoretical concepts' indicators;
2. **Deriving New Hypotheses:** Identify additional variables and new hypotheses;
3. **Exploring Causal Mechanisms:** Detailed examination of the mechanisms of operation; and

4. **Modelling and Assessing Complex Causal Relations:** Allow equifinality by producing narrower and more contingent generalizations.

In addition, Rowley (2002, p. 18) confirm that "the ability to undertake an investigation into a phenomenon in its context" is considered a strength of applying case studies. Thus, this method is chosen to describe the importance of AML and how the bank under study implement it properly to understand one of ethical consumerism factors that is ethical business policies.

THE CASE STUDY

At the beginning a brief highlight of the Kingdom of Bahrain financial services – more specifically banking sector – is clarified.

Kingdom of Bahrain Banking Sector

The Kingdom of is a regional financial center where the banking sector considered the largest non-oil contributor to GDP (Central Bank of Bahrain, 2018). The Economic Development Board announce that banking sector is the biggest in Bahrain financial services sector. According to Bahrain Association of Banks (BAB) economic and banking bulletin of the first quarter 2018, there are 395 financial institutions in the Kingdom that are regulated by the Central Bank of Bahrain. There are one hundred banks in the Kingdom that include 29 retail banks and 71 wholesale banks (Central Bank of Bahrain, 2018). The Central Bank of Bahrain (2018) clarify that there are four segments of banks in Bahrain, they are: conventional retail, conventional wholesale, Islamic Retail, and Islamic wholesale. In KPMG 2017 report, 'Shifting Horizons', the Central Bank of Bahrain (CBB) work toward improving the quality of the banking business in Bahrain by encouraging transparency obligations.

The Bank

The bank under study has headquarter in Manama, Bahrain with 25 branches and 61 ATMs which make it the largest network and highest market share in the commercial banking sector. It is one of the leading conventional retail banks in the Kingdom. The bank Annual Gross Revenue is BD96.87 million (US$257.65 million). The Bank was established in 1957 as the first locally owned bank and has grown nationally and internationally ever since. The bank is publicly-listed on the Bahrain Bourse and at year end of 2016, the bank reported profits totaled to BD58.24 million (US$154.88 million). The bank has 585 employees working in its branches which are located in Bahrain, Abu Dhabi and Riyadh and providing various personal and business banking services for its customers.

Anti-Money Laundering (AML)

Anti-money laundering is a policy under the corporate governance framework designed by the Bank that implements the programs against any activities related to money laundering and terrorist financing as required by the laws and regulations of the Central Bank of Bahrain. Bahrain Anti Money Laundering Law was established in 2001 by Decree No. 4 (Central Bank of Bahrain, 2019). Going through the law, it is noticed that it did not specify how institutions should apply it. It is true that this law should be compelled by all the banks in the Kingdom of Bahrain, but the bank under study take the initiation to implement this law in an accurate way. Therefore, the bank main driver to anti-money laundering policy is to design and implement certain systems and procedures that would limit the possibility of any financial crime as a result of the money laundering and terrorist financing. By doing so, the bank is following banking ethics that as stated by Jalil, et al. (2010) will enhance the bank reputation and consequently customer satisfaction. Expertly, the bank is working hard to avoid unethical practices that may cause harm to business stakeholders more precisely customers and the Kingdom government. The compliance to these regulations and legislation stated by the Central Bank of Bahrain in the Financial Crime Module (FCM) and the Customer Due Diligence (CDD) Rules is a key requirement to gain and maintain a legal banking license. Jalil et al. (2010) realize that business code of ethics has been stressed by governments and stakeholders. Thus, governments of different countries forced business organizations to prepare and accurately implement their code of business ethics (Jalil et al., 2010), and the Kingdom of Bahrain is one of these countries. No doubt that this anti-money laundry law is a must for all the financial institutions in the Kingdom including banks and money transfer agencies. However, not all of these financial institutions success in following and applying the law. What distinguish the bank under study their systematic plan and correct implementation of this plan as it will be shown in the coming sections.

AML Policy Development

The policy has been developed as part of the corporate governance framework at the bank which is mainly aimed to protect the interests of all stakeholders and promote the proper functioning and practices of the board of directors and other committees. As explained in the chapter first section, this is an important factor to ethical consumerism phenomenon. The board of directors through its two committees;

the Audit Committee and the Corporate Governance Committee, developed the policy and translated the regulations and laws of the Central Bank of Bahrain into a system designed to monitor and detect any case of financial crime related to money laundering and terrorist financing.

The development of this policy required the application of several factors such as: proper procedures for customer identification, the ability to determine beneficial ownership, accurate and appropriate record keeping and reporting, regular and effective monitoring efforts to detect any suspected events or transactions. This required extensive efforts among all bank's executives and employees, along with massive financial, human and technological resources in order to collaboratively and coordinately implement the system.

Process for Embedding AML Within the Bank

In order to embed the practice of anti-money laundering, the bank followed certain processes which are:

- The establishment of an anti-money laundering department to handle all reporting and actions taken in the case of any suspected transactions and the communication with relevant authorities.
- Special procedures for customer identification called "Know Your Customer" which are implemented on an on-going basis to screen and observe the transactions made by customers, the sources of funds, and due diligence on customers based on their risk.
- Implementing systems for compliance, inspections and records which are needed by the audit committee and other regulatory authorities. This is done through adequate and proper procedures to make sure the effectiveness and efficiency of those systems are maintained.
- Regular monitoring of PEP accounts.
- Regular training for all employees at the bank to raise their knowledge and awareness regarding the identification of any anti-laundry activities, what actions to take and how to report them. This is done without the identification of employee's name to ensure a high level of confidentiality and protect them against adverse actions. The in-house training was done with the help of Emirates Institute for Banking and Financial Studies "EIBFS" which comprised eight modules for banking activities including anti-money laundering.
- Internal and external audit is also conducted on a regular basis to ensure the fulfillment to the rules and laws pertaining the anti-money laundering actions.

While implementing the anti-money laundering practice, the bank faced some challenges which were handled later on. This included the lack of competency or capability of employees to detect any suspected activities through the verification of documents and identification of their genuineness which required additional training to them on a regular basis especially for newly-hired ones. Another challenge is the reluctance of bank to share personal information of its major customers who might affect negatively the bank status in the country.

Identification and Reporting of AML

In order to identify and report the issues related to anti-money laundering, the bank developed a "whistle blower policy" which is mainly aimed to allow its employees to reach the Audit Committee or the CEO if they detect any unethical or improper acts or wrongful practices within the bank of any financial or legal nature. All employees under this policy are protected from adverse actions that might be taken against them by managers if they do so which can affect negatively their employment status or terms.

An employee should whistle blow in "good faith" which means that he should have a reasonable basis for making such claims that are based on personal knowledge and facts without any false or malicious statements. Wrongful conduct and unethical or improper acts are those which do not conform to standards and laws of social or professional conduct. This include, among other: any violation of law or duty of care, breach of code of conduct, misuse of money, abuse of authority, morally offensive behavior or fraud.

By using this mechanism, an employee can report to the CEO or the Chairman of the Audit Committee through an email or a hard copy report. Then, an investigation to the allegation is raised without making any contact to the suspected party. The whistle blower cannot make any personal investigation or questioning if not instructed by the CEO or the Chairman. The HR department is responsible to send a notice to the whistle blower to inform him that the allegation has been received, to advise him of the results of the investigation, and to maintain all related records and reports of the issue in hand.

Enforcement

The bank enforces the anti-money laundering practice through the adherence to the laws and regulations as applied by the Central Bank of Bank against any anti-money laundering and terrorist financing activities. This includes the Financial Crime Module, Customer Due Diligence (CDD) outlined by the Basel Committee, Financial Action Task Force (FATF), and Foreign Account Tax Compliance Act (FATCA).

In order to ensure the enforcement of the practice, independent audits are conducted internally and externally on a regular basis. The board of directors, through the Audit Committee and the Corporate Governance Committee, is responsible to develop, implement and assess the anti-money laundering policy and make sure its adequacy and effectiveness in complying to the laws and regulations and detecting any suspicious actions.

On an external level, KPMG Fakhro is assigned by the bank to perform external independent audit to its financial statements, identify any material misstatement, detect any case of suspected activities such as money laundry, fraud, error, forgery, intentional omission, misrepresentation, or override the internal audit of the bank. The external auditors are also responsible to obtain audit evidence in case of the detection of any suspected activities and evaluate the appropriateness of the accounting policies used by the internal audit committee and provide assurance that those audit efforts are made in accordance to the ISAs.

Final Thoughts

Since the bank under study is a conventional retail bank, customers satisfaction is crucial to its success and development. Acting ethically by following the law and appropriately implement is a key for the bank reputation that will lead to satisfy customers. Ethical consumerism is customers believe on the business – that is in this case the bank – and how the business is behaving ethically. As a result, the above explanation of the implementation of anti-money laundry law will positively affect ethical consumerism and motivate customers to choose the bank under study to get their required banking services.

The adherence to the laws and regulations of the Central Bank of Bahrain by all banking and financial institutions can increase the operational efficiency on the whole banking industry in terms of limiting any possible financial abuse in the banking system and minimizing the money laundering and terrorist financing activities by such criminals. This would also strengthen the reputation of the bank itself and the banking industry in general and enhance customers' trust and retention.

Internal control and auditing efforts are the first step towards guaranteeing the effectiveness of anti-money laundering system and the proper practice to detect and monitor any suspected activities. There should be coordinated and well-managed efforts among all stakeholders of the bank (board of directors, committees, executives, managers, employees, etc.) in order to effectively and efficiently implement anti-money laundering measures and practices within the bank.

Other companies, especially financial institutions and banks can benefit from these anti-money laundering policies by implementing appropriate risk management procedures that help in the prevention of anti-money laundering activities and other terrorist financing. They will be able to identify any large transactions, unusual financial dealings, source of finance, determination of clients, and any suspicious or unlawful financing. Companies can also implement procedures of due diligence in order to identify their clients, and determine their relationships, transactions, and their activities.

Through anti-money laundering systems, companies can have in place effective internal control procedures, risk management systems, effective communication, monitoring and compliance assessment. This combined will help in minimizing any financial risks and unlawful practices. Moreover, employees and managers will be trained and aware of the relevant procedures to recognize and deal with such practices and communicate them to the appropriate personnel.

REFERENCES

Ali, A. J., & Wisniesk, J. M. (2010). Consumerism and ethical attitudes: An empirical study. *International Journal of Islamic and Middle Eastern Finance and Management*, *3*(1), 36–46. doi:10.1108/17538391011033852

Bahrain, C. B. (2018). *Financial Stability Report.* Manama: Financial Stability Directorate, Central Bank of Bahrain. Retrieved from https://www.cbb.gov.bh/wp-content/uploads/2019/01/FSR-Sep-2018.pdf

Bahrain, C. B. (2019, July 12). *Bahrain Anti Money Laundering Law 2001: Contents*. Retrieved from Central Bank of Bahrain: cbb.complinet.com/cbb/display/display.html?rbid=1863&element_id=4

Bahrain Association of Banks. (2018). *Economic and Banking Bulletin.*

Barnett, C. C., Cloke, P., Clarke, N., & Malpass, A. (2005). Consuming Ethics: Articulating the Subjects and Spaces of Ethical Consumption. *Antipode*, *37*(1), 23–45. doi:10.1111/j.0066-4812.2005.00472.x

Baxter, P. a. (2008). Qualitative Case Study Methodology: Study Design and Implementation for Novice Researchers. *Qualitative Report*, *13*(4), 544–559. Retrieved from http://www.nova.edu/ssss/QR/QR13-4/baxter.pdf

Bray, J. J. (2010). An Exploratory Study into the Factors Impeding Ethical. *Journal of Business Ethics*, 1–17. doi:10.100710551-010-0640-9

Bray, J. J., Johns, N., & Kilburn, D. (2011). An exploratory study into the factors impeding ethical consumption. *Journal of Business Ethics*, *98*(4), 597–608. doi:10.100710551-010-0640-9

Callejas-Albiñana,, F.E. (2017). Assessing the Growth of Ethical Banking: Some Evidence from Spanish Customers. *Frontiers in Psychology*, *8*(782). doi:10.3389/fpsyg.2017.00782 PMID:28596742

Carrigan, M., & Attalla, A. (2001). The myth of the ethical consumer - do ethics matter in purchase behaviour? *Journal of Consumer Marketing*, *18*(7), 560–578. doi:10.1108/07363760110410263

Cho, S. a. (2009). hat Makes us Care? The Impact of Cultural Values, Individual factors, and Attention to Media Content on Motivation for ethical Consumerism. *International Social Science Review*, *86*(1&2), 3–23.

Cooper-Martin, E. a. (1993). Ethical Consumption Experiences and Ethical Space. *Advances in Consumer Research. Association for Consumer Research (U. S.)*, *20*(1), 113–118.

d'Astous, A., & Legendre, A. (2009). Understanding Consumers' Ethical Justifications: A Scale for Appraising Consumers' Reasons for Not Behaving Ethically. *Journal of Business Ethics*, *87*(2), 255–268. doi:10.100710551-008-9883-0

George, A. a. (2005). *Case Studies and Theory Development in the Social Science*. Cambridge, MA: MIT Press.

Govind, R. S., Singh, J. J., Garg, N., & D'Silva, S. (2019). Not Walking the Walk: How Dual Attitudes Influence Behavioral Outcomes in Ethical Consumption. *Journal of Business Ethics*, *155*(4), 1195–1214. doi:10.100710551-017-3545-z

Harrison, R. N. (2005). *The Ethical Consumer*. London: Sage Publications Inc.; doi:10.4135/9781446211991

Jalil, M. A., Azam, F., & Rahman, M. K. (2010). Implementation Mechanism of Ethics in Business Organizations. *International Business Research*, *3*(4), 145–155. doi:10.5539/ibr.v3n4p145

Komninou, M. (2014). *Ethical Consumption: Identities, Practices and Potential to Bring About Social Change*. The University of Edinburgh.

KPMG. (2017). *GCC listed banks results: Shifting horizons*. Manama: KPMG.

Low, W., & Davenport, E. (2007). To boldly go…exploring ethical spaces to re-politicise ethical consumption and fair trade. *Journal of Consumer Behaviour*, *6*(5), 336–348. doi:10.1002/cb.226

Malone, S. (2012). *Understanding the Role of Emotion in Ethical Consumption; a Tourism Context*. University of Nottingham.

Micheletti, M., & Stolle, D. (2008). Fashioning Social Justice Through Political Consumerism, Capitalism, and The Internet. *Cultural Studies, 22*(5), 749–769. doi:10.1080/09502380802246009

MoneyGram. (2008). *Latin America and the Caribbean Anti-Money Laundering Compliance Guide.* Author.

Parihar, B. B. (2014). Consumer's Perception and Willingness Towards Business Ethics. *Elk Asia Pacific Journal of Marketing and Retail Management*, 1-14.

Peretti, J. (2004). The Nike Sweatshop Email: Political Consumerism, Internet, and Culture Jamming. In M. F. Micheletti (Ed.), Politics, products, and markets: Exploring political consumerism past and present (pp. 127–142). London: Academic Press.

Rowley, J. (2002). Using Case Studies in Research. *Management Research News, 25*(1), 16–27. doi:10.1108/01409170210782990

Schott, P. A. (2006). *Reference Guide to Anti-Money Laundering and Combating the Financing of Terrorism.* The World Bank.

Starman, A. B. (2013). The Case Study as a Type of Qualitative Research. *Journak of Contemporary educational. Studies*, 28–43.

Yeow, P. A., Dean, A., & Tucker, D. (2014). Bags for Life: The Embedding of Ethical Consumerism. *Journal of Business Ethics, 125*(1), 87–99. doi:10.100710551-013-1900-2

Chapter 3
Ethical Consumerism in Financial Institutions:
Evidence From Bahrain

Yomna Abdulla
University of Bahrain, Bahrain

ABSTRACT

There has been a rise in the concept of ethical consumerism in various sectors of the economy. This chapter examines ethical consumerism in the Bahrain banking sector by analyzing customer surveys and annual reports from seven commercial banks. The findings show limited evidence of ethical consumerism in supply and demand. This chapter also documents challenges faced by banks and customers in ethical, social, and environmental decision making and operations. Finally, the results enhance the understanding of ethical consumerism in financial institutions.

INTRODUCTION

Ethical consumerism involves positive ethical behaviors and consumer responsibility toward negative actions (Davis, 1979; Wilkes, 1978). It was initiated in 1970s along with the first green consumerism movement concerning changes in business ethical issues (Sebastiani, Montagnini & Dalli, 2013). Muncey and Vitell (1992) documented that the investigation of consumers' ethical behaviors is overlooked in the literature. Several studies have more recently been developed, especially after the concept spread throughout many sectors of the economy.

The financial sector in included in this trend, with some banks and financial institutions providing ethical finance to cope with recent customer demands. The

DOI: 10.4018/978-1-7998-0272-3.ch003

importance of satisfying customer demands became more significant due to the increase in their market power. This may be due to the globalization of markets and a loss of government regulations in multinational corporations (Brown, 2008).

The history of ethical finance started in 18th century religious organizations. These organizations, located in the United Kingdom and United States, opposed investments in tobacco, alcohol, and gambling. In the late 1980s, the initiation of ethical consumerism coincided with the launch of *Ethical Consumer* magazine. Prior literature indicates that ethical consumption is not a niche. Instead, it represents a large group of consumers who are concerned with social and environmental issues.

Ethical finance includes both the areas of ethical banking and ethical investment (Brown, 2008). The first consists of products like ethical current accounts, ethical savings, ethical loans, and ethical insurance. The second includes investment funds and social investments.

Ethical customers are interested in financial products that satisfy the standard selection criteria of risk and return. They also seek products with ethical features. In other words, financial products must accomplish a reasonable return along with consideration of social, environmental, and ethical concerns. Ethical financial products range from green bonds, renewable energy-related financial products, and social financial instruments. For instance, in 2019, Citibank issued a €1 billion green bond to finance renewable energy, sustainable transportation, water quality and conservation, energy efficiency, and green building projects (Euromoney, 2019). In another example, Noumra holdings offers financial products for sustainable growth. This includes agriculture, environment, medical, and water (Noumura, 2019).

This chapter investigate ethical consumerism in the Bahrain banking sector. It uses a review of prior customer surveys. It also includes a narrative analysis of annual reports from seven Bahraini commercial banks listed in Bahrain Bourse.

LITERATURE REVIEW

The following section starts by defining and discussing ethical consumerism, vision, mission and corporate social responsibility terms. We then review relevant studies to investigate the role of ethics in the process of a bank selection.

Ethical Consumerism

Ethical consumerism (or ethical consumption) is defined as "the moral principles and standards, which guide individual or group behavior as they obtain, use, and dispose of goods and services" (Muncy & Vitell, 1992). A more recent definition was developed by Ferrell & Fraedrich (2014, p. 341) as "the conscious and deliberate choice to make certain consumption choices due to personal moral beliefs and values". While, consumerism is a choice made based on an ethical decision-making process (Al A'ali and Al-Sarraf, 2016).

Several papers suggest that ethical consumerism is a choosing process reflecting various concerns of the consumer, for instance, moral, ethical, and social concerns (Szmigin and Carrigan, 2006), social values (Carey, Shaw and Shiu, 2008), moral beliefs (Gill, 2012) and interaction with market place and reference groups (Fullerton, Kerch & Dodge, 1996).

Vision

Vision can be defined as "a mental picture of a compelling future situation which is initiated from creative imagination, the act or power of observing imaginative mental images, sort of foresightedness" (Abiodun, 2010). Papulova (2014) argues that a vision should cover new issues and connections in the environment.

Mission

A mission defines the space of the business operations, moreover, it includes present and future directions, is not constrained by time frame and should be developed before the strategy (Papulova, 2014). According to Henry (2008), a mission seek to "answer the question of why an organization exits".

Corporate Social Responsibility

Carroll (1979) defines corporate social responsibility as "the social responsibility of business as encompassing the economic, legal, ethical, and discretionary expectations that society has of organizations at a given point in time".

The theories of corporate social responsibility can be divided into four groups, each discussing an aspect of its definition (Eller, 2017). The first group entails the theories related to economic side of the relationship between the business and the society. The second group discusses the responsibility of the business towards the political issues. The third group, called integrative theories, considers the responsibility of the business towards the social demands of the economy. The ethical theories represent the last group which deals with the ethical side of a business operations (Garriga and Melé, 2004).

Role of Ethics in the Process of a Bank Selection

Most decisions made by ethical customers, whether related to consumption, finance, investment, or even tourism, rely on normative and descriptive ethical philosophies (Malone, 2012). A normative philosophy uses a moral system of discipline to understand ethical decisions (Reidenbach & Robin, 1988). A descriptive philosophy explains ethical decisions based on psychology, sociology, and anthropology (Fukukawa, 2003).

Ethical consumerism in the banking sector can be observed from the supply side or demand side. The banks' customers represent the demand; banks are the suppliers. This chapter reviews the literature on criteria for bank selection to identify whether ethical consumerism is used in the decision of bank selection. Several papers have focused on investigating the reasons clients choose banks across different countries. In Turkey, customers choose banks according to friendliness of bank employees, location of bank branches, speed of service, and availability of financial advice (Kaynak et al., 1991). In Sweden, service quality, availability of credit, price, distribution system, promotion, and reputation are the most important factors for bank choice (Zineldin, 1996). Using market survey, Jahiruddin and Haque (2009) found that convenience, economic, promotion, and influence are the main drivers for bank selection in Bangladesh. Similarly, Katircioglu et al. (2011) showed that convenience is the most important factor for Romanian consumers. In Nigeria, size of bank assets and number of branches are factors on which customers rely when choosing a bank (Maiyaki, 2011). Tan and Chua (1993) showed that the influence of family and friends plays an important role in bank choice in Singapore.

In the Gulf Cooperation Council (GCC), customers in the United Arab Emirates (UAE) prefer Islamic banks over conventional banks due to higher service quality, as well as the religious impact and positive image of Islamic banks (Al Tamimi et al., 2009). In another study on UAE customers, reputation was not a determinant for bank selection (Sayani & Miniaoui, 2013). In Kuwait, businesses believe that financial stability of a bank, efficiency, and helpfulness of bank staff help in financial emergencies. Therefore, the reputation of a bank is the most important criteria for bank selection (Edris, 1997).

Gilani (2015) gave three reasons why Islamic banks are more ethical than conventional banks. The first is the prohibition of interest in Islamic banks. The second is the ban of investments in immoral acts like gambling, alcohol, weapons, or other activities directly or indirectly impacting humans. Third, Islamic banking is based on a religion which addresses the good deeds and propensity of human beings.

Several papers have identified the religious factor as a main driver of customer bank selection in the Arab region. This was documented in Jordan, Kuwait, Egypt, and Tunisia (Abou-Youssef et al., 2015; Al-Sultan, 1999; Hegazy, 1995; Naser et al.,

1999; Souiden & Rani, 2015). Similarly, Malaysian customers choose Islamic banks due to their religious and financial reputation, as well quality of service (Dusuki & Abdullah, 2007). Several studies find that the choice of Islamic banks is based on religious preferences. However, there is evidence that does not support this claim (Abbas et al., 2003; Awan & Bukhari, 2011; Gerrard & Cunningham, 1997).

Overall, most research finds that ethics is not a determinant of bank selection. Instead, the religious aspect seems to be an important motive. This finding suggests confusion between ethical finance and Islamic finance. Therefore, customers consider religious rather than ethical aspects. This finding is consistent with the results of Basgoze and Tektas (2012) who document that the lack of information and knowledge about the ethical and unethical behavior of a corporation make it hard for consumers to involve in ethical consumerism.

Furthermore, the literature investigates ethical consumerism from a consumer point of view. This chapter also examines the supply side, which has been given little attention in the literature. This chapter examines whether Bahraini banks consider ethical, social, or environmental aspects in their operations and decisions.

BAHRAIN BANKING SECTOR

The financial industry is one of the main sectors in Bahrain. As of 2017, it contributed to the gross domestic product (GDP) by 16.7%. In addition, it employs 14,093 individuals. As of 2018, the assets of the banking sector reached $192.1 billion with 382 financial institutions. Ninety-eight were retail banks and 14 were locally incorporated banks (CBB, 2019).

This chapter uses two approaches to investigate ethical consumerism in Bahrain's banking sector. In the first approach, the chapter reviews studies on customer bank selection in Bahrain to examine whether ethics is considered when customers choose a bank. This provides an initial step in testing the existence of ethical consumerism in Bahrain's banking sector. It indicates whether customers rely on moral principles and standards in the process of their selection.

Metawa and Almossawi (1998) found that the religious feature is one of the most significant reasons impacting Bahraini customers' bank selections. According to Al Mossawi (2001), reputation, friendliness of staff, and convenience are the main reasons for Bahraini students to choose banks. Al-Ajmi et al. (2009) summarized the factors for bank selection into six motives: (1) economic; (2) convenience; (3) influence of others; (4) satisfaction with bank's products and services; (5) reputation; and (6) social responsibility. The social responsibility motive is measured by variables like support of scientific, social, and cultural activities, environmental practice and impact, and respecting the right of bank staff. The results show that customers in

Bahrain find quality of service as the most important motive in their selection. Environmental practice and impact are the least important motives.

In short, customer surveys of previous research papers conducted in Bahrain indicate that customers neither rely on ethical nor moral principles when they choose a bank. Therefore, there is no evidence of ethical consumerism since the process of bank choice is not made based on an ethical decision.

In the second approach, the chapter studies whether the suppliers (Bahraini banks) are concerned with the ethical aspects in their operations, products, and decisions. The discussion of data collection and findings are presented in the next two sections.

Data and Research Methodology

The sample consists of seven commercial banks in Bahrain Bourse. It uses listed commercial banks due to the ease and availability of data, as well as their larger customer base as compared to investment banks. The banks are: (1) Ahli United Bank; (2) Al-Salam Bank; (3) Bahrain Islamic Bank; (4) BBK; (5) Ithmaar Bank; (6) Khaleeji Commercial Bank; and (7) National Bank of Bahrain. The chapter utilizes annual reports from the banks for the year 2018. This information was available on the banks' and the Bahrain Bourse Websites. Annual reports are used because they represent the main source of public information available to bank stakeholders. To examine whether Bahraini banks consider the ethical, social, and environmental aspects, the chapter conducted a narrative analysis of the banks' annual reports.

Analysis of Collected Information

Table 1 presents an overview of the seven banks, including number of employees, number of local branches, number of foreign branches, and market value.

Table 1 provides information about the size and international access of the banks. Based on the available information, BBK has the largest number of employees; Ahli United Bank has the highest market value. International presence may indicate the significance of ethical considerations as the bank deals with a broader customer base with various cultural and demographic backgrounds. Therefore, ethical consumerism may be substantial. Ahli United bank has the highest number of foreign branches (approximately 108 branches). The National Bank of Bahrain has the leading local presence (24 local branches). The high number of local branches may suggest that the bank will be more affected by local culture, norms, and traditions to satisfy its large customer base.

Table 2 presents the investigation of the mission, vision, objectives, and values of the banks. The chapter examines whether ethics, society, or environment are

Table 1. Overview of banks in Bahrain Bourse

	No. of Employees	No. of Local Branches	No. of Foreign Branches/Subsidiaries	Market Value (BD)
Ahli United Bank	615	22	108	2,765,459,153
Al Salam Bank - Bahrain B.S.C.	194	7	0	188,348,382
Bahrain Islamic Bank	394	14	0	125,558,913
BBK	1,077	15	4	573,226,151
Ithmaar Holding B.S.C.	NA	16	0	75,411,247
Khaleeji Commercial Bank B.S.C	219	11	0	66,150,000
National Bank of Bahrain	570	24	2	987,707,253

Table 2. Ethics in mission, vision, objectives, and values

	Mission, Vision, Objectives, and Values
Ahli United Bank	Objective: Contribute to the social and economic advancement of the communities in which the group operates
Al Salam Bank - Bahrain B.S.C.	-
Bahrain Islamic Bank	-
BBK	-
Ithmaar Holding B.S.C.	-
Khaleeji Commercial Bank B.S.C	-
National Bank of Bahrain	Values: Ethics

mentioned in the mission, vision, objectives, and values of the banks. The results show that only two of the seven banks have these terms in their mission, vision, objectives, or values. Ahli United Bank lists an objective as "contribute to the social and economic advancement of the communities in which the group operates." National Bank of Bahrain lists ethics as a value.

As discussed earlier, vision is a picture of future direction and since the vision of Bahraini banks do not include ethics as one of its elements, this show that there is neither a current nor a future concern about ethics.

Similarly, ethics appears not to be a part of the banks' mission. Based on the definition of mission discussed above, this suggests that ethics is not an essential component of the space where a bank operates. In other words, ethics seems to be not one of the reasons of the establishment of a bank.

Table 3 shows whether Bahraini commercial banks have a code of ethics and business conduct. Results show that all seven banks have an existing code of ethics and business conduct. This indicates that the banks consider ethics in dealing with their day-to-day operations, customers, and employees. This is considered a positive signal to ethical stakeholders.

Table 4 summarizes an investigation of ethical, social, and environmental considerations in the banks' annual reports. The second column shows the number of times the term "ethics" was mentioned in the annual reports. Findings show that Ithmaar Bank has the highest number of the term (15 times); Al-Salam Bank has the lowest number (3 times). The number of mentions may suggest the significance of signaling the importance of the ethics concept to a bank's stakeholders.

The third column presents social responsibility. The results show a range of diversity in reporting information about social responsibility activities. Some banks reveal detailed information. Others use a concise, conservative approach. Ahli United Bank did not disclose information about their social responsibility activities. Al-Salam Bank and Khaleeji Commercial Bank were conservative in discussing their social responsibility activities, limiting their discussion to funds donated to charity organizations. The remaining four banks provided relatively detailed information about their social responsibility. For instance, National Bank of Bahrain was unique in declaring the financial budget of the donation and social committee, which represents 5% of the bank's annual net profits. BBK presents the

Table 3. Code of ethics and business conduct

	Code of Ethics and Business Conduct
Ahli United Bank	✓
Al Salam Bank - Bahrain	✓
Bahrain Islamic Bank	✓
BBK	✓
Ithmaar Holding B.S.C.	✓
Khaleeji Commercial Bank	✓
National Bank of Bahrain	✓

Table 4. Ethical, social, and environmental terms in the annual report

		Ethical	Social	Environmental
1	Ahli United Bank	8	-	• Established a social and environmental management system (SEMS) that details the policy, procedures, and workflow in respect of environmental risk. • Implemented effective social and environmental management practices on environmental, health, safety, and social issues. • Adopted the Equator Principles (EP), a globally recognized benchmark for managing social and environmental risks in project finance. • Finances projects only when they are expected to be designed, built, operated, and maintained in a manner consistent with applicable national laws.
2	Al Salam Bank - Bahrain B.S.C.	3	• The social responsibility committee supports medical assistance, culture initiatives, and care for the less fortunate.	• Supports environmental activities.
3	Bahrain Islamic Bank	5	• Assists the less fortunate and areas affected by rainfall. • Provides financial support to cover education, Eid, and Ramadan month needs. • Sponsors events, conferences, and forums. • Launched a corporate responsibility program in 2019, investing in initiatives to foster education in a digital age, creating a positive and sustainable impact on local communities.	• A guiding principle listed as friendly ecosystem.
4	BBK	9	• Activities include backing the Bahrain financial sector, supporting employees, empowering women, and addressing community needs, special needs, education, healthcare, sports, culture, and the environment.	• Seeks and implements new ways to reduce its carbon footprint and contribute to environmental sustainability. • Refines digital services along with energy-saving practices and recycling of paper. • Supports the Supreme Council for Environment in its annual conservation work with Al Areen Wildlife Park.
5	Ithmaar Holding B.S.C.	15	• Contributions given to charity organizations.	-
6	Khaleeji Commercial Bank B.S.C	4	• Contributions given to charity organizations.	-
7	National Bank of Bahrain	11	• Allocated BHD 49.2 million since the inception of its donations and contributions program. • Program covers education, health, social welfare, development programs, etc. • Allocates annual budget of the donation and social committee equal to 5% of the bank's annual net profit.	-

most detailed information. Its social responsibility activities include backing the Bahrain financial sector, supporting employees, empowering women, and addressing community needs, special needs, education, healthcare, sports, culture, and the environment. On the other hand, Bahrain Islamic Bank indicates the establishment of their corporate responsibility program. This program will focus on education in a digital age, as well as its positive and sustainable impact on local communities.

Based on the definition of social responsibility discussed earlier, a bank social responsibility activities should cover four elements, i.e. economic, legal, ethical, and discretionary. The results show that the not all of Bahraini banks are concern with these four aspects, especially that some of them do not indicate the details of their social responsibility activities in the annual reports.

Finally, four of the seven banks discuss environmental aspects in their annual reports. For instance, Bahrain Islamic lists "friendly ecosystem" as a guiding principle. Al-Salam Bank supports environmental activities. Furthermore, BBK supports local initiatives related to the Supreme Council for Environment, as well as energy saving programs, recycling initiatives, and reduction of carbon. Ahli United Bank seems to have the most systematic approach in dealing with the environment through a SEMS. This details the policy, procedures, and workflow regarding environmental risks. In addition, they adopted the EP, a globally recognized benchmark for managing social and environmental risks in project finance.

DISCUSSION OF THE FINDINGS

According to the definition of ethical consumerism developed by Muncy and Vitell (1992) and Ferrell and Fraedrich (2014), we do not find a significant evidence of ethical consumerism in Bahrain banking sector. The choosing process of a bank seem not to reflect customers' ethical, social, or moral beliefs and values. We direct this finding mainly to the challenges faced by both the customers and the banks. From a demand side, customers question the meaning of ethical finance, confusing it with Islamic finance which makes it challenging for them to base their decision of choosing a bank on ethical or moral principles.

From a supply side banks suffer from various issues, including lack of innovative ethical financial products and weak marketing of ethical finance. Overall, the findings show that international access of banks plays an important role in strengthening ethical considerations. This may be due to a greater presence in other countries. Moreover, the increase in local presence, measured by number of branches, appears to enhance the importance of ethical and social considerations. Findings also suggest that Bahraini banks do not signal ethical finance in their annual reports. There was no evidence promoting ethical financial products. Banks may be conducting ethical-related attempts. However, these attempts need further emphasis.

Based on the results, this chapter proposes recommendations for both banks and customers to encourage ethical consumerism. Banks may introduce simple ethical financial products, enhance their marketing activities related to ethical financial products, and engage in more activities with an added value to the society and environment. Customers can boost their financial literacy regarding ethical finance to distinguish it from Islamic finance. They can also act as active stakeholders by informing the banks with their ethical needs.

RECENT TRENDS IN THE BANKING SECTOR

Fintech, a recent trend in the banking sector, can be defined as:

Technologically enabled financial innovation that could result in new business models, applications, processes or products with an associated material effect on financial markets and institutions and the provision of financial services. (Navaretti et al., 2017)

Fintech, a global phenomenon, has had several significant and successful attempts in Bahrain. This chapter proposes several ways in which Fintech can enhance ethical consumerism. First, digital technology will encourage fairness and equality in dealing with customers, which is one intentions of ethical finance. Second, the reduction of operating costs may enhance available funds for social responsibility activities. Third, marketing, public relations, customer feedback, and reviews will be easier with a digital system. Using the system, banks can consider customers' ethical views in their operations. Fourth, digital technology can create innovative ethical financial products.

CONCLUSION

This chapter explores ethical consumerism in the Bahrain banking sector using an analysis of prior literature and a narrative examination of annual reports of commercial banks listed on Bahrain Bourse. Prior market surveys found that Bahraini customers did not consider ethical, social, or moral aspects when selecting a bank, therefore, it seems that there is no a significant evidence of ethical consumerism. Based on the banks' annual reports, there is no evidence of ethical financial products and instruments which makes it challenging for customers to consider ethical or moral principles in their bank selection decision. There are some positive attempts of ethical, social, and environmental considerations. However, attempts do not exist in all banks. The limited scope of ethical finance could be due to the complexity of financial products, lack of customer awareness, and weak marketing by financial institutions.

The results contribute to the literature in several ways. First, it provides a new angle in investigating the concept of ethical consumerism by examining the supply side. Second, it adds to the limited literature on ethical consumerism in financial institutions. Third, it sheds light on the need for further development of ethical products by Bahraini banks and improvement of customers' financial literacy on ethical finance.

This research can be extended by including a larger sample and employing various data analysis techniques. Future research may consider using qualitative methods, including interviews with banks managers and employees, to better understand their view of ethical consumerism.

REFERENCES

Abbas, S. Z. M., Hamid, M. A. A., Joher, H., & Ismail, S. (2003). Factors that determine consumers' choice in selecting Islamic financing products. *International Islamic Banking Conference*, Prato.

Abiodun, A. (2010). Interface between corporate vision, mission and production and operations management. *Global Journal of Management and Business Research, 10*(2), 18–22.

Abou-Youssef, M. M. H., Kortam, W., Abou-Aish, E., & El-Bassiouny, N. (2015). Effects of religiosity on consumer attitudes toward Islamic banking in Egypt. *International Journal of Bank Marketing*, *33*(6), 786–807. doi:10.1108/IJBM-02-2015-0024

Al A'ali, E. A., & Al-Sarraf, A. R. (2016). Ethical Consumerism: Contextual Issues of Ethical Decision-Making Processes: An Exploratory Study. In Ethical and Social Perspectives on Global Business Interaction in Emerging Markets (pp. 133-149). IGI Global.

Al-Ajmi, J., Abo Hussain, H., & Al-Saleh, N. (2009). Clients of conventional and Islamic banks in Bahrain: How they choose which bank to patronize. *International Journal of Social Economics*, *36*(11), 1086–1112. doi:10.1108/03068290910992642

Al-Tamimi, H. A. H., Lafi, A. S., & Uddin, M. (2009). Bank image in the UAE: Comparing Islamic and conventional banks. *Journal of Financial Services Marketing*, *14*(3), 232–244. doi:10.1057/fsm.2009.17

Awan, H. M., & Bukhari, K. S. (2011). Customer's criteria for selecting an Islamic bank: Evidence from Pakistan. *Journal of Islamic Marketing*, *2*(1), 14–27. doi:10.1108/17590831111115213

Başgoze, P., & Tektaş, O. O. (2012). Ethical perceptions and green buying behavior of consumers: Across-national exploratory study. *Journal of Economics and Behavioral Studies*, *4*(8), 477–488.

Brown, J. (2008). *Going green? How financial services are failing ethical consumers*. New Economics Foundation (NEF).

Carey, L., Shaw, D., & Shiu, E. (2008). The impact of ethical concerns on family consumer decision-making. *International Journal of Consumer Studies*, *32*(5), 553–560. doi:10.1111/j.1470-6431.2008.00687.x

Carroll, A. (1979). A Three-Dimensional Conceptual Model of Corporate Performance. *Academy of Management Review*, *4*(4), 497–505. doi:10.5465/amr.1979.4498296

Central Bank of Bahrain (CBB). (2019). *Factsheet*. Retrieved from https://www.cbb.gov.bh/fact-sheet/

Davis, R. M. (1979). Comparison of consumer acceptance of rights and responsibilities. In Ethics and the Consumer Interest (pp. 68-70). Academic Press.

Edris, T. A. (1997). Services considered important to business customers and determinants of bank selection in Kuwait: A segmentation analysis. *International Journal of Bank Marketing*, *15*(4), 126–133. doi:10.1108/02652329710189393

Eller, H. (2017). Corporate Governance and Corporate Social Responsibility: Research on the Interconnection of Both Concepts and Its Impact on Non-Profit Organizations. *International Journal of Economics and Management Engineering*, *11*(4), 869–873.

Ferrell, O. C., & Fraedrich, J. (2014). *Business ethics: Ethical decision making & cases*. Cengage Learning.

Fukukawa, K. (2003). *Understanding Ethically Questionable Behaviour in Consumption. An Empirical Investigation* (PhD Thesis). University of Nottingham.

Fullerton, S., Kerch, K. B., & Dodge, H. R. (1996). Consumer ethics: An assessment of individual behavior in the market place. *Journal of Business Ethics*, *15*(7), 805–814. doi:10.1007/BF00381744

Garriga, E., & Melé, D. (2004). Corporate social responsibility theories: Mapping the territory. *Journal of Business Ethics*, *53*(1-2), 51–71. doi:10.1023/B:BUSI.0000039399.90587.34

Gerrard, P., & Cunningham, B. (1997). Islamic banking: A study in Singapore. *Journal of Bank Marketing*, *15*(6), 204–216. doi:10.1108/02652329710184433

Gilani, H. (2015). Exploring the ethical aspects of Islamic banking. *International Journal of Islamic and Middle Eastern Finance and Management*, *8*(1), 85–98. doi:10.1108/IMEFM-09-2012-0087

Gill, K. (2012). College Students Altitudes towards Ethical Consumerism – An Indian Perspective. *IOSR Journal of Business and Management*, *4*(5), 1-13.

Hegazy, I. A. (1995). An Empirical Comparative Study between Islamic and Commercial Banks' selection Criteria in Egypt. *International Journal of Commerce and Management*, *5*(3), 46-61.

Henry, A. (2008). *Understanding Strategic Management*. Oxford University Press.

Jahiruddin, A., & Haque, R. (2009). Bank selection criteria of retail customers in Bangladesh: A study on Khulna city. *Journal of Business and Management*, *15*(2), 159–169.

Katircioglu, S. T., Tumer, M., & Kılınc¸, C. (2011). Bank selection criteria in the banking industry: An empirical investigation from customers in Romanian cities. *African Journal of Business Management*, *5*(14), 5551–5558.

Kaynak, E., Küçükemiroglu, O., & Odabasi, Y. (1991). Commercial bank selection in Turkey. *International Journal of Bank Marketing*, *9*(4), 30–39. doi:10.1108/02652329110004249

Maiyaki, A. A. (2011). Factors determining bank's selection and preference in Nigerian retail banking. *International Journal of Business and Management*, *6*(1), 253–257.

Malone, S. (2012). *Understanding the role of emotion in ethical consumption: a tourism context* (PhD Thesis). University of Nottingham.

Metawa, S. A., & Almossawi, M. (1998). Banking behavior of Islamic bank customers: Perspectives and implications. *International Journal of Bank Marketing*, *16*(7), 299–313. doi:10.1108/02652329810246028

Muncy, A. J., & Vitell, J. S. (1992). Consumer Ethics: An Investigation of Ethical Beliefs of the Final Consumer. *Journal of Business Research*, *24*(4), 297–311. doi:10.1016/0148-2963(92)90036-B

Naser, K., Jamal, A., & Al-Khatib, K. (1999). Islamic banking: A study of customer satisfaction and preferences in Jordan. *International Journal of Bank Marketing*, *17*(3), 135–151. doi:10.1108/02652329910269275

Navaretti, G. B., Calzolari, G., Mansilla-Fernandez, J. M., & Pozzolo, A. F. (2017). Fintech and Banking. Friends or Foes? European Economy. Europeye srl.

Nomura Holdings. (2019). *Social Finance Products*. Retrieved from https://www.nomuraholdings.com/csr/sustainable/products.html

Papulova, Z. (2014). The significance of vision and mission development for enterprises in Slovak Republic. *Journal of Economics, Business and Management*, *2*(1), 12-16.

Reidenbach, E. R., & Robin, P. D. (1988). Some Initial steps towards improving the measurement of ethical evaluations of marketing activities. *Journal of Business Ethics*, *7*(11), 871–879. doi:10.1007/BF00383050

Sayani, H., & Miniaoui, H. (2013). Determinants of bank selection in the United Arab Emirates. *International Journal of Bank Marketing*, *31*(3), 206–228. doi:10.1108/02652321311315302

Sebastiani, R., Montagnini, F., & Dalli, D. (2013). Ethical consumption and new business models in the food industry. Evidence from the Eataly case. *Journal of Business Ethics*, *114*(3), 473–488. doi:10.100710551-012-1343-1

Souiden, N., & Rani, M. (2015). Consumer attitudes and purchase intentions toward Islamic banks: The influence of religiosity. *International Journal of Bank Marketing*, *33*(2), 143–161. doi:10.1108/IJBM-10-2013-0115

Szmigin, I., & Carrigan, M. (2006). Exploring the dimensions of ethical consumption. *European Advances in Consumer Research*, *7*, 608–613.

Tan, C. T., & Chua, C. (1993). Intention, attitude and social influence in bank selection: A study in an oriental culture. *International Journal of Bank Marketing*, *4*(3), 43–53.

Wajdi Dusuki, A., & Irwani Abdullah, N. (2007). Why do Malaysian customers patronise Islamic banks? *International Journal of Bank Marketing*, *25*(3), 142–160. doi:10.1108/02652320710739850

Wilkes, R. E. (1978). Fraudulent behavior by consumers. *Journal of Marketing*, *42*(4), 67–75.

Zineldin, M. (1996). Bank strategic positioning and some determinants of bank selection. *International Journal of Bank Marketing*, *14*(6), 12–22. doi:10.1108/02652329610130136

Chapter 4
The Role of Auditing Firms in Promoting Ethical Consumerism:
Ethical Programs for Business Companies

Ebtihaj Al-A'Ali
University of Bahrain, Bahrain

ABSTRACT

This research examines the roles of auditing firms to spread ethical awareness. Auditing firms' roles can also enhance understanding of business companies regarding ethical consumerism. This can be accomplished by assisting businesses to develop their own ethical programs. The programs can enable companies to achieve profit and maintain desirable reputation in relation to investors, employees, and customers. Qualitative research is employed in this research. Based on snowballing technique, six in-depth interviews and two more telephone interviews were conducted. The findings of the research show that auditing firms are not familiar with the issue of ethical consumerism to promote. Businesses have not approached auditing firms to aid them in developing their own ethical programs. Such aid is not seen by auditing firms however as prohibited non-auditing services.

DOI: 10.4018/978-1-7998-0272-3.ch004

INTRODUCTION

As a result of unethical acts of businesses attributed to their involvement with auditing firms, the role of the later have been transformed in USA since 2002. Ethics is a major focus for auditing practices in general and in relation to business clients in specific. The later acknowledges the importance of being ethical in leading to attract more customers and therefore to develop positive reputation inducing profits. Auditing firms can assist their business clients to develop their own ethical programs which will be beneficial to all stakeholders. This research examines the practices and the roles of auditing firms to promote ethical environment and culture for businesses. It also investigates the issue of ethical consumerism as perceived by auditing firms. This perception can guide firms in helping their business clients to develop their own ethical programs as a non-auditing service. Issues studied are associated to the definition of ethical consumerism, the definition of non-auditing services by firms examined, and finally whether businesses have sought assistance from auditing firms to help developing their own ethical programs.

AUDITING FIRMS' CULTURE, NON-AUDITING SERVICES AND ETHICAL CONSUMERISM

In this section definitions of non-auditing services, culture of auditing firms, ethical consumerism, and corporate governance is discussed first. Literature review concerning auditing firms in relation to non-auditing services then is elaborated.

Definitions of Non-Auditing Services, Ethical Culture, and Ethical Consumerism

Non auditing services are defined by what factors they stand for. These factors are related to decision making and management, services related to taxes, payroll tax and human resources related to recruitment and compensation, legal services including negotiation and the resolution of litigation, services related to internal auditing and services concerned with shares of audited entities (ey, 2016; Pwh, 2016; KPMG, 2017; Deloitte, 2015). These stated factors are constituting the definition of NAS. The factors are the same to auditing firms due to the global nature of auditing industry. If these services are offered, the firm's independence will be compromised. According to literature of auditing firms and their non auditing services, the issue of providing assistance to business companies to develop their ethical frameworks is not stated. Such frameworks can enable business companies to meet different aspects of ethical consumerism. Ferrell, Fraedrich and Ferrell (2015) explain that business ethics and ethical culture can lead to profit through enhancing employees' commitments and trust, promoting trust and loyalty of investors and gaining satisfaction and trust of customers. The later can be defined in term of complex behavior based on decision making processes leading to choose between goods, services and products (Al A'Ali & Al-Sarraf, 2016). To enhance customers satisfaction, trust and ethical consumerism, auditing firms have to promote ethical cultures through following specific decision-making processes. The decision -making processes is based on interaction between two main influences. The first influences are related to decision makers themselves. The factors related to these influences are moral integrity, cognitive moral development, personal integrity and values, moral imagination, gender and age, cultural and national beliefs and education and employment. The second influences are termed contextual and issues related. The elements of this second influences are moral framing and intensity pertaining to issues examined, and systems related to authority and ethical practices, impacts of bureaucracy on ethics, work roles as being structured or non-structured, values representing organizational culture and its impacts on ethical decisions, values of national culture varying geographically and finally focus of reward system to promote or to neglect importance of ethical decisions (Crane & Matten, 2016) . The decision processes lead firms, i.e auditing to promote ethical culture inducing ethical decisions. This can nurture the definition of ethical consumerism which includes ethical, environmental, learning social values based on interactions between consumers with marketplace. This is to say that auditing firms play two roles to develop ethical consumerism. The first is related to stimulating of an internal ethical environment and culture through two aspects. The first aspect is concerned with the auditing firms' unique culture reflected through values, beliefs, code of conduct and customs. The second aspect is related to perpetuating of ethical environment and culture through training. The second role is pertaining to help businesses designing their ethical programs.

Ethical consumerism differs from corporate governance. Corporate Governance refers to the fundamental values and principles in relation to the objective of businesses. Corporate Governance, according to Ferrell, Fraedrich and Ferrell (2015), can be based on one of the following approaches.

1. The shareholder model assumes that maximizing profit is the main objective of business companies. This is based on classical economics perspective. The model is directed to serve the interest of investors. The model is criticized for ignoring the importance of other groups having stake in the same businesses.
2. The second approach is called stakeholder model. The model refers to businesses' responsibilities toward governments, communities, interest groups, suppliers, employees and consumers. These stakeholders are classified as primary and

secondary. Corporate Governance are geared toward serving the interest of primary stakeholders first. This is due to the limited resources available.

The above definitions of internal culture, non-auditing services and ethical consumerism guide this research to examine the perceptions of auditing firms in relation to the same definitions. This can assist in understanding practices of auditing firms to create ethical culture which in turn helps to aiding businesses to develop their own ethical programs.

Auditing Firms in Relation to Business Ethics and Non-Auditing Services NAS: Literature Review

Ethics can be viewed from two different but complementary perspectives in relation to auditing firms (Ferrell, Fraedrich & Ferrell, 2015; Crane & Matten, 2016). The first perspective is related to internal ethics followed and practiced by auditors themselves (Al qtaish, Baker & Othman, 2014). The second is concerned directly with business clients as a resultant of implementation of the first perspective (Cohn, 2004). Crane and Matten (2016) state that auditing has major impacts on different stakeholders. They add that there are four types of codes of ethics which can be related to all professions including auditing. These codes are as follows:

1. Ethics related to a specific organization are focusing on the behavior of individuals e.g. integrity, respect etc. i.e. every auditing firm has different values and principles guiding behaviors of its employees.
2. Professional ethics are referring to guidelines and procedures followed by a specific professions such as auditors, accountants and other professions (Boatright, 2003).
3. Ethics for a given industry is evolving based on its needs. Large global companies develop such ethics i.e. International Air Transport Association.
4. Ethics for groups or for programs refer to coalitions of organizations working together to establish code of ethics for participants. Using a label or getting accreditation requires conforming to code of ethics of a given program e.g. Fair-trade, Association of International Accountants and other groups.

Group ethics I.e. auditing firms can be defined in term of the professional code of conduct developed by the American Institute for Certified Public Accountants in 1988 . This code of conduct is "based on six principles: responsibilities, the public interest, integrity, objectivity and independence, due care, and scope and nature of services" (Stanwick & Stanwick, 2009, page 170). Al qtaish, Baker and Othman's

(2014) findings however, show that impacts of ethics or code of conduct on auditing quality vary based on factors ranked as follows:

1. Auditors' independence and objectivity
2. Honesty
3. Commitment to professional conduct
4. Efficiency of auditors
5. Confidentiality of information related to customers

Ballwieser and Clemm (1999) explain that there are five problems encountering financial intermediaries 's job i.e. accounting firms and Credit Rating Agencies in general (Crane & Matten, 2016). These problems make these intermediaries i.e. accounting and auditing firms to experience ethical situations regardless of the earlier stated code of conduct i.e. professional, industry, ethics of an organization and ethics stemmed from coalitions. These problems are:

1. **Influence on the Market:** This refers to the power intermediaries exert on players in the market through rating by Credit ratings agencies. BIG4 auditing firms play a major role on procedures and laws development.
2. **Conflict of Interest:** This occurs as accounting firms involve more with clients through providing non auditing services. Conflict of interest experiences by credit rating agencies as a result of providing consultancy to companies to structure and to design their financial product. Stanwick & Stanwick (2009) state that there are three types of conflict of interest which might occur in the process of auditing. a) conflict of interest between the auditing firm and companies as a resultant of pressuring the first to sign financial statements regardless of any other concerns related to auditing processes. Doing this Due to financial interest in companies, auditing firms might encounter conflict as they have to abide to accounting standards and regulations. b) Lack of of objectivity in the financial statements due to the desire of management to present clean statements to their shareholders. This is because of shareholders-management conflict. c) Conflict is due to incompatibility between self and professional interests. Auditors might give priority to their own self-interest.
3. **Long - Term Relationship:** This relationship is based on confidentiality of information that intermediaries are exposed to. Laws in some countries do not allow such relationship to develop however, its problems still exist due to its personal nature. This jeopardize independence and objectivity of intermediaries 's job.

4. **Bureaucratic Oversight and Control:** Credit rating agencies and accounting firms develop standard procedures leading to economies of scale. Standard procedures make individual auditor to lose personal responsibility of the task.
5. **Competition Between Intermediaries**: Public interest might be jeopardized in the process of competition between intermediaries. Auditing and evaluation functions might be affected in order to win competition. Crane and Matten (2016) state that the above illustrated problems might have negative impacts on auditing ethics in relation to objectivity, independence and quality.

Khasharmeh and Desoky (2018) illustrate that auditors independence is impaired as result of providing non audit services. Audit quality and objectivity are improved for providing non audit services, however. This is based on their research on a sample of listed companies in Bahrain Boursa, auditors, accountants and financial managers. Zulkanian & Sori & Karbhari & Shamsher (2012) argue that audit and NAS should be rendered by two different departments or entities. These departments or entities should be separate and no cooperation of whatsoever take place between them. This is to minimize or to eliminate having negative impact on auditors' independency. Joshi, Bremerton, Hamalatha and Al-Mudhaki (2007) argue that there are three perspectives, based on literature, in relation to impacts of NAS on auditor's independence. These perspectives are as follows: 1-NAS if rendered impairs auditors 's independence. 2- NAS improves audit quality and enhances audit independence and audit objectivity. 3- There is no effect of NAS on auditor independence. The findings show that independence may be affected by NAS to a certain extent as NAS fees is very limited in Bahrain. This, according to business companies, can enhance quality of work, achieve cost effectiveness and understanding of businesses in better ways. Besides, the same research of Joshi & others (2007) illustrates that BIG4 firms arguing that NAS such as legal services, recruitment, personnel and management services and management discussions do not compromise independence. However non BIG4 audit firms explain that management discussions might have limited impact on independence. Internal audit and internal control according to BIG4 auditing firms will compromise independence. Joshi, Bremerton, Hamalatha and Al-Mudhaki (2007) highlight the issue that business companies have no NAS policy. Bahrain also does not have a law equivalent to SOA (Sarbanes-Oxly Act).

The impacts of NAS on independence, quality and objectivity are debatable according to the above researches reviewed. None of the earlier researches mention that assisting business companies to develop their own ethical programs as an NAS. Such assistance is not referred to as NAS by BIG4 and other smaller size auditing firms.

This research. therefore, explores the following issues in the context of auditing firms in Bahrain:

1. The definitions of NAS, ethical consumerism and ethical culture
2. Auditing firms' role in assisting business companies to develop their ethical programs.

Auditing Firms and Their Environment: Bahrain Context

Secondary information about auditing firms and their environment is not readily available. an interview with the official in charge of financial analysis and economical information has become a need. The official states that the commercial companies' law Decree No (21) discusses the types of companies having to file their annual financial statements. He added that 25 auditing firms are registered in the Ministry of Industry and Commerce at the present time. The first firm to enter Bahrain is SABA & CO (date of entry is June,1961); followed by Ernst & Young - Middle East (entering date is Nov, 1961). Since then many firms have entered the auditing industry in Bahrain. However, the first legislative Decree in respect to auditors and auditing firms is No 26 of 1996. A new Decree is to be issued concerning auditing firms and auditors. The official explains that the new Decree will be more thorough and concrete in relation to practices of auditors and auditing firms. Joshi, Bremerton, Hemlatatha and Al-Madhaki (2007) explain that Bahrain adopted international accounting standards IAS and IFRS international financial reporting standards. Bahrain joins international federation of Accounting in 2004. However, there is no legislation similar to the Americans Sarbanes-Oxly Act that control and regulate accounting and auditing practices.

RESEARCH METHODOLOGY

The above literature review shows that aiding business companies to develop their ethical programs is not stated in BIG4 's prohibited NAS list. Research concerning the role of auditing firms to fostering ethical environment and culture is not found in relation to Bahrain. Besides, there is no research about the role of auditing firms to assisting business companies to develop their own ethical programs in general. This represents the uniqueness of the issue being examined due to its contemporary nature. The lack of previous similar researches characterizes the research as being exploratory. This justifies the reasons underlying the use of qualitative research. Qualitative research aims to capture, understand and manifest perceptions and meanings of individuals i.e. participants in this research (Alaali & Alzzali (2018), Cooper and Schindler (2008)). There are about 25 auditing firms including BIG 4. In-depth interviews are the method to collect information from participants in this research. Partners or Directors in charge of ethics in auditing firms are the participants. Partners and Directors at BIG4 were chosen firstly for two reasons. Firstly, these BIG 4 firms dominate the auditing and accounting industry. Secondly snowballing technique was used to seek participants. Based on this technique no more interviews are to conduct if no new information is generated. After the first four interviews with participants of BIG 4 firms were conducted, four more interviews with partners or directors of relatively smaller firms were arranged in order to triangulate information based on size. However, no new information was still generated. Questions asked are as follows:

1. Definitions of ethical culture, ethical consumerism and roles of auditing firms to promote
2. Definition of NAS
3. Would assisting clients to develop their own internal ethical programs is an prohibited NAS violating auditors 'independence and objectivity.
4. Did clients ever ask their auditing firms for such assistance to designing their ethical programs.
5. If the answer for question number 4 is no or yes then explanation is required

DISCUSSION AND ANALYSIS OF INFORMATION COLLECTED

The following section presents the analysis of collected information for the above stated questions based on interviews conducted.

Analysis of Collected Information for Question One

Question one investigated participants' definitions of ethical consumerism.

Themes evolved based on collected information are as follows:

1. Auditing firms have their own periodic ethical training programs for their auditors to act ethically. There are values and codes of conduct that auditors have to abide
2. Auditing firms have a passive role in ethical consumerism. It's consumers' duty to be ethical
3. Ethical consumerism can be manifested through many indicators i.e. fair fees, caring for environment, suppliers and contractors' relationships as a reflection of fair trade, employees' competencies and other values.

All participants express the first theme (theme no. 1) as a definition for ethical consumerism. This indicates that auditors have to be trained to act ethically in order to abide to internal values and codes of conduct. This is partially compatible to the definition of ethical culture stated above by Ferrell, Fraedrich and Ferrell (2015). Though auditors' competency and ethical acts are indicators of having ethical culture inducing ethical consumerism, it is not the cornerstone of ethical consumerism. Participants highlight the importance of professional ethics as it's explained by Crane and Matten (2016). No participant referred to the need for ethical decision-making processes as a requirement for establishing ethical culture. One participant representing a global auditing firm however states that ethical consumerism is related to consumers' acts and decisions. Auditing firms have no role in promoting ethical consumerism (theme no. 2). Themes one and two illustrate lack of awareness of the issue of ethical consumerism despite the existing of code of ethics held by auditing firms examined. This unawareness can be attributed to two reasons. Firstly, the issue of ethical consumerism as a phenomenon is relatively new and is a complex issue. Though students of college of business was taught a course in business ethics, they provided no definitions for the issue of ethical consumerism (Al A'ali & Al-Sarraf (2016)). Secondly the first regulatory Decree concerning auditing firms and auditors was issued in 1996 in Bahrain. This illustrates that the conducts of auditing firms were not regulated before that year. In addition, issues pertaining to unethical conduct of firms were not well examined in that first Decree. The last theme (theme no.3) is expressed by two participants. The theme is compatible to the definition of ethical consumerism stated above. However, the ethical decision-making processes leading to achieve ethical standard of practices, environmental concerns and learning social values are not stated in relation to the answer for this question. As stated above ethical consumerism can be a resultant of ethical culture based on ethical decision-making processes (Ferrell, Fraedrich & Ferrell, 2015). One of these two participants oversees ethics standards and practices in the firm that he works for. This may explain his awareness of the issue of ethical consumerism. The second is a partner in charge of auditing service. The lack of perceptions of ethical consumerism may lead auditing firms to exhibit passive role in promoting ethical culture based on ethical decision making processes. This passive role is accentuated by the absence of regulations monitoring the practices of auditing firms.

Question Two Concerning Definition of NAS (Non-Auditing Services)

Information collected related to the second question reveal the following themes:

1. NAS are services not related to auditing but are related to other services provided by the auditing firms i.e. consultancy
2. Being an international firm there is a list of prohibited NAS

3. The firm abides by the values and codes of conduct of international standards of international federation of Accounting (IFAC) and International Ethics Standards Board for Accountant (IESBA).
4. The firm offers both auditing and non-auditing services to the same clients assuming that some countries allow such offerings. Both services however are offered by different departments
5. The auditing firm does not offer non-auditing services to the same clients as per their codes of conduct regardless of location
6. The auditing firm does not have a prohibited NAS list. The firm may refrain from providing non auditing services to a client based on a judgmental decision made.

Theme one (no.1) is stated by all participants in this research. However, except for one participant, others have provided no written documents to illustrate their non auditing services list. Participants did not provide NAS list due to the confidentiality as explained. The websites of firms are examined. It is found that five of websites explicitly and publicly exhibit the lists of prohibited non auditing services. The remaining websites mention nothing about such prohibited non auditing services. Theme number two (2) is expressed by seven. These seven firms state that being global indicates the existence of prohibited NAS services lis but websites of two firms have no such list. Theme number three (3) is argued by seven firms. Based on their global operations, international standards of IFAC and IESBA regulate their services. Theme number five (5) is claimed by five firms. It is contended by firms that no offering of NAS to the same client as it is obligatory by their code of conduct (theme no. 5). The remaining two global and the domestic firms state that they offer NAS to the same business clients. The offering though is provided by two different departments (theme no.4). The eighth firm abides to regulations followed in Bahrain due to its domestic nature regardless of its affiliation to international firm. Doing so, offering NAS to the same clients, according to these three firms (two global and one domestic) does not jeopardize independence as auditing and non-auditing services are provided by different departments. This is compatible to the arguments of Joshi and others (2007), Zulkanian et al. (2012). Theme 6 (theme no.6) however is expressed only by the domestic firm. Participant representing the domestic firm explains that no compromise is allowed on independence. But due to the lack of objective guidelines to make decisions concerning offering of NAS, judgmental decisions are employed. Guidelines for such decisions are contextual based. It means guidelines change as the situation requires. The themes of this question supports literature findings of Joshi & others (2007) that there are different perspectives in relation to NAS and auditors independence as discussed above.

The Analysis of Collected Information for Questions Three, Four, and Five

All participants argue that assisting business clients to develop their own ethical programs would not compromise independence and objectivity. The assistance to the contrary will enhance ethical practices and is not related to any of prohibited non auditing services specified by auditing firms (answer for question no. three).

Question four is concerned with auditing firms aiding business companies to develop their own ethical programs. Seven firms affirm that no businesses approached them to assist in developing their own ethical programs (question no.4). This is attributed, according to participants, to business environment and culture. The existing environment and culture does not highlight the importance of such ethical programs. Participants explain that no regulations existing to accentuate the need for having such programs. All participants add however that large businesses have their own corporate governance systems enabling them to maintain ethics. Smaller businesses are aided by auditing firms to develop their own corporate governance systems. This illustrates that participants do not differentiate between corporate governance and ethical programs for businesses. For ethical programs can correspond to dimensions of ethical consumerism as explained above (Al A'ali & Al-Sarraf, 2016) while corporate governance is to create formal system targeting certain stakeholders (Ferrell, Fraedrich & Ferrell, 2015). Only one participant explains that his/her firm has offered services to businesses to develop their own ethical programs (question no 4). This later participant has given no definition for ethical consumerism and has provided no numbers and details for businesses receiving such service. He adds that such information is confidential and not to reveal (question no.5).

CONCLUSION, LIMITATIONS AND FUTURE RESEARCH

This research investigates the roles of auditing firms to promote ethical environment and culture at one hand and to help business clients to design their ethical programs at the other hand. The research shows that auditing firms have some values reflecting dimensions of ethical consumerism. These values are stated in their vision, mission and code of ethics. However, the definition of ethical consumerism is not conceptualized and is not perceived by participants. The majority of participants are unable to give a definition for the issue of ethical consumerism. The lack of such conception of the issue of ethical consumerism and its dimensions explains the passive role of auditing firms in relation to developing ethical culture. This as well justifies the findings illustrating that no business companies requested auditing firms to aid in developing their own ethical programs. Though such programs are not seen by auditing firms as elements of prohibited non auditing services NAS

This research is exploratory in nature based on qualitative methodology. Interviews are the methods to collect information. This methodology is compatible to the unique nature of the issue studied. However, there is a need to replicate this same research employing quantitative research methodology. Quantitative research can reach a larger sample size. Objectivity assumed in such research can lead to enhance understandings of the roles of auditing firms in promoting ethical environment and culture. Besides it can shed light on the roles of auditing firms in helping business companies to develop their ethical programs.

Future research can investigate the factors underlying judgmental decisions of domestic auditing companies for rendering NAS. Such decisions are made due to the absence of objective lists of prohibited NAS similar to those of BIG 4 and some international auditing firms. There may be a need as well to explore and investigate the reasons for lacking of ethical consumerism orientation among auditing firms.

REFERENCES

Al A'ali, E. A., & Al-Sarraf, A. R. (2016). Ethical Consumerism: Contextual Issues of Ethical Decision-Making Processes: An Exploratory Study. In Ethical and Social Perspectives on Global Business Interaction in Emerging Markets (pp. 133-149). IGI Global.

Al A'ali, E. A., & Alzzali, R. M. (2018). Gender Differences in Relation to Organizational Sources of Power. In *Arab Women and Their Evolving Roles in the Global Business Landscape* (pp. 1–25). IGI Global. doi:10.4018/978-1-5225-3710-6.ch001

Al Qtaish, H. F., Baker, A. A. R. M., & Othman, O. H. (2014). The ethical rules of auditing and the impact of compliance with the ethical rules on auditing quality. *International Journal of Research and Reviews in Applied Sciences*, *18*(3), 1.

Amiri Decree no 26 for 1996 in relation to public auditors. (n.d.). Retrieved from http://www.legalaffairs.gov.bh (in Arabic)

BDO. (2014). *Code of conduct and business ethics*. Retrieved from http://www.bdo.com.co

BDO. (2019). *Mission, Vision and Values*. Retrieved from http://www.bdo.com.co

Blumberg, B., Cooper, D. R., & Schindler, P. S. (2008). *Business research methods* (Vol. 2). London: McGraw-Hill Higher Education.

Boatright, J. R. (2000). *Ethics and the Conduct of Business, 6/e*. Pearson Education India.

Crane, A., & Matten, D. (2016). *Business ethics: Managing corporate citizenship and sustainability in the age of globalization*. Oxford, UK: University Press.

Deloitte. (2008). *Code of Conduct*. Retrieved from http://www2.deloitte.com

Deloitte. (2015). *Non-audit services: Restrictions and fee cap*. Retrieved from http://www2.deloitte.com

EY. (2016). *Audit reform*. Retrieved from http://www.ey.com

EY. (2017). *Global Codes of Ethics*. Retrieved from http://www.ey.com

Ferrell, O. C., Fraedrich, J., & Ferrell, L. (2015). *Business ethics: Ethical decision making & cases*. Stamford, CT: Cengage Learning.

Geneva Group International. (2015). *Objectives*. Retrieved from http://www.ggi.com/oboist/objectives

Gordon Cohn. (2004). *Auditing and Ethical Sensitivity*. Available at http://academic.brooklyn.cuny.edu/economic/cohn/ind.htm

Grant Thornton. (2016). *Non-audit services*. Retrieved from http://www.grantthornton.ie

Grant Thornton. (2018). *Code of Conduct*. Retrieved from http://www.grantthornton.com

Joshi, P. L., Bremser, W. G., Hemalatha, J., & Al-Mudhaki, J. (2007). Non-audit services and auditor independence: Empirical findings from Bahrain. *International Journal of Accounting. Auditing and Performance Evaluation*, *4*(1), 57–89. doi:10.1504/IJAAPE.2007.012595

Khasharmeh, H., & Desoky, A. M. (2018). Does the Provision of Non-Audit Services Affect Auditor Independence and Audit Quality? Evidence from Bahrain. *Asian Academy of Management Journal of Accounting & Finance*, *14*(1), 25–55. doi:10.21315/aamjaf2018.14.1.2

KPMG. (2005). *KPMG Global Code of Conduct*. Retrieved from http://homekpmg

KPMG. (2017). *KPMG Specimen non-audit Services Policy*. Retrieved from http://home.kpmg.com

Price Waterhouse Coopers. (2008). *Code of Conduct*. Retrieved from http://www.pwc.ru

Price Waterhouse EU Audit Legislation. (2016, October). *Guidance on non-audit service and fees cap.* Retrieved from http://www.pwc.com

Sori, Z. M., Karbhari, Y., & Mohamad, S. (2010). Commercialization of accounting profession: The case of non-audit services. *International Journal of Economics and Management*, *4*(2), 212–242.

Stanwick, P., & Stanwick, S. D. (2013). Understanding business ethics. *Sage (Atlanta, Ga.).*

Talal Abu-Ghazaleh & Co. Consulting. (2019). *Our Codes of Ethics.* Retrieved from http://www.tag-consultants.com

Chapter 5
Ethical Programs for Patients in Bahrain

Gardenia AlSaffar
Royal Hospital of Bahrain, Bahrain

ABSTRACT

2030 vision for the kingdom seeks to promote Bahrain as a healthcare destination. New private hospitals have entered the health service industry. This leads competition to soar. Patient care has become a priority. The need to acquire accreditation for health services rendered by hospitals accentuates the importance of maintaining international standards in term of quality and cost. The purpose of the study is to reflect on the development of ethical resolutions, procedures, policies, and programs to enhance and to improve healthcare by National Health Regulatory Authority (NHRA). The study employs qualitative analysis of literature in relation to the evolution of ethical programs for health professionals in general and for patients at hospitals in Bahrain.

INTRODUCTION

Article 25 of the Universal Declaration of Human Rights of 1948 illustrates the human right to wellbeing, medical care and health services. This 1964 constitution of the World Health Organization defines health as "the enjoyment of the highest attainable standard of health" (WIKIPEDIA, from en.m.wikipedia.org, Right to Health). Principles related to the right for health include spread of medical knowledge, adequate health services, and child health. Therefore, this paper examines the theoretical evolution of ethical programs, elaborating on ethical programs frequently discussed in the literature. It also highlights the differences between doctor-patient

DOI: 10.4018/978-1-7998-0272-3.ch005

models in the USA, the UK, and Canada. Finally, this study reflects on NHRA's (National Health Regulatory Authority) "attempts to promote and develop ethical programs by health providers in the Kingdom of Bahrain."

PATIENT ETHICAL PROGRAMS: LITERATURE REVIEW

According to Moorhead and Griffin (2102), there are four stages of group development: mutual acceptance of members, open communication and establishing norms, members' cooperation and creativity, and finally, working as team based on the ability to self-reflect and self-correct. Groups made of professionals and work teams develop their own norms and values at the second stage of group development. Norms and values assist in defining expected behavior, differentiating a given group from others, aiding the group to avoid unexpected situations, and finally helping the group to survive.

The Law Society (1986) outlines the differences between professional and occupational groups in term of four factors.: professional members are identified by register or record; members need to abide by ethical standards; membership indicates having skills and learning in a given field; being responsible for actions and behavior towards they serve. (Picker Institute, 2006).

A professional body is constituted of members of the same profession and has five objectives the first of which is to illustrate codes of ethics related to a given professional i.e. physicians demanded in a professional capacity by regulatory authorities. The second is to specify to future members how to behave. The third is to outline the consequences of violating such codes. The fourth is to assist in clarifying the needs for medical education, trading, and solving problems. The fifth is to maintain and improve the public's image of physicians (Picker Institute, 2006).

Kaba and Sooriakumaran (2006) state that there are three models for the doctor-patient relationship. Stanwick and Stanwick (2009) added a fourth model. The first according to Stanwick and Stanwick (2009) is the "Engineering" model. In this model "the doctor provides factual information.....but the patient makes all relevant decisions." (p.105). This relationship of patient domination is argued by Kaba and Sooriakumaran (2006) to prevail in the 1700s. In the second model, the doctor takes on a "Priestly" role that assume that the doctor will do their best for a patient who plays a passive role. This to Kaba and Sooriakumaran (2006) exists in the 1000s. The third model is "Collegial", which states that the doctor and patient make all decisions based on trust. This is partially compatible with the model of "mutual participation" of 1956 as explained by Kaba and Sooriakumaran (2006). The last and fourth model discussed by Stanwick and Stabnwick (2009) is the "Contractual" model, in which the doctor and patient are said to pursue a mutual objective. Any party of the doctor-patient relationship based on this model can withdraw at any time.

At present, patient-centered medicine revolves around four principles. The first principle views a patient as a person in a totality perspective. The second states an equal relationship through shared power and responsibility, where patients are encouraged to participate more in their treatment. The third is that doctor-patient relationship is based on therapeutic alliances. The fourth is views the doctor as a person. The doctor and patient are in an interactive relationship, which leads each party to influence, and be influenced by the other. This makes the patient the focus of the doctor, not the illness.

Stanwick and Stanwick (2009) state that the health care industry is based on the following ethical values: "beneficence" in health decisions centered around the best interest of patients; "non-malfeasance" of health service workers to cause no harm to patients; the "autonomy" of patients to accept or reject treatment; "justice" implying that decisions made by health workers are fair to all patients; the preservation of patient "dignity" in their treatment; "truthfulness"vand honesty in which doctors should inform patients about their treatment in order to get their consent.

Riddick, Jr, (2003) states "The Oath of Hippocrates" in the fifth century was the first to determine the conduct of physicians. It mentions that the physician is to have an altruistic attitude toward patients. It also claims that 11th century principles of physicians are used as a starting point to enter medical school or to guide physicians after graduation. Violato (2013) argues that Hammurabi, the Babylonian, discussed the issues related to professional life of physicians earlier in 1740 B.C.E. He adds that after Hippocrates, Galen in 161 A.D. came was the first in Rome and then returned to Greece. Riddick, Jr. (2005) explains that Tomas Perceval, a philosopher and a physician in England in 1803, "published a Code of Medical Ethics describing professional duties and ideal behavior to hospitals and other charities". He expounds that the American Medical Association (AMA) has focused on two items, since its inception in 1847. The first was to establish a code of ethics and the second, was to state the minimum requirements for the education and training of physicians. Since then, many revisions have taken place in 1903, 1912, and 1947. The 1980 revision attempted to balance the tension between professional standards and legal requirements.

The first code of ethics for the Canadian Medical Association in 1868 was taken verbatim from the American Medical Association's Codes of Ethics. Since then, many revisions took place to differentiate the AMA Code of Ethics from that of the CMA (Naylor,1983). In the United Kingdom, the General Medical Council was established in 1858. It aims to promote and sustain public safety and health. It also governs and methodizes standards for schools of medicine and other national agencies

(Wikipedia, http://en.m.wikipedia.org). The Picker Institute (2006) published a review comparing the professional standards for doctors in the USA, the UK, and Canada.

The examination focused on two elements in the aims of those Codes. The first is to analyze standards for being general or specific. The second is to investigate the Codes' impacts on education and implementation. The review illustrated similarities, differences, strengths and tensions between the reviewed Codes. There were 3 major similarities. First, the doctor must be competent and possesses technical skills. The assessments of competency and skills varies, however, especially for routine assessment against standards of competence. Second, the Codes elaborated on the doctor-patient relationship. Non-discrimination against patients and confidentiality are common themes, with stipulations of situations in which confidentiality can be breached. Third, most codes require patients' consent ahead of any investigation and treatment.

The Pickers Institute report (2006) discusses the differences between the investigated Codes of Ethics. The major difference found is that the Canadian Codes induce doctors to enhance patients' learning empower them to be responsible for their health. Second, it is also exhibited that trust and communication are emphasized more in codes related to primary care. Psychiatrists' code of ethics gives heavy weight to trust and communication, due to the long term treatment of patients. Confidentiality, patient consent and patient's autonomy are dealt with differently by codes of psychiatry when a patients' capacity is compromised. The Pickers review asserts that Good Medical Practice for GPs provides detailed procedures to report colleagues who underperform. The issue encountering doctors is methods of gathering evidence to justify these reports as well as ways to deal with them. It also explained that the most prominent tension between codes is related to the doctor's use of resources concerning individual patients, or in relation to the doctor's responsibility to patients and collective access to resources.

The National Health Regulatory Authority in Bahrain published their first comprehensive code of conduct for all medical professions in September 2017. This Code of Professional Conduct is based on two major references: The International Code of Medical Ethics of the World Medical Association and the Code of Ethics of Canadian Medical Association. In this section a review of the latest versions of these codes is presented.

WORLD MEDICAL ASSOCIATION

In 1949, the World Medical Association (WMA) adopted the the International Code of Ethics. This Code of Ethics outlined the duties of doctors to the sick and to colleagues. It explained practices that are considered to be unethical, once they were exhibited by doctors. The amendments in 1968 and in 1983 stated the physicians' the code of ethics required for members of the medical profession. It discussed physicians' responsibility to humanity and their role as teachers. It also stated the physician's responsibility to maintain dignity and confidentiality, to prioritize patients, and not discriminate against them (Illinois Institute of Technology, 2011). The fourth amendment for the code of ethics of the World Medical Association was in 2006 and added further detail to the previous code. In addition to earlier codes, this amendment discussed issues focusing on resources used to provide treatment, colleagues' rights, the importance of continuous training and education for doctors, respect for different cultures, and doctors' physical and mental health to provide the right health service, and collaboration with colleagues as needed. The Canadian Medical Association journal published an article by Collier (2017) stating that the World Medical Association approved revision of their own Code of Ethics. The new Codes highlight the importance of patient dignity and confidentiality. Instead of using the word "shall" the new Code use the phrase "the physicians pledge". Physicians health should be attended. Respect is due to medical students, teachers and colleagues. Bullying and harassment is a widely spread issue due to the hierarchical nature of the profession. This explained the new statement mentioned in the Code of Ethics related to bullying and harassment. These Codes of Ethics are to guide National Medical Associations.

THE CANADIAN MEDICAL ASSOCIATION CMA

The Canadian Medical Association was formed in 1867 (Wikipedia, http://en.m.wikipedia.org). The first Code of Ethics was published in 1868 which was taken verbatim from the codes of Ethics of the American Medical Association (Naylor,1983). Since then many revisions were made to the Code of Ethics of CMA. The revisions of 1965, 1984, 1996, 2004, and December 2018 are examined. This is because the Canadian Code of Ethics is a major reference for the Code of Professional Conduct in Bahrain. A review of the amendments shows that all of them contain introductory sections. These sections are called General Duties (1965 & 1996), Brief Code of Ethics (1984), Fundamental Responsibility (2004), Virtues Exemplified by the Ethical Physician, and Fundamental Commitments of the Medical Profession

(Dec. 2018). The later version lists the virtues of promoting trust in all aspects of a physicians' duties. These virtues include compassion to patients, maintaining honest behaviors and attitudes, humility in acknowledging the limitations of their knowledge, integrity implying consistency in behaviors and intentions regardless of situations, and finally prudence in the use of all knowledge, using your judgement and reasoning to make decisions.

These virtues guide the Fundamental Commitments of the Medical Profession. These Commitments focus on patients: respect for humans, using justice in dealing with patients, sustaining the integrity and competence of the profession, contributing to academically and empirically enhance professional excellence, both academically in collaboration with others, encouraging a training culture and maintaining self-care, and finally personal and professional development through inquiry and research. These virtues and commitments exist explicitly or implicitly to varying degrees in the previous Codes of Ethics. It is found that two issues are stated explicitly in the 1965 version of the Codes of Ethics. These issues are 'induction of abortion' and 'sterilization'. These same issues are not referred to in the following revisions.

The issues of discrimination, integrity and confidentiality are stated explicitly in the revisions of 1984, 1996, 2004 and 2018. The 1965 version elaborates on issues of advertising and the differences between physicians and nurses, which is not discussed in following versions. These two issues are discussed in all versions but not to the same depth of the 1965 version. In addition, the differences between physicians, referred to as responsibilities to colleagues and the profession, are more specific and concrete. Physician's fees are an issue highlighted by all all versions.

The 2018 Code of Ethics elaborates on the responsibilities of physicians through two aspects. The first refers to the doctor-patient relationship. This relationship entails that the physicians should be free of sources of discrimination, continues treatment until notified otherwise, acknowledges and respects differences of conscience, communicates information to patients in an understandable way, avoids the overuse of resources by employing evidence-based treatment, attends emergency cases for others, limits treatment for oneself and close relations to emergency treatment. It also stipulates that conducted research should be ethically and scientifically evaluated, and that research participants have the right to continue or to withdraw. Physicians are also required to not contribute to inhuman or cruel procedures.

The second aspect pertains to physicians' decisions. This aspect states that physicians should attempt to empower patients to make their own health decisions, to respect competent patients' decisions concerning their treatment. It stipulates that physicians should deal with minors on a case-by-case basis, respect the values of incompetent patients, encourage patients with cognitive impairment to decide make decisions about their own health care with the support of their families, and act in the best interests of incompetent patients, and allow patients to seek second opinions.

The second issue that the Code of Ethics of 2018 focuses on is physicians and the practice of medicine. This issue is illustrated through two indicators. The first deals with privacy and confidentiality issues. The second relates to conflicts of interest and methods of minimizing them. These conflicts of interest stem from physicians' various roles and relationships, including communicating with patients, relationships between research participants, relationships with associations, agreement and contracts. The 2018 Code of Ethics then discusses the responsibilities of physicians to themselves, demonstrated by three issues. These are: to spread and advance "wellness services", to search for qualified professionals to aid in your professional and health matters, to induce an environment of training to promote psychological and safety. Responsibilities toward colleagues are then outlined. These responsibilities revolve around respect of others, treating others in the same way one would like to be treated, assuming responsibilities for ones' actions, making decisions without harming other colleagues, acting as mentors and leaders for juniors and other lower level physicians, and finally promoting interdisciplinary teams to improve patient care. The final responsibilities referred to by the Code of Ethics for 2018 draws attention to the responsibilities of physicians toward their society. This is achieved through maintaining professional standards, identifying factors affecting public health, acting for promoting health knowledge, legislation enacting related to health, assisting in the development of accessible health and resources. It also stipulates that physicians' opinions should be consistent with present and accepted ones and any physician stating otherwise should state it explicitly. Physicians are also to contribute to collaboration between different professions to enhance health systems. Physicians are to respect and collaborate with "indigenous patients" as well as work towards improving the general health care of vulnerable and disadvantaged groups.

THE HISTORY OF HEALTH SERVICES IN BAHRAIN

The discussion of the history of the codes of ethics and the regulation of practices in the health care sector in Bahrain can be split into two factors. The first is the agency for promoting such codes and regulations. The second is the comprehensiveness of such codes and regulations relative to content and implementation procedures. Therefore, such history in Bahrain can be described as having gone three phases as follows.

Pre and Post-Independence Era Up to 2009

The first health services rendered in Bahrain were provided in 1892 by a missionary by the name of Samuel Zwemer from a rented room (http://amh.org.bh, American

Mission Hospital, history). The American Mission Hospital was established in 1902. The Victoria Hospital was established two years later by the British Government in India. In 1925, the government of Bahrain opened a small clinic to provide treatment for pearl divers. In this same year, the Bahraini government set up a Directorate for Public Health. After the discovery of oil in Bahrain in 1932, the Bahrain Petroleum Company established a private hospital for their staff in 1937 (Bahrain Medical Bulletin, Vol. 24, No. 4, December 2002). Al-Naim Hospital, the first government hospital, "was inaugurated in intervals from 1940 to 1942" (WHO, 2002, p19). A police force hospital was opened in 1936 and closed in 1941. Salmaniya Medical Complex was inaugurated in 1957 due to population changes and the evolution of the economic sector. Salmaniya Medical Complex is now a teaching and training hospital for the Arabian Gulf University, after being renovated in 1978. Bahrain became of the World Health Organization in 1967 after and has since implemented all its resolutions. The Bahrain Medical Society was formed in 1972, and was registered in 1992, based on resolution No. 1 of 1992, issued by the Minister of Labor and Social Affairs. The resolution stated the objectives of the Society. These objectives are to regulate and monitor the profession, maintain a code of ethics, assist members to find jobs and solve their problems, help to improve and enhance health services, promote health awareness among citizens, cooperate with other societies and clubs, encourage scientific research, cooperate with regional and Arabic medical societies, and promote relationships with medical doctors globally (Resolution No.1 1992, for licensing and re-registering of the Bahrain Medical Society). However, no Code of Ethics was issued by the Society as it was the responsibility of the Ministry of Health at the time.

The Amiri Decree No. (6) of 1972 addressed issues related to practicing medicine in Bahrain. It discussed the issues of licensing and the conditions for a person to grant a license. It stipulated that no patients to be admitted at private clinics which are not a part of a hospital, no general anesthesia operations can be conducted at clinics. It detailed the issues of conflicts of interest for being a doctor and a representative of a pharmaceutical company, and the keeping of patient records. Cases of infectious disease are to be reported to the Ministry of Health in 24 hours. Abortions are to only be allowed when the mothers' life is at risk. It also discussed the attending and management of emergency cases, the passing of medical records upon ending a doctor-patient relationship. It also detailed the doctor's responsibility toward patients in cases of malfeasance, ignorance, and experimenting with no prior approval of ministry of health. This last responsibility, according to the Decree, could lead the physician receiving a warning or a suspension from practice, or to the rescinding of his/her license.

The Amiri Decree No. 7 of 1989 was issued to replace the Amiri Decree No. 6 of 1972 and the Amiri Decree No. 23 of 1986 in relation to private hospitals. In addition to general articles, the Decree of 1986 discussed issues relating to methods of the establishment and management of private hospitals, and the roles and methods of inspection of private hospitals. If a hospital was found to be violating the articles stated, it would suffer punishment. The Decree No. 7 of 1989 consisted of 37 articles, with an overlap between the two Decrees of 1972 and 1989. Articles 1 through 7 were concerned with physicians' license, procedures, and requirements. Articles 8 through 13 explained methods to grant licenses to private clinics. Articles 14 through 34 discussed issues related to a code of ethics but in a simplistic manner and similar to those of Amiri Decree No. 6 of 1972. It added further detail to the articles listed in the 1972 Decree, which included Articles 32, 33, and 34. Article 32 stated that punishment toward a physician should be approved by the Minister of Health and not the Director of Health as there was no minister at that time. An appealing would be allowed in the first two weeks from the date of the verdict. Such period was also referred to in the Decree of 1972. A physician receiving punishment could only re register after two years of the verdict being issued.

The World Health Organization stated that there were many attempts to enhance the role of the Ministry of Health in policy making and regulations. However, there was a plan to establish an independent regulatory body at that time in 2007. This was due to the lack of a national policy dealing with all health issues.

Establishment of a National Health Service NHRA in Bahrain

Due to the lack of a national policy as mentioned by the Health System Profile of Bahrain published by World Health Organization in 2007, an independent body was established by Law Decree No. 38 for 2009. Based on this, the National Health Regulatory Authority assumes the responsibilities related to private hospitals, lawsuits related to practitioners of allied health services and pharmacists, issues governing the practice of medicine and dentistry, the organization and regulation of pharmaceutical centers, and the profession of pharmacy. Royal Decree No. 20 of 2012 reorganized the Board of Directors to consist of seven members: three from the Ministry of Health, three from the private sector, and one representative from the Bahrain Defense Force Hospital. In 2013, after restructuring the Ministry of Health, the Directorate of Pharmacy and Control of Medicine and the Registering and Licensing Office were assigned to the NHRA. The tasks of NHRA can be divided into three categories (NHRA, Annual Report, 2013):

1. Implementation tasks related to licensing and relicensing of health facilities:
    a. Registration of pharmaceutical companies and regulation of prices and licensing of medicines.
    b. Registration of health food and health supplements.

c. Inspections of pharmaceutical centers.
d. Regulation of import and export of chemical ingredients classified as drugs.
e. Licensing and re licensing individuals working in health services.
f. Professional exams to grant licenses for all individuals working in health service.
g. Examining patients' complaints to check on malpractice.
h. Disciplinary acts for violation of the professional laws of health services.
i. Approval of research.

2. Organizational tasks concerned with setting the broader strategy and internal policies for the authority for the period 2011-2014. It involves cooperating with Gulf Cooperation Countries in relation to medicine, setting criteria for importing and using drugs in cooperation with ministries of interior and health. Developing criteria for inspection of hospitals, and criteria for licensing of professionals in the health services and standards to check on patients' complaints.
3. Legal tasks focusing on enacting laws and procedures to cope with the latest international developments, especially pertaining to patients' rights.

The annual 2013 NHRA report explains that there were many challenges encountered by the Authority. The Authority can question private hospitals' practices, but it was unable to investigate practices of public hospitals. Physicians' malpractice was dealt with individually by clearly defined laws but there were no laws to deal with malpractice of health systems and medical teams. There was a lack of laws to regulate the growing alternative medicine sector. The issue of conflicts of interest pertaining to health professionals was not addressed. Previous laws did not address continuous training and education as a requirement for granting licensing. Other challenges included issues relating to pharmacists and pharmaceutical centers, experimental medical research, human resource management, and budget allocated to the Authority.

One of the strategic achievements of 2013 was the collaboration between the Authority and the International Development Ireland (IDI). IDI offered training programs for inspecting staff at the Authority. This collaboration led to the development of criteria, standards, and rules related to general and specialized hospitals. These included inspections of health institutions, primary health care centers, alternative, and traditional medicine centers. It also encompassed licensing for all health service workers including physicians and dentists, and licensing for pharmaceutical centers, as well as the registration of medications in line with GCC criteria. The collaboration further developed the professional code of conduct for physicians and allied services, clinical research, and finally developed steps for dealing with patients' complaints.

The Authority reviewed the earlier laws, regulations, and decrees in relation to private hospitals, and the practice of medicine by non-physicians and non-pharmacists in the allied health services. It regulated the profession of pharmacy and pharmaceutical centers and focused especially on controlled drugs that could impacts mental abilities. The Authority concluded that there was a need for unified licensing, follow-up, inspection, and disciplinary procedures. It stated a need to update and to enact laws and regulations in line with international standards.

The annual report of 2013 summarized their future plans. The first plan was related to allocated budget. The second focused on preparing drafts for improving and updating laws related to the professions of medicine, dentistry, and allied health services. It proposed new laws for private hospitals, pharmaceutical issues, and regulations of medicine. It planned training programs for all individuals working in health services, to be offered starting from January 2015, and to be mandatory in January 2016. At this time the Authority implemented new criteria as prerequisites for licensing and accreditation.

The annual report of 2015 referred to law No. 38 of 2015 decreeing the Supreme Council of Health headed by His Excellency Lieutenant General (Doctor) Sheikh Mohamed Bin Abdulla Al-Khalifa to replace the Board of Directors of NHRA.

The 2015 report reflected the development of the NHRA in terms of their structural progress on one hand, and their future plans on the other. The report was different from the 2013 report. The vision and mission of NHRA were stated clearly in the 2015 report. The vision is stated as "safe, trusted, high quality and effective health care" (Annual Report, 2015, p3). The mission elaborated on the vision and explained that international and scientific standards are applied to governmental and private hospitals to achieve the vision stated. The new organizational structure of NHRA showed the six departments of NHRA. These are: the consultants office, the department of regulations for health services, the department of regulations for health facilities, the department of regulations for pharmaceutical, human and financial, complaints and lastly the department of clinical trials. The 2015 report stated that challenges encountered by NHRA were due to limited budget, lack of human resources and the need for new organizational units e.g. inspection, as well as the need for new for updated resolutions and to develop NHRA's information technology. Opportunities for NHRA stemmed from political support, resolutions differentiating between responsibilities of NHRA and the Ministry of Health, technical expertise, partnerships with private and public institutions, including academic ones, generating financial resources from the services rendered, and finally an audit report defining gaps to be used as opportunities.

Internal work in NHRA was organized by resolutions from the Supreme Council of Health and the Chief Executive. This included a thorough examination of all departments regulating health facilities and their pharmacies centers if any, pharmaceutical issues, health professions in relation to licensing of health workers, the complaints department to develop rigorous procedures for reviewing complaints, the medical devices and equipment department to approve the importing of devices and equipment to meet national standards, clinical research trials and the human resource department to assess current and future staffing requirements.

Based on this examination, NHRA came up with plans to deal with two groups of recommendations to implement. The first group was concerned with the Audit Court of Financial and Administration. The plans for the first group are to review licensing procedures, restudy the NHRA's structure to cope with the needs of the health services improvement, improve inspection capacities, to follow up patients' complaints, activate disciplinary accountability through devising a mechanism to coordinate with prosecution, development of accreditation criteria through registered standards, plan for annual inspections, policies for dealing with complaints, internal rules, and procedures to regulate the work of committees, collaboration with waste companies to organize the disposal of drugs and pharmaceuticals, and finally to expedite drug registration.

The second group of plans focused on 30 items. The most important plans were concerned with developing a strategic plan for NHRA for the coming five years, to spread awareness about NHRA in the media, the establishment of an accountability committee for private health facilities, the proposal of a system to link hours of continuing development for health professional to license renewal, and the issuance of licenses to monitor and regulate alternative and complementary professionals and their centers. One of the major plans was to regulate and develop a code of ethics for health professionals. The annual report of 2015 stated that similar reports will be prepared on a yearly basis to measure progress.

The annual NHRA report of 2016 declared the publication of its strategic plan for 2016-2020. The strategic plan discussed challenges encountered by the NHRA and opportunities to seek. These challenges and opportunities are similar to those listed in the annual report of 2015. The researcher explained that the changes required time to be implemented. However, the vision and mission of NHRA were cultivated leading to the development of its own values. These values are best practices, accountability, fairness, transparency, and independence. The new vision is stated as "Safe and High Quality in the Delivery of Health Care" (page10). The goals of the NHRA were grouped into three categories. The first goal is to regulate accountable health care facilities. Procedures to measure the first goal are concerned with professional licensing, developing a code of ethics, professional development linked to license renewal, regulatory standards in health facilities, pharmaceutical facilities, drug warehouses, factories, and specialized health centers, and the registration and categorization of medicine. The second goal focuses on promoting safe and trusted health services. The indicators for the second goal included accreditation programs, subjecting drugs for testing, regulating clinical research, and developing a committee for ethical research conduct. The last goal concerns health rights relating to malpractice reporting systems, disciplinary committees for different professions and regulations for malpractice insurance.

The report links NHRA goals to the economic vision of the Kingdom of Bahrain for 2030, since the goals and their measures can contribute to achieving the economic vision of 2030. Improving health services for citizens in general and for women and children can contribute to the improvement of the quality of life, and in turn the achievement of Women National Plan. It is important to note that the report of 2016 is the first to explicitly mention the rights of patients. Many resolutions were issued in 2016 related to the NHRA's internal procedures, licensing of professionals, linking continuing development to license renewal, medical device policies, drug registration procedures, developing committees to investigate violations of health professionals, electronic systems for drug registration, and finally, the establishment of National Accreditation for health care. The code of ethics for professionals in health services was still not crystallized in 2016 despite its relationship to NHRA's goals.

NHRA Strategic Goals From 2017-Till Present

The 2017 and 2018 Annual Reports are discussed in this section. The 2017 report is by far the most structured and goal directed in comparison to earlier reports. It is stated that by the end of 2017 NHRA had implemented 84% of initiatives related to the goals identified in 2016. Resolutions issued were related to the renewal of medicine guidelines, pharmaceutical manufacturing, procedures for manufacturing pharmaceuticals locally, pricing guidelines, medical complaints, dental services, a reporting policy for medical complaints, clinical trials and research proxies, an accreditation policy, a privilege policy for neurology, and a professional code of conduct and consent policy. The efforts of previous years are cultivated especially in the professional code of conduct. That is a major target of this research.

16 policies and guidelines were issued according to the report. These included: collaboration and agreements with international companies pertaining licensing, medical devices, and drugs, in order to exchange knowledge, expertise, and services. The number of applications for licensing of new health care facilities was 234 and only 103 received preliminary approval. NHRA issued 51 licenses for new pharmacies. The total applications processed for new licenses were for 82 pharmacies, 504 allied health care professionals, 946 nursing professionals and 492 medical professionals. The procedures for linking continuing development to licensing renewal were implemented. NHRA demanded that it would be mandatory by December 2019 for all medicine in Bahrain to print a barcode on the packaging stating the Global item number, expiry date, and batch number. NHRA approved 6861 out of 8178

applications for medical device licenses. 13 Complementary and alternative medicine centers were registered offering Chinese Medicine, Homeopathy, Chiropractic, Cupping, Naturopathy, and Ayurveda in 2017. NHRA also approved 3022 programs for continuous professional development as requirements for the renewal of health care professionals' licenses. 12 clinical trials were approved.

The 2016 report showed an increase in the numbers of complaints received by NHR: 86 complaints in 2013, 116 complaints in 2014, 137 complaints in 2015, and 171 in 2016. In 2017 the number of complaints reached 237. In 2018 complaints received by NHRA were 228 cases. This is attributed to the efforts of NHRA to spread awareness about NHRA's roles in the media (Annual Report of 2015). This led citizens and patients to realize their rights to investigate malpractices in health services.

The recommendations resulting from an evidence-based review of NHRA's Accreditation Program's principles to promote relationships with health facilities based on "just-culture values, attitudes and practices, continuous partnership, and peer evaluations" were value-added revolving around situations and patients and cost-effectiveness. The first visit for the implementation of the Accreditation program was in May 2017, followed by a subsequent 14 visits. This Accreditation Program seeks to sustain the public trust in health services and to maintain international standards.

One of the future initiatives according to the 2017 Annual Report is to strengthen and develop NHRA's relationship with its stakeholders of clients, pharmaceutical centers, hospitals, professionals and private insurance companies to prepare for a national health insurance system. The NHRA continues to improve procedures and policies to sustain the trust of its stakeholders.

Reviewing version number one of the Code of Professional Conduct issued in 2017 by NHRA shows the following in comparison to the Canadian Code of Ethics of 2018:

The 2017 Code of Professional Conduct issued by NHRA is very comprehensive. It examines seven types of duties. It is the first to elaborate on a code of conduct for health professions and their relationships to patients. It starts with the general duties related to physicians' conduct toward patients, colleagues, themselves, and equipment used. The general duties are divided into ten sections. The first is titled safe care. The second refers to methods to manage adverse events. This is comparable to both the WMA and the CMA code of ethics as discussed above. These codes mandate physicians to prevent harm. However, phrasing and depth of discussion varies. Emergency calls is the third section, which is similar to those of the CMA and the WMA as discussed above. The difference is that NHRA's code gives the right to provide treatment with the no consent for organ protection. The CMA of 2018 states that any sort of help should be provided in case of emergency. The fourth section examines issues related to respect of patients.; discrimination on any basis must be avoided. Physicians are required to protect patients' dignity, provide honest treatment, and allow a second opinion, provide medical reports, continuous care, and respect of views. Conflicts of interest of physicians should be discussed and solved for the interest of patients. The latter should not be a source for personal gain.

The fourth section is referred to in all codes of ethics of the WMA and the CMA as illustrated above. Section five deals with the issue of confidentiality of patient information. Section six elaborates on patients' consent, requiring physicians to provide patients with all relevant information, to empower them to make decisions about treatment and provide consent. Respecting the views of competent patients is highlighted as well. Sections five and section six are well outlined in Codes of WMA and CMA. The Code of CMA however added the methods to deal with cognitive impairment and minor patients. Section seven is called "Beginning of life". Abortion is prohibited legally based on religious principles except in the case of danger to a mothers' life. This was specified in the 1965 Code of ethics of the CMA. However, it is overlooked in the amendments of following years. According to NHRA's Code of Conduct, cloning is prohibited and created embryos should be dealt with respect. This latter statement is not declared in the codes of WMA and CMA.

Section eight pertains to the termination of life. The wishes of dying patients should be treated with respect. The CMA 2018 indicates that patients' life should be respected even when there is no cure. NHRA adds that a member of a team of physicians should explain to family members the situation of the deceased person. Section nine is concerned with infectious diseases and the treatment of carriers with respect. In those cases, the lack of competency of the physician or the lack of health care equipment by a health care provider entails the transfer of the patients to another qualified care provider. Precautions should be taken by physicians, colleagues and others to protect themselves. There is no article referring to such patients explicitly in the Codes of Ethics of the WMA and the CMA. These latter codes emphasize importance of patients' care regardless of illness.

The last section for the first general duties is about transferring patients to another health care provider. This section differentiates between three types of transfer. Delegation means that the physician will remain responsible while another provides health care. The second is referral, which means getting an opinion of an expert. The third stipulates the handover of all responsibilities to the new health care provider. The CMA requires that all information about the patient must be transferred to the new health care provider. Continuous collaboration is demanded as well in referral cases.

The second type of duties focuses on colleagues. NHRA's Code of Professional Conduct is for all professionals in the health services. This section is about relationships between colleagues. Relationships should be based on respect, honesty, maintaining team spirits, avoiding discrimination, bullying, or harassment. Belittling or underestimation of colleagues or their services is unacceptable. This is compatible to the 2017 code of ethics of the WMA. Besides, this second type of duties points out the importance of reporting colleagues for performing poorly, unethically, or unprofessionally to NHRA. There is no similar article for reporting colleagues in the CMA's 2018 code of ethics. However, it is present in the1965 version of the Code of Ethics for the CMA.

The third type of duties is applicable to health care professions. This is congruent without Codes of the WMA and the CMA. The last two codes, as well as that of the NHRA, exhibit the significance of physicians' roles as teachers, learners, peer reviewers, and the exchange of information, and collaboration with colleagues to improve health care. It also explains that there is no financial incentives for patient referral and to testify for verified knowledge. It also accentuates the need for health professionals to seek assistance in case of suffering from physical or psychological problems.

All indicators of these types of duties are in harmony with the Codes of WMA and the CMA in general. These types of duties have three sections. The first section is about the use of social media that results in limiting privacy. This requires professionals to review privacy settings at all times. However, educating the public can be achieved through social media only in one's own professional field of expertise, and professionals should avoid misrepresentation of themselves. Social media is not elaborated on in the Codes of Ethics of the WMA and the CMA. Advertisement is discussed in detail in the 1965 version of the CMA Code of Ethics and referred to in the subsequent versions. This is section two of the third type of duties. Advertising about professions should comply to NHRA guidelines and represent factual information. It should not include fake statements, or patient photos and information. In all instances, advertisements should protect the dignity of the profession.

The third section pertains to the prescription of drugs. It states that drugs prescribed should serve patients, be safe and registered in Bahrain, and addictive drugs should be cautiously prescribed. It discusses the availability of trained professionals and facilities to deal with patients having drugs dependency, and if no such availability is possible, referral of patients is required. The 2018 Code of Ethics of the CMA states that treatment should be evidence-based. Drugs and treatments should neither be overused or underused.

The fourth duty is that of NHRA toward society. It describes the role of professionals in the use of resources, educating the public and providing equitable access to resources. These are some of the roles of physicians cited by the codes of ethics of the CMA and the WMA. The fifth duties are concerned with professionals themselves. This implies that professionals should not over exhaust themselves with work, should limit their work to their expertise, report situations when assistance is not provided, and not perform procedures with no supervision if not competent. They should also seek help if there are problems affecting their capacity to fulfill their duties. The Codes of Ethics of the WMA and the CMA name these duties.

The sixth type of duties is connected to clinical trials. These duties limit participation in research which is officially accepted by the NHRA and its related research committees. In these cases it must be explained to participants the purpose of the research, and to provide enough information to enable them to accept or reject decisions. It requires researchers to provide consent forms signed by participants before launching a trial, to discuss unexpected risks of such trials which might affect their consent, and finally to prioritize the wellbeing of participants over gaining knowledge. These trial duties are reviewed by the CMA Codes of Ethics of 1984 and 2018.

The seventh duty outlines the duties of professionals toward NHRA. These are procedures related to licensing professionals, license renewal, cooperation with NHRA staff and inspectors, acquiring approval of the NHRA for sub-speciality practice, license categories limiting practices, continuous training and education for license renewal, informing the NHRA in case of changes in health care facilities, stopping practice, or any other required changes. The 1965 CMA Code of Ethics explains that physicians should associate with the domestic, regional, and national medical associations like Canadian Medical Associations to advance medicine as a science and an art.

The 2018 Annual Report exhibits the progress in the different sections of NHRA. This progress presents the operational plan to achieve NHRA's goals. The 2018 Annual Report shows that most of the regulations pertaining to the above stated strategic goals were issued in 2017 by the Professional Regulation Section. The system concerned with malpractice insurance is not yet finalized. Regulations to sustain the efficiency and the quality of health care facilities are completed. With respect to pharmaceutical products, NHRA publishes regulations to ensure quality of medicine and health services. However, a system for pharmacovigilance is not yet ready to implement. Regulations for the accreditation of health care facilities are complete and were implemented by 2017. Licensing of health care facilities, however, was completed in 2017 and a second version was published. Committees for ensuring medical accountability and disciplinary investigations for all health care professionals are set and working. However, systems for surveillance of reporting medical errors are incomplete. These are tasks of the Complaints section. Guidelines and committees to permit safe clinical trials, and to manage and run development programs, are issued by the section of Clinical Trials and CPD. The safety and quality of medical supplies are continuously examined. Regulations for medical supplies and device registration were completed in 2017. A surveillance system for medical supplies and devices is slated for readiness by the end of 2019.

The national database system for registering medical devices is still being built. Internal procedures concerning human resources relating to staff performance, budget-based employment, planning for risk assessment, and NHRA's internal policies and procedures are completed. However, organizational structure is still being reviewed by the Civil Service Bureau. The IT system and training programs for NHRA employees are in progress. NHRA completed the systems and regulations for payments for committees and for consultants' visits.

This review of the 2018 Annual Report indicates that the Code of Professional Conduct remains the same. Although, the 2018 report states that NHRA seeks to optimize all tasks performed including the evolution of guidelines, procedures and policies, the review of Code of Professional Conduct is not referred to. This might be ascribed to the fact that the Code developed by NHRA is new. Implementation of this Code may reveal needs for improvement and changes.

CONCLUSION AND RESEARCH PROSPECTIVES

The above review of literature highlights the importance of developing patient-centric relationships. The dimensions of such relationships are based on viewing patients from a totality perspective. This perspective leads to the promotion of equal relationships between patients and doctors, humanizing doctors, and developing therapeutic alliances. The totality perspective does not correspond to the Code of Professional Conduct of NHRA. This can be attributed to the prevailing hierarchical nature of health care professions. However, the six values of the Annual Report of the Health Care Industry (beneficence, non-malfeasance, autonomy, justice, dignity, and trustfulness) are referred to in the 2017 Code of Professional Conduct of NHRA. The review of the latter code illustrates the compatibility to the Codes of Ethics of the WMA and the CMA to a great degree. The 201& Code of Ethics of the CMA exhibits some articles not mentioned by NHRA' s Code of Professional Conduct. These unmentioned articles are related to acknowledging the different conscience of colleagues, realizing the conflicts of interest stemming from competing roles i.e. financial, administrative, research, leadership, organizational and clinical, supporting interdisciplinary team practices, recognizing factors that affect the health of populations and patients. They also omit those articles that go beyond health care and its related practices, discussing collaborative models between physicians to providing health care, focusing attention on the underprivileged, and collaborating with and respecting indigenous patients. The last two articles might not be of context to Bahrain. This is due to the fact that health care at present is free or subsidized.

The above review of the Code of Professional Conduct seems to be comprehensive to a great degree, but it is applicable to all health service workers without specificity, which is necessary in some circumstances. Many of its articles and duties are compatible to the codes of the WMA and the CMA. This explains the need to develop codes of ethics just for physicians, similar to the other codes of ethics reviewed. This is important for two reasons. The first is to highlight the importance of physicians' work as a cornerstone of health services. The second is for the new suggested code of ethics to include points which are underestimated or overlooked by the present codes of professional conduct, based on Pickers' review of 2006. Some of these points are related to the following:

1. Describing and outlining the dimensions of a patient-centric model for physicians to follow. This model is promoted globally. This leads to the second point.
2. Investigating the extent to which patients are practicing autonomy as it is assumed by all codes of ethics reviewed including that of NHRA.
3. Examining the proposition of viewing a person in totality and how patients' practices can reflect such proposition.
4. Elaborating on evidence-based health management.
5. Refining and designing specific codes for professions of different specialties.
6. Involving patients in the development of codes of conduct.

The above stated points can serve as focuses for future research, leading to the enhancement of the present code of professional conduct. The limitations of this can be its strengths. Although it is comprehensive, it might be said to be general as it is applicable to all professions of healthcare. The contribution of IDI in the development of the codes of ethics for health is not found. This does not illustrate the progress of establishing a code of ethics in Bahrain. However, earlier Amiri Decrees discussing the practice of medicine and dentistry are still available.

REFERENCES

Amiri Decree no (6) of 1971 concerning practicing medicine and dentistry. (n.d.). Retrieved from http://www.legalaffirs.bh (in Arabic)

Amiri Decree no(23) of 1986 in relation to private hospitals. Retrieved from http://www.bahrain.net/post1330.html (in Arabic)

Amiri Decree no(7) of 1989 for practicing medicine and dentistry. (n.d.). Retrieved from http://www.legalaffairs.gov.bh (in Arabic)

Canadian Medical Association. (1984). *CMA Code of ethics*. Retrieved from http://www.royalcollege.ca/documents/bioethics/CMA-code-ethics-1984

Canadian Medical Association. (2004). *CMA Code of Ethics*. Retrieved from http://www.ucalgary.ca

Canadian Medical Association. (2018). *CMA Code of Ethics and Professionalism*. Retrieved from http://policy base.cma.ca

Canadian Medical Association Code of Ethics. (1965). Retrieved from http://www.royalcollege.carcsite.bioethics/CMA-code-ethics-1965

Canadian Medical Association Code of Ethics. (1996). Retrieved from http://royal college.ca/rcsite/documents/bioethics/CMA-code-ethics-1996

Canadian Medical Association. (n.d.). Retrieved from en.m.wikipedia.org

Collier, R. (2017). World Medical Association updates ethical code for physicians. *Canadian Medical Ass Journal*. Retrieved from http://cmajnews.com/2017/10/17/world-medical-association-updates-ethical-code-for-physicians-CMAJ-109-5513/

Declaration of Geneva. (1968). Retrieved from http://ethics.iit.edu/encodes/node/4170

General Medical Council. (n.d.). Retrieved from en.m.wikipedia.org

Griffin, R. W. & Moorhead, G. (2014). *Organizational Behavior, Managing people and organization*. Mason, OH: South-Western Cengage Learning.

Illinois Institute of Technology. (2011). Retrieved from http:www.wma.net

Kaba, R., & Sooriakumaran, P. (2007). The evolution of the doctor-patient relationship. *International Journal of Surgery*, *5*(1), 57–65. doi:10.1016/j.ijsu.2006.01.005 PMID:17386916

Ministry of labor and social affairs, resolution no (1) for 1992, in relation to licensing and re registering Bahrain Medical Society. (n.d.). Retrieved from http://www.legalaffairs.gov.bh (in Arabic)

National Health Regulatory Authority. (2013). *Annual report of 2013*. Retrieved from www.nhra.bh (in Arabic)

National Health Regulatory Authority. (2015). *Annual report of 2015*. Retrieved from www.nhra.bh

National Health Regulatory Authority. (2016). *Annual report of 2016*. Retrieved from www.nhra.bh

National Health Regulatory Authority. (2017). *Annual report of 2017*. Retrieved from www.nhra.bh

Picker Institute A review of professional codes and standards for doctors in the UK, USA and Canada. (2006). Retrieved from http://www.picker.org

Riddick, F. A., Jr. (2003). The Code of Medical Ethics of the American Medical Association. *The Ochsner Journal, 5*(2), 6-1.

Stanwick, P. A., & Stanwick, S. D. (2009). *Understanding business ethics.* Pearson Prentice Hall.

Violate, C. (2013). Doctor-patient relationships, laws, clinical guidelines, best practices, medical errors and patient safety. *Canadian Medical Education Journal, 4*(1), e1–e6. PMID:26451192

World Health Organisation Constitution for 1946. (n.d.). Retrieved from en.m.wikipedia.org

World Health Organization. (2007). *Health System Profile Bahrain.* Retrieved from http://apps.who.int/medicinedocs/documents/s17291e

World Medical Association. (1949). *Internationally Code of Ethics.* Retrieved from http://www.cirp.org/library/ethics/intel ode/

World Medical Association, International Code of Medical Ethics. (2018). Retrieved from http://www.wma.net/policies-post/s

Chapter 6
Ethical Green Consumerism of Energy in Bahrain:
The Responsibility of Reducing Energy Use and GHG Emissions

Hanan Naser
https://orcid.org/0000-0002-9062-0603
American University of Bahrain, Bahrain

ABSTRACT

Since ethical green consumerism plays a vital role in stemming global warming, the vast amount of greenhouse gas emissions (GHG) produced in Bahrain has started to bring several ethical and moral issues. As a developing country, the population of Bahrain has lately increased rapidly driving more consumption for energy. In addition, as a tiny economy that aims at improving human quality of life, the use of energy has also been doubled in order to boost economic growth, where the focus on energy efficiency and conservation have been neglected. To tackle this issue, this study provides a review on energy consumption behavior and GHG emissions in Bahrain including sulphur dioxide (SO_2), nitrogen oxides (NO_x), carbon dioxide (CO_2), and particulate matters (PM). The key findings empathize that Bahrain's per capita CO2 emissions were twice the average of the high-income country, and almost five times higher than the world average. Therefore, a significant technological and mental shift towards ethical green consumerism is required.

DOI: 10.4018/978-1-7998-0272-3.ch006

INTRODUCTION

It is argued in literature that the developed countries have not only taken governmental responsibility towards ethical energy consumerism through energy conservation policies, however, the use and daily demand of energy by individuals are decreasing due to their awareness and ethical accountability to reduce greenhouse emission.

On the other hand, this is not the case in most of the developing countries. It is considered that the main duties of these governments are different at this stage where they are still keen about improving human quality of life, which means greater use of energy. In addition, some studies such as Asafu-Adjaye (2000) and Lee (2005), have found that using energy conservation policies are harmful for developing countries' economic growth. This has in fact not only affected the countries' policies, but also individual use of energy and the use of energy efficient technology in the industrial sector.

The human impact on the environment has often been expressed as a product of population, per capita consumption, and technology. In mathematical terms, the equation may be represented as follows: I (impact) = P (population) x A (affluence, or per capita consumption) x T (technology).[1] The core message of this equation is that three factors contribute to our environmental impact-population, consumption, and technology-and that no effort to reduce that impact is likely to succeed unless all three-including consumption-are addressed.

Under the light of the above, the important message that can be grasped is focusing on the relevancy to the global warming and climate change. Precisely, the latest estimation of the United Nations (UN) reveals that the global population has almost reached more than six billion and will peak at a point of time after 2050 to be between nine and ten billion. Although it will decline slowly after that, this huge change in population is making the climate change harder to be addressed (United Nations, 2004). Therefore, the challenge of feeding, clothing, housing, and employing this many people are enormous. It is at least plausible to envision the end of global population growth.

Accordingly, there is a high demand not only on having innovated technology that aim at reducing greenhouse gas emissions, but also having aware people that consume energy ethically in order to help in controlling this crucial problem. People need to understand and deeply believe that their individual ethical consumerism does really matter (Kok et al. 2008). In December 2008, the European Parliament approved legislation to reduce greenhouse gas emissions by 20% from 1990 levels by 2020, to increase renewable energy usage by 20%, and to cut energy consumption through improved energy efficiency by 20%.[2] Even in the United States, unstable energy prices and the current recession have created an environment where it is possible to discuss reduced energy consumption (Dernbach, 2007).

Although there are many gases that may together harm the environment, the most greenhouse gas that has received the most attention is carbon dioxide (CO2). This in fact is due its level in contributing to the increasing problem of global warming and climate change as reported the Intergovernmental Panel on Climate Change (IPCC) in 2001 (Houghton et al., 2001). Another reason is that CO2 emissions have a relatively long residence time in the atmosphere in the order of a century or more (IPCC, 1995).[3] This means that even if net emissions were to be stabilized at current levels there would still be a constant rate of increase for at least two centuries. The reasons why CO2 emissions continue to increase are: (1) the carbon cannot be efficiently filtered or captured as can most other pollutants, (2) the global energy supply relies heavily on fossil fuels (80%) as its main energy source and, (3) while economic growth has been a prerequisite for the reduction of many types of environmental problems the correlation between CO2 emissions and economic growth is the opposite. The latter is problematic and a source of obvious conflict as the reduction of CO2 is not the only target for the international community, governments and individuals. Increasing income levels, improving the quality of the education system, care for the elderly and reducing unemployment, etc. are in many instances considered a higher priority or at least more urgent. There are two principal ways of reducing CO2 emissions by reducing energy consumption. One is energy conservation which aims at reducing the consumption of energy, preferably while maintaining or even increasing utility and performance, the idea behind the Factor 4 and Factor 10 concepts as discussed by Weizsäcker et al., 1998. A second is energy efficiency which involves doing the same amount of work or producing the same amount of goods or services with less energy. These two are different from what is called mitigation options, such as renewable energy and carbon sequestration, because they offer an opportunity for payback of the initial investment through cost savings. They also reduce the demand for fossil fuels, the fastest growing source of greenhouse gas emissions, and can be implemented right away by adopting the ethical green consumerism by industries and individuals.

While there is a growing recognition that a global solution to climate change is necessary to assure that atmospheric concentrations of greenhouse gases do not exceed dangerous levels, nations will need to limit their emissions based upon equity rather than national interest alone to assure that global atmospheric goals are achieved. In fact, climate change raises many civilization-challenging ethical issues (Brown, 2007). Climate change must be understood as creating these ethical challenges because: (1) those who are most responsible for climate change are often separated by great time and space from those who are most vulnerable to climate change impacts; (2) the harms to some may be catastrophic; and (3) achievement of a global solution will require consideration of the interests of others. The ethical dimensions of climate change are also becoming more prominent. The goal of the United Nations Framework Convention on Climate Change is stabilization of greenhouse gas concentrations in the atmosphere at a level that would prevent dangerous anthropogenic interference with the climate system.[4]

While ethical issues associated with energy consumption have received less attention especially in developing countries, this chapter argues that energy efficiency, conservation and mitigation are not simply more options that countries can employ to address climate change; they are entitled to particular ethical consideration for ethical green consumerism by industries and individuals in the world. A whole range of underlying driving forces, including institutions, individual preferences, technologies and economic policies all help to determine not only the consumption patterns but also whether it is ethical or not (Poortinga et al., 2004). According to Liverman et al. 1988, further quantitative analyses and qualitative case studies of specific consumption activities are needed for different regions to understand the patterns and to find out the best solutions for promoting ethical green consumerism for energy. In addition, the Intergovernmental Panel on Climate Change (IPCC) has recently pointed out that there is an obvious need for immediate short-term action.

As Bahrain is one of the developing countries that aims at improving human quality of life and boosting the economic growth of the country by using extra energy, this chapter provides a review on energy consumption behavior in Bahrain with a specific focus on the level of greenhouse gas emission taking into account both technological and ethical challenges.

The study provides at first the background and literature review, followed by a review on energy sector in Bahrain. Then, greenhouse gas (GHG) emissions in Bahrain are discussed. Data and results are provided, where the last section drive the recommendations and policy implications for Bahrain.

BACKGROUND AND LITERATURE REVIEW

Although the ethical consumerism has started to revolute from 1950s, it is still argued that the term is much beyond than what the literature has found yet. To make it easier, the simplest definition of ethical consumerism can be found in making the connections between a product, where that product originated and in what context it has been produced. In another word, consumers need to think before buying any good or service about how their own lifestyle may affect the other people and communities, as well as the environment. This doesn't mean that the consumers should deprive themselves rather than compete with each other to find out the most worthy shopping list among the others. It is about recognizing the power those individual consumers have, as consumers of goods and services, in influencing business to be more sustainable, ethical and accountable.

Accordingly, many studies such as Carrigan et al., 2004; and Low and Davenport, 2007, have investigated the ethical intention of consumers and found that although most consumers are having common sense about the ethical consumption, older consumers should be considered as the target of promoting the ethical consumerism as they share more sensitive social obligations. On the other hand, articles published by Auger and Devinney, 2007, Bray et al., 2011, Carrigan and Attalla, 2001, Carrigan et al., 2011, d'Astous and Legendre, 2009, and Papaoikonomou et al., 2012, have reported that there is a `significant difference between what consumers say about the importance of consumption-related ethical issues and their actual behavior' (d'Astous and Legendre, 2009). This phenomenon has been confirmed by Cowe and Williams (2000), who have built their model using data from the UK. While 30% of UK consumers claimed to espouse ethical standards, only 3% of the examined purchases could reflect those standards! This phenomenon has been labeled the attitude behavior gap (e.g., Boulstridge and Carrigan, 2000).

In addition, Moser and Dilling (2007) have demonstrated that just convincing people that there is a serious environmental problem and providing them with more information did not necessarily lead to have more actions towards ethical consumerism. This implies that although people may make statements indicating an awareness of the arguments in favor using 'bags for life', they will not necessarily do so. Auger and Devinney, 2007 and Carrigan and Attalla, 2001 have suggested that the reason of this gap may be contributed to the social desirability bias which leads to inflated measures of consumers' intentions. Moreover, Griskevicius et al. (2010) found that some people espoused `green' behavior because they wished to appear superior to others and were thus status motivated. However, Carrington et al. (2010) argue that social desirability bias only partially explains the gap. Bray et al. (2011) identify two theoretical approaches to understanding ethical decision making. The first is based on philosophical principles (Vitell et al., 2001) in which individuals make an ethical judgment based on rules/obligations and the consequences of taking action (Bray et al., 2011). This judgment informs both intention and behavior. The second is based on the theory of reasoned action (Ajzen and Fishbein, 1980) and the theory of planned behavior (Ajzen, 1991). Briefly, the theory of reasoned action argues that, in a given situation, behavior is a direct function of intention, which in turn is a function of individual attitudes and subjective (social) norms (Ajzen and Fishbein, 1980).

Later, Ajzen's (1991) has included a further factor that may explains the behavioral control their actions by investigating the individual perceptions of societal pressure and individual control over the action. But the meta-analysis done by Armitage and Conner (2001) has confirmed that the theory of planned behavior was a good predictor of behavioral intentions and a reasonably good predictor of actual behavior. However, even they concede that 80% of the variance in people's behavior was unexplained by factors in the theory. Later authors such as Shaw et al., 2000 has added additional factors to attitude such as ethical obligation and self-identity; however the basic premise of a direct functional link remained. Bray et al. (2011) argued that theory of planned behavior models failed to take into account the attitude-behavior gap which has been identified by earlier empirical studies. A number of more recent studies such as that of Chatizidakis et al., 2007, have attempted to explain the attitude behavior gap by considering not simply the attitude-intention gap, but by also considering the intention-behavior gap. Specifically they have looked for causes and impediments that may prevent the translation of intention into action. Chatzidakis et al. (2007) explored the justifications used by consumers to explain the discrepancy between their attitude and behavior, categorizing them on the basis of Strutton et al's (1994) classification of rationalizations of norm-violating behavior. They identified four types of behavior. The first type named denial of responsibility, which means that there are factors outside the consumer's control that affect consumer's behavior such as cost. The second is the lack of information, where inadequate availability of information or extra promotion can affect the consumption pattern. In addition, appeal to higher loyalties that may be contributed to the financial constraints, convenience, and inferiority of products. Denial of injury or of benefit is also another challenge where many consumers find that changing behavior would overall have little effect on the problem it was intended to solve or would make little difference. D'Astous and Legendre (2009) have attempted to develop a scale for appraising why consumers do not behave ethically used different types of justification: economic rationalism; economic development reality; and government dependency. An economic rationalism argument is one in which consumers think that to behave in a socially responsible manner is more costly to them than the benefits they receive; an economic development reality argument is one in which consumers think that to achieve economic growth and improve / maintain acceptable standards of living, ethical considerations have to be put aside (so costs outweigh benefits at a macro-level); a government dependency argument is one in which consumers take their lead from government cues, in other words if there is no government action to enforce socially responsible behavior it is not viewed as having important consequences. Both Chatzidakis et al. (2007) and d'Astous and Legendre (2009) argue that inclusion of the moderating effect of neutralisation techniques increases the explanatory power of the theory of planned behavior (Ajzen, 1991). D'Astous and Legendre's (2009) framework treats lack of knowledge and perceived ineffectiveness as antecedents to economic rationalization, economic development reality and government dependency justifications for not adopting socially responsible behavior. They argue that these antecedents have a moderating effect on the adoption of such justifications such that they were found to be used less where knowledge about socially responsible behavior and/or consumers' perceived effectiveness (belief their actions would make a difference) were greater. Whilst the studies above are concerned with cognitive justifications stemming from personally constructed rationalizations, other studies suggest more externally influenced barriers. Bray et al. (2011) used focus group data to identify factors impeding ethical behavior despite ethical intentions (i.e., barriers to behaving ethically). They identified seven barriers: price sensitivity, personal experience, ethical obligation, and lack of information, quality of goods, inertia, and cynicism (Bray et al., 2011). In our view, these factors represent a combination of external barriers (for example, price and quality) and neutralization techniques (for example, ethical obligation).

The importance of barriers to ethical consumerism is also demonstrated by Moser and Dilling (2007) who argue that "for communication to facilitate a desired social change, it must accomplish two things: sufficiently elevate and maintain the motivation to change a practice or policy and at the same time contribute to lowering the barriers to doing so". Both Chatizidakis et al. (2007) and d'Astous and Legendre (2009) suggest that an understanding of how consumers use neutralization techniques to justify not changing behavior can be used to formulate appropriate communication strategies which directly address those techniques themselves. Bray et al. (2011) suggest that by developing strategies to reduce the barriers between intention and action sustained behavior change is easier to achieve. They argue that taking this intention-behavior stage into account increases the predictive power of attitude-behavior models.

The term `Green' has become an established concept and is today widely used as a label for a seemingly divers set of products, ideas and phenomena: usually for types of consumption and consumption patterns that from an environmental perspective is considered to be better compared to some alternative, but also for products that from an ethical perspective, for example the welfare of animals is preferred or for phenomenon that fits into the perception of a green sustainable society. Examples of the latter are to purchase locally produced food, recycling, etc. Green is also used as a label for consumers that try to consume in an environmentally conscious manner. In many cases the label is used without any `hard evidence' that the alternative is superior from the point of view that is claimed (Wagner, 1997). Instead of evidence of the end of the line effects on the environment, the use of the term green can rather be derived back to a fundamental idea, an idea which is one of the cornerstones of the `deep ecologists': That humanity is one component in the ecological system and one that does not have special rights over other life forms (Arne Naess, 1984; Castells, 1997). Related to or rather a logical consequence of this postulate spring a whole set of rules for how individuals should live their lives and how society should be organized (Castells, 1997). A radical view is that humans should first of all live by the rules of nature. This in itself means that this green ideology is in opposition to many of the dominant trends in society. Being based on the idea of every life forms equal value for example mean an opposition against the patriarchal society but also in opposition with technocracy, industrialism and even central governance. The green ideology advocate an economy primarily based on domestic production, a focus on quality of life rather than quantitative growth, local rather than central governance but also global thinking. The fundamental version of the green ideology is however only in rare cases the ideology of those who consider themselves environmentally friendly. For most `being green' are only one part of their identity and lifestyle and a part, which is given higher or lower priority, depending on what it is set against – Environmental evolvement is sensitive to the state of the economy. For others, although implicit and sometimes even unconscious, this is the fundamental ideology and driving force but which for practical reasons is not advocated, instead the explicit focus is on smaller components that are considered a positive step towards this utopia.

Being more precise, the ethical green consumerism is an accessible way to engage in pro-environmental, sustainable behavior for a significant portion of the Western industrial population. An operational definition of ethical green consumerism subsumes a list of behaviors that are under- taken with the intention of promoting positive environ-mental effects. Some prototypical behaviors that fall within this rather vague definition are purchasing appliances with energy star labels, buying organic products, or turning off electrical appliances when not in use, and taking shorter showers. Considering consumers' pro-environmental motivations, it is worth asking what effect their green behaviors have on environmental sustainability. If one considers a free market perspective, purchasing `greener' products may be a means for consumers to vote with their pocketbooks, leading to large-scale environmental benefits via systemic policy changes (e.g., car-makers self-instituting policies to manufacture more fuel-efficient cars (see, MacEachern, 2008). From a psychological perspective, recent evidence suggests that relatively low-cost green behaviors such as buying green products might act as a gateway to more significant and more committal pro-environmental behavior, such as habitual recycling or expressing support for alternative energy sources (Thøgersen & Noblet, 2012).

To sum up, the ethical issues with green consumerism, particularly with energy, can be divided into three categories: producers, consumers and policy. Although these categories are not solid and some of the issues will overlap between two or all categories, they are very crucial and can together make a significant impact on environment. Energy producers face ethical issues in the way energy is extracted and produced. All energy sources will involve the transformation of nature. Several energy industries (oil and gas production, mountaintop removal coalmining, uranium mining) contain significant risks such as: toxic chemicals, water contamination, irreversible environmental degradation, destruction of ecosystems, and relocation of communities. These raise important ethical issues that environmental philosophy deals with, such as:

- Are there important values in nature?
- Should we respect nature?
- What is the relationship between humans and nature?
- Is human's part of nature?
- Can we justify extinction of a species to satisfy human desires or needs?

Therefore, as Bahrain is a tiny country that is mainly depending on oil and gas for its revenues and economic growth, taking diversification of economy into account in not the only main concern at this stage, however, government, industry and individual consumers need to pay extra attention to the level of consuming energy in the country and thus maintain the greenhouse gas emissions.

OVERVIEW ON ENERGY SECTOR IN BAHRAIN

Although Kingdom of Bahrain is a small country within the GCC group, it appears to be an interesting case study due to the clear increase in its CO2 emissions which have grown exponentially over the last 30 years. The levels of CO2 emission and fossil fuel consumption over the period 1980 - 2007 increased by 172% and 212%, respectively (calculated based on WDI, 2011). Currently, per capita energy consumption among Bahraini's is one of the highest in the world - it uses two folds more energy per capita than Japan and even more in comparison to some European countries.

In 2007, an average Bahraini consumed 9456 kg oil equivalent of energy. By comparison, Japan and the US have per capita energy uses of 4033 and 7747 kg, respectively. Figure 1 shows per capita energy consumption in Bahrain as compared with neighboring countries (Oman and UAE) and selected developed countries. Such a high consumption rate of energy in Bahrain may have contributed to a high per capita emission level.

Looking at Figure 2, it is clear that energy sector still represents the biggest contribute or to the kingdom's GDP, although its share of the economy has been falling as non-oil sectors continue to drive growth. The kingdom's financial sector represents the second largest contributor to GDP, accounting for 16.5% in 2014, with Bahrain recognized as a pioneer in Islamic finance, having been the first country in the world to introduce and implement rules specific to Islamic banking in 2001. Manufacturing is the third-largest GDP contributor, at 14.4% of the total in 2014, with the kingdom home to one of the world's largest aluminum smelters.

Figure 1. Energy consumption per capita for Bahrain and other selected

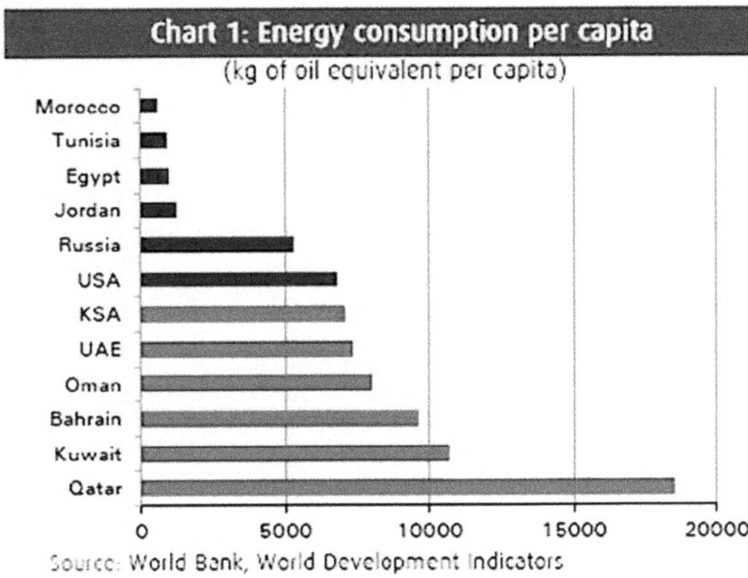

Meanwhile, Bahrain continues to invest in consider able infrastructure upgrades, and these are expected to enhance the kingdom's logistics offerings, as well as help facilitate greater tourism numbers. For its part, tourism has been identified as an area with significant potential for growth, with the Supreme Council for Tourism created to help guide and develop the sector.

Although the global drop in crude oil prices is a concern, the early adoption of economic diversification efforts has created positive growth trajectories in non-oil sectors in Bahrain, such as construction and transport. Hydrocarbons continue to form the bulk of government revenues in Bahrain, with oil and gas accounting for 24.1% of Bahrain's GDP in 2014. Neighbouring Saudi Arabia remains a vital energy partner for the kingdom, and recent Saudi investments in its Eastern Province have benefitted both countries in terms of hydrocarbons processing. Meanwhile in June 2014 Bahrain opened its first solar energy facility in the town of Awali. The 5-MW facility relies on the concept of a smart grid that harvests energy through photovotaic panels dispersed around the city. The most important measure in the energy balance of Bahrain is the total consumption of 11.69 billion kWh per year, where it is with an average of 8,681 kWh per capita.

Bahrain could provide itself completely with self-produced energy. However, the local demand of energy has been increased recently due to many factors such as population growth and increase in electricity demand as summarized in Table 1.

Figure 2. Share of Bahrain's GDP

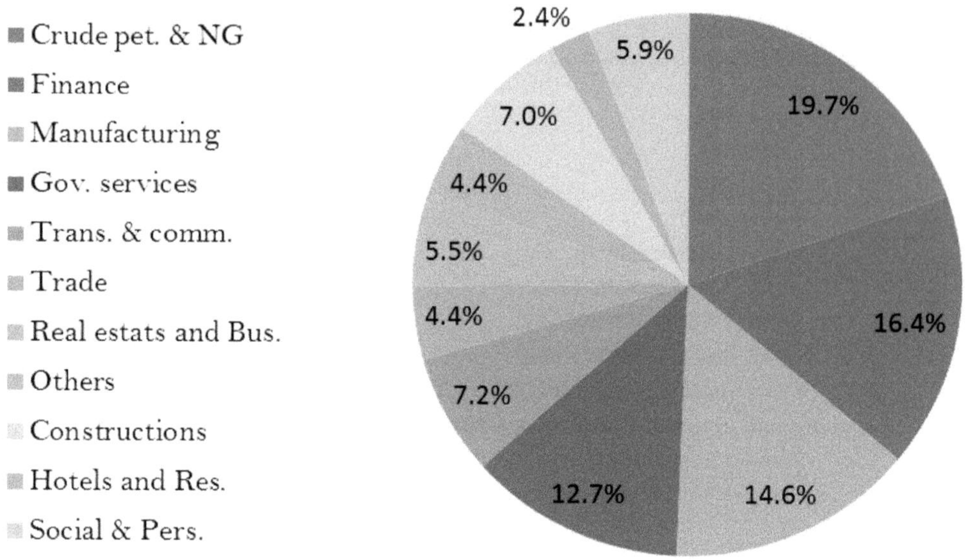

The total production of all energy producing facilities is 13 bn kWh. That's 113% of the countries own usage. Despite this Bahrain trades its energy with foreign countries. Along with pure consumptions the production, imports and exports play an important role. Total per capita energy consumption is 10.8 toe (including about 19 400 kWh of electricity) (2014). Consumption has almost doubled since 2000 and reached 14.8 Mtoe in 2014.

Looking at energy companies, the gas exploration and exploitation activities in the country are managed by Bahrain National Gas Company (BANAGAS), which is owned by the State (75%), Chevron Bahrain (12.5%) and Boubyan Petrochemical Company K.S.C. (BPC) (K.S.C, 12.5%). In general, energy Consumption per capita is 10.8 toe (including about 19 400 kWh of electricity) (2014). Therefore, government of Bahrain is considering developing renewable energies to diversify its power supply.

Despite this, Bahrain is trading energy with foreign countries. Along with pure consumptions the production, imports and exports play an important role. Other

Table 1. Energy statistics for Bahrain

Variables	1990	2013
Energy production (total million metric tons of oil equivalent)	14.3	22
Energy use (fossil fuels \% of total energy use)	100	100
Energy use growth (\%)	4.5	

energy sources such as natural gas or crude oil are also used. The most important measure in the energy balance of Bahrain is built on the macro level where the total consumption is the most and almost main measure. With a glance on the data provided by Electricity and Water Authority provided in Table 2-6, it is revealed that the total consumption of 26.11 billion kWh of electric energy per year.[5] Per capita this is an average of 17,493 kWh.

Bahrain could provide itself completely with self-produced energy. The total production of all electric energy producing facilities is 27 bn kWh, which is 103% of the countries own usage.

In 2013 countries around the world saw particularly high average temperatures. Indeed, 2013 was one of the hottest years on record, with the combined global land and ocean surface temperature 0.62°C above the 20th century average, according to the US National Oceanic and Atmospheric Administration. Despite the warm weather and increased use of air conditioning, Bahrain was able to avoid a prolonged energy crisis. Peak usage for 2013 in Bahrain occurred in September, when electricity demand reached 2917 MW. During the previous summer, peak demand also reached

Table 2. Energy balance in Bahrain

Electricity	Total	Bahrain/ Capita	Compared to Europe/ Capita
Own Consumption	26.110 bn kWh	17493.15 kWh	5514.73 kWh
Production	16.810 bn kWh	17962.14 kWh	5929.23 kWh
Import	276.00 m kWh	184.91 kWh	730.42 kWh
Export	213.00 m kWh	142.71 kWh	708.32 kWh

Table 3. Energy balance in Bahrain - Electricity

Electricity	Total	Bahrain/ Capita	Compared to Europe/ Capita
Production	16.81 bn kWh	17962.14 kWh	5929.23 kWh
Import	276.00 m kWh	184.91 kWh	730.42 kWh

Table 4. Energy balance in Bahrain – Crude Oil

Crude Oil	Barrel	Bahrain/ Capita	Compared to Europe/ Capita
Production	45000.000 bbl	0.030 bbl	0.005 bbl
Import	226200.00 bbl	0.152 bbl	0.020 bbl

Table 5. Energy balance in Bahrain – Natural Gas

Natural Gas	Cubic meters	Bahrain/ Capita	Compared to Europe/ Capita
Production	15.89 bn m^3.	10645.97 m^3.	904.00 m^3.
Import	15.89 bn m^3.	10645.97 m^3	456.91 m^3

over 2900 MWh, according to World Bank figures. However, peak usage is a fraction of the kingdom's 6600 MW of electrical power generation capacity. Bahrain relies on 4000 MW of public sector power generation and 2000 MW from independent power producers (IPPs). A final 600 MW worth of electricity is imported from the GCC's interconnection grid, which allows for member states to swap electricity with one another to help meet peak demand. Thus, the k's total power generation and importation capacity is still roughly twice its demand. The brief power outages speak to the need for an upgrade to transmission lines, rather than a lack of power generation cacity. Yet, with Bahrain's economy growing steadily and an array of new industrial projects in the planning stage, the country is moving ahead with plans to build more power plants to stay on top of future demand.

The World Bank data shows that by 2020 energy demand within the kingdom will reach 19,706 GWh. Until then, Bahrain is expected to experience a monthly peak demand of 4312 MW. Domestic electricity demand is growing by 7-10% per annum, which is driven by a housing program, population growth and the needs of the industrial sector. To meet the growing demand, Bahrain has launched ambitious plans to expand power generation capacity, which calls for phase two of the Al Ddur independent water and power project (IWPP), as well as the construction of new, smaller power plants. When the Al Dur expansion is completed in 2016, where another 1200-1500 MW of power is generated by this expansion. Bahrain also has three new power plants in where Figure 3 shows the yearly power generation by each of them.

From here, it is very important to analyze the usage of the energy in even more details. Therefore, the Sustainable Energy Unit of Bahrain has attempted to collect more data on the micro level and found that most of the electricity is used by the households with approximately 46%, where the commercial and industrial sectors use around 34%, and 17%, respectively, see Figure 4.[6]

Buildings consume nearly 40% of energy demand and account for around one third of greenhouse gas emissions globally. Energy efficiency initiatives deployed in buildings have long lasting implications because buildings last for 40-50 years or more. As such, if known energy efficiency best practices are implemented, global building energy demand could be reduced by one-third by 2050.

Figure 3. Yearly Power Generation per Station in Bahrain

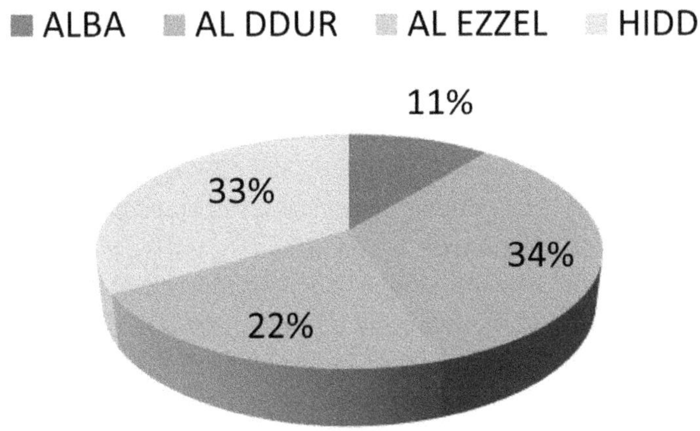

Residential properties represent around 76% of Bahrain's housing stock, with commercial buildings accounting for around 17%. Total housing demand (Bahraini and non-Bahraini) is expected to increase to 263,536 housing units in 2020 and to 346,718 in 2030, from a current stock of 145,181 in 2013. The residential and commercial sectors therefore have high potential for significant energy efficiency improvements.

There are two major energy efficiency opportunities for the residential and commercial sectors in Bahrain; first to significantly reduce the electricity used in buildings and second, to improve the thermal efficiency of buildings. The two are inextricably linked. Inefficient appliances and lighting generate heat, and inadequate

Figure 4. Grid Electricity Consumption by Sector, 2014

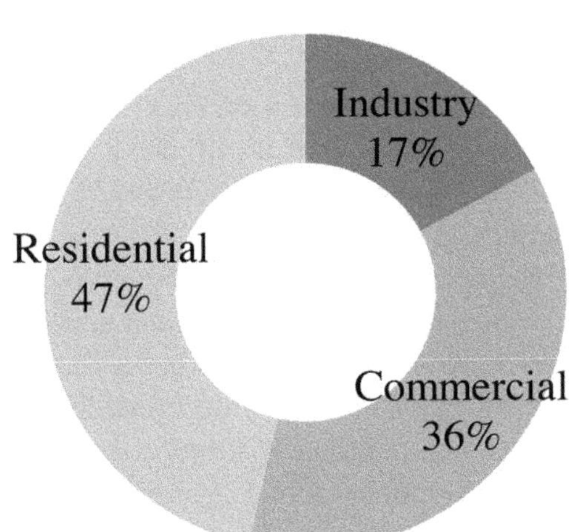

thermal insulation allows heat from outside to enter the building. These three sources of heat place an extra load on the air conditioning system, which requires significant electricity during the summer months.

New build, or renovation, creates the opportunity to improve efficiency by building to a higher standard, and by introducing more efficient equipment. Alternative modes of cooling can also be considered, where technically and economically feasible, such as converting to district cooling instead of using standalone air conditioning.

The residential sector used most of the grid electricity, at 49.5% of total grid consumption, during the baseline period. The commercial sector was the second-largest user, accounting for 36.6% during the same period.

This massive use of energy on the local level has obviously increased the level of greenhouse gas emissions (GHG) in the country, and therefore, intensive works have been done to investigate the level of many different emissions in Bahrain in order to find the right solutions towards the ethical green consumerism of energy, which includes both concerns: energy conservation and energy efficiency.

GOVERNMENT INITIATIVES FOR SUSTAINABLE ENERGY

Government of the Kingdom of Bahrain is in line with the United Nations Development Program (UNDP) by being committed to the sustainability of the country's natural resources for future generations, as well as the protection of the environment.[7] There is considerable potential for undertaking energy efficiency and renewable energy initiatives in Bahrain, which will extend the lifetime of oil and gas reserves, and enable long-term sustainable development. Bahrain's Economic Vision 2030 puts special emphasis on providing incentives for reducing and managing electricity demand and investing in clean energy technologies; promoting energy efficiency standards to ensure sustainability; and ensuring better energy and water demand management.

Indeed, Bahrain has been a pioneer on the way to a more sustainable future. The Kingdom was one of the first countries to install utility-scale wind turbines on a new commercial development, the iconic World Trade Center in 2008; and Bahrain was the first country in the GCC to have a district cooling system. There are already several private sector renewable energy systems in operation; and a number of initiatives are underway to facilitate more efficient energy use.

In order to unify and consolidate efforts on energy efficiency and renewable energy, the Sustainable Energy Unit (SEU) was established in November 2014. The Sustainable Energy Unit is mandated to develop strategies and policies for the integrated planning of energy sources in the Kingdom, as well as the rationalization of energy use, and to raise efficiency in all sectors through coordination with all concerned parties. To this end, the Sustainable Energy Unit, in consultation with key stakeholders, has formulated the National Renewable Energy Action Plan and the National Energy Efficiency Action Plan, which were endorsed by the Cabinet (resolution no. 2384-08).

These plans are an important milestone in setting out Bahrain's national targets for renewable energy deployment and the adoption of energy efficiency initiatives. As such, they represent the Kingdom's efforts to deliver the sustainable energy transition envisioned in the Economic Vision 2030 and the Government Action Plan 2015-2018. The plans also represent the implementation of the Kingdom's regional and international commitments under the Paris Agreement, the United Nations Sustainable Development Goals, and the League of Arab States Renewable Energy Framework and Guidelines on Energy Efficiency.

The initiatives within the plans, with the support of leadership across all ministries, and from key stakeholders and members of society, will enable the Kingdom's sustainable future. By working together, Bahrain can achieve its sustainable energy objectives, which will benefit the Kingdom economically and environmentally.

GREENHOUSE GAS EMISSIONS IN BAHRAIN

Energy production and consumption throughout the world are facing serious environmental crisis and which create challenges for growing in most countries, especially for developing countries like Bahrain. The main two important environmental consequences for electricity production are global warming and acid deposition. Examples of health effects are decrease respiratory resistance to infections and heart disease.

Thermal power plants are one of the most significant sources of pollutant producer as a result of burning fossil fuels. Thus, from green ethical point of view, thermal power plant must be equipped with proper control emission systems in order to reduce pollutions. However, emission reduction is adding costs, but considering environmental and maintenance of equipment losses, then the cost is reasonable.

In Bahrain, approximately 77% of the emissions are associated with the combustion of fossil fuels or the release of fugitive emissions from oil and gas operations. Industrial processes accounted for about 11% of all GHG emissions, followed by the waste sector, which accounted for about 12% of total emissions.

The environmental emissions associated with fossil fuels combustions are considered the worst where the main harmful are Carbon Mono Oxide (CO), Sulphur dioxide (SO_2), Nitrogen Oxides (NO_x), Carbon dioxide (CO_2), Hydro Carbon (HC) and Particulate Matters (PM), as shown in Figure 4, where has different negative environmental and health impact as shown in Table 6.

Figure 5. GHG associated with fossil fuel combustion

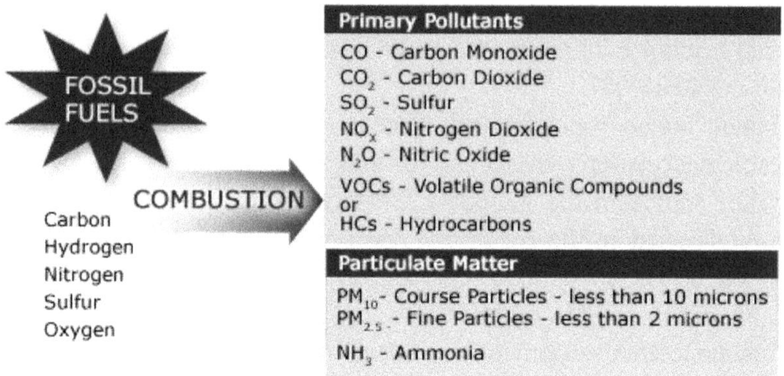

While greenhouse gas emissions (GHG) that contribute significantly to the climate change is a serious risk to the Kingdom of Bahrain, as well as the rest of the world, the most greenhouse gas that has received the most attention from scientists and researchers is the carbon dioxide (CO2). This in fact is due to its level in contributing to the increasing problem of global warming and climate change as reported the Intergovernmental Panel on Climate Change (IPCC) in 2001.[8]

Although Bahrain makes relatively minor contributions to global greenhouse gas emissions, Bahrain's per capita emissions are amongst the highest in the world and continue to trend upwards as shown in Figure 6 below. In 2013, Bahrain's per

Table 6. Environmental and health impact of Emissions

Pollutant	Health Concerns	Environmental Effects
CO	Decreases Oxygen amount to human body as it enters the blood. High content can cause, visual loss, slow learning capability and reduced physical skills.	
NOx	Irritate lung and decrease respiratory resistance to infections.	Contributes to ozone distortion and can have negative effects to earth and marine systems.
SOx	Breathing, sicknesses, reduction in lung resistance and heart disease.	Contributes in acid rains, monuments and buildings corrosions, decrease visibility
PM	Damage respiratory systems and lung, cancer, and death.	Damage materials in the form of acids and decreases visibility.

(Azidet et al., 2000)

Figure 6. Comparison of CO2 emission

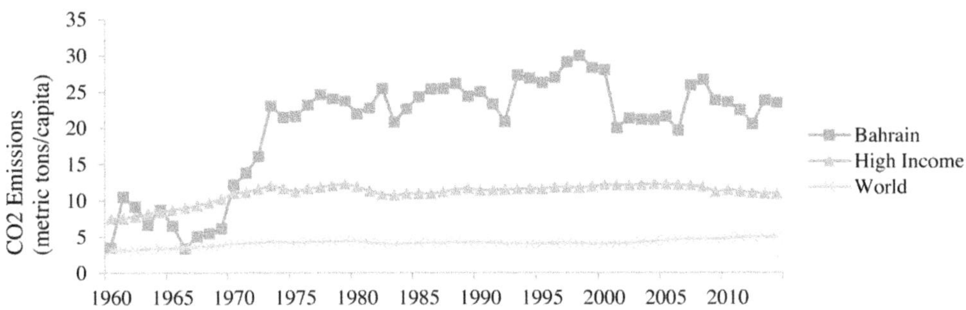

capita CO2 emissions were twice the average of the high-income country, and almost five times higher than the world average. Relatively high per capita emissions are attributed to Bahrain's small land size, population density, harsh climate conditions, scarcity of water resources, and heavy reliance on energy intensive desalination plants. Implementing energy efficiency and renewable energy policies has high potential to reduce the Kingdom's greenhouse gas emissions.

Where the latest records shown in Table 7 show the comparison records of Bahrain's and Europe per capita of carbon footprint:

Reducing the growth in Bahrain's CO2 emissions requires resources to be consumed as efficiently as possible taking into account both energy conservation and energy efficiency tips among all industries and households, which is in another words; thinking more ethical towards green consumerism. Being green consumerism can help the Kingdom will not only help in stimulating more efficient use of electricity, but also optimizing the use of indigenous gas resources, decreasing peak electricity demand, and promoting investment, employment and innovation in energy efficient products and services. For more investigation, this research collected and analyzed hourly data on the major pollutants in Bahrain as shown in the nest section.

Table 7. Carbon footprint in Bahrain

Carbon Footprint	CO_2 in 2014	Bahrain/ Capita	Compared to Europe/ Capita
Total	31.34 m t	21.00 t	5.39 t
• of which diesel + gasoline	2.210 m t	1.480 t	2.23 t
• of which natural gas	28.38 m t	19.01 t	1.31 t
• other sources	748068.00 t	0.500 t	1.86 t

DATA AND RESULTS

In order to achieve the goal of this study, a set of data is collected from an independent power station for a number of major pollutants in Bahrain including: Sulphur dioxide (SO_2) in ppm, Nitrogen Oxides (NO_x) in ppm, Carbon dioxide (CO_2) in ppm, and Particulate Matters (PM) in mg/ m3. Since CO_2emissions contribute largely to global warming, which is considered the major cause of all other changes in earth's climate, this study pay a selective attention to this critical measure. To be precise, data is collected from one running gas turbine after machine startup. It is not similar to experimental data collection where all influencing independent variables kept constant and changing one of them to see the effect on dependent variable. All variables are collected on hourly basis for 24 hours per day for 301 days (July, 2016), which accounts for over 700 observations. All the series were transformed into natural logarithm to stabilize variances and reduce heteroscedasticity. Table 8 shows the descriptive statistics of the data.

By plotting the collected time series data as shown below in Figures 7, 8, 9, and 10 it is clear that there are periods where the GHG reach its peak level. These peaks are specifically in the afternoon, and late night, where the demand for electricity becomes very high. This is in line with the report of the Sustainable Energy Unit (2017) where the report suggests that Bahrain has two daily peaks in consuming electricity: the first peak occurs between 11:00 and 16:00, and the second occurs between 18:00 and 19:00. On a typical summer day (30 August 2015), the first peak consumption occurred at 13:39 reaching 3,441 MW, and the second peak occurred at 18:36 reaching 3,189 MW. These numbers are compared with electricity consumption during a typical winter day (30 January 2015), when the first peak occurred at 12:06 reaching 1,137 MW, and the second peak occurred at 18:09 reaching 1,208 MW. This in fact has a significant impact on environmental challenges that faces Bahrain and the rest of the world. Therefore, many tips are needed in order to increase the

Table 8. Descriptive Statistics

Variables Description	SO_2 Emissions (ppm)	NO_x Emissions (ppm)	CO_2 Emissions (ppm)	PM Emissions (m/m3)
Mean	34.289	11.376	2.9710	15.201
Std. deviation	14.289	2.3440	6.0280	9.1760
Minimum	9.8620	0.0000	1.0155	0.0000
Maximum	100.00	29.230	100.00	48.519
obs	720	720	720	720

Figure 7. Plot of SO2 emissions in Bahrain (July, 2016)

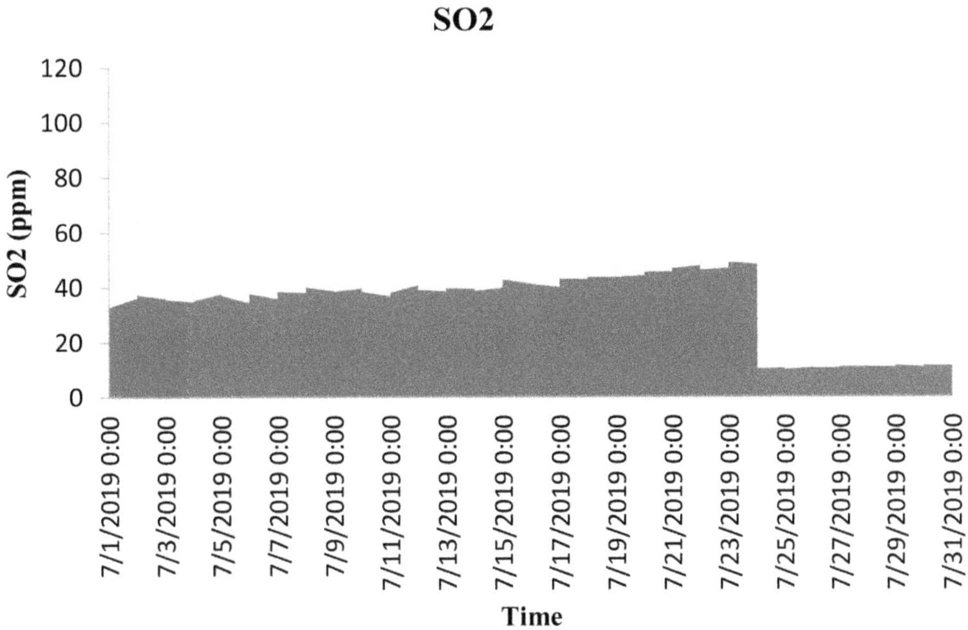

awareness among the households and industries in order to consider the efficient use of energy for sustainable development.

RECOMMENDATIONS AND POLICY IMPLICATIONS

This study has shown that developed countries in particular have an obligation to be more ethical towards green consumerism and thus reduce energy consumption. However, we argue that although developing countries have an obligation to reduce energy consumption from existing uses of energy, the use and the consequences on environment are still high. The Convention and traditional ethics begin from somewhat different starting points. The Convention would have countries reduce greenhouse gas emissions to avoid or minimize dangerous human interference with the climate system. A basic touchstone for traditional ethics, at once more general and more challenging, is to do no harm. Neither the Convention nor traditional ethics provides an exact statement of the required reduction in energy consumption. Still, an outline of required efforts under the Convention is discernible.

As a tiny developing and high income country, Bahrain should focus on the ethical green consumerism and reduce energy use through efficiency and conservation to the extent it is cost effective. They should help foster models of the good life that are

Figure 8. Plot of NOx emissions in Bahrain (July, 2016)

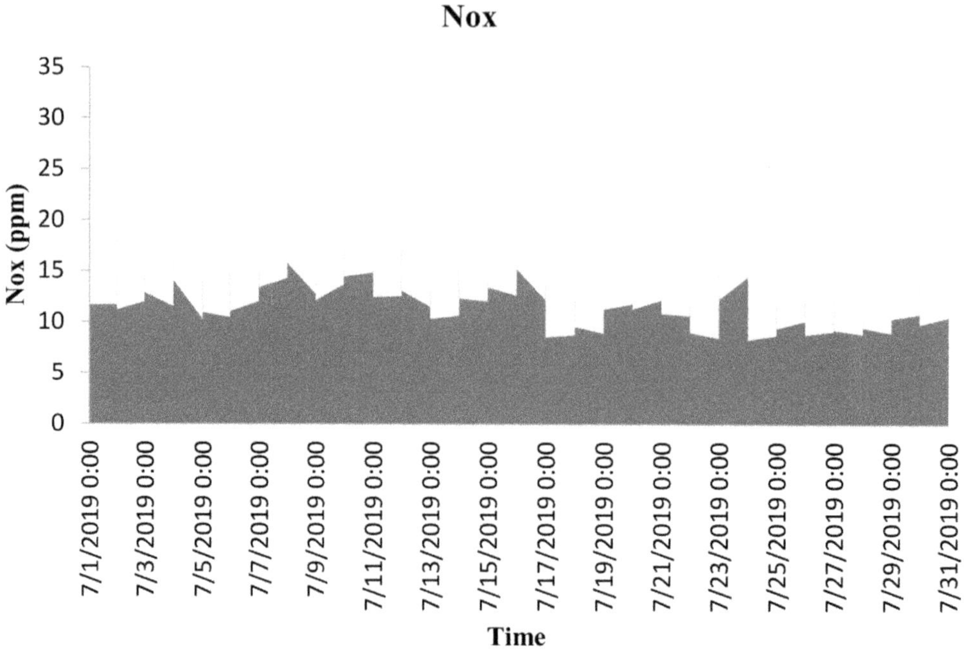

Figure 9. Plot of CO2 emissions in Bahrain (July, 2016)

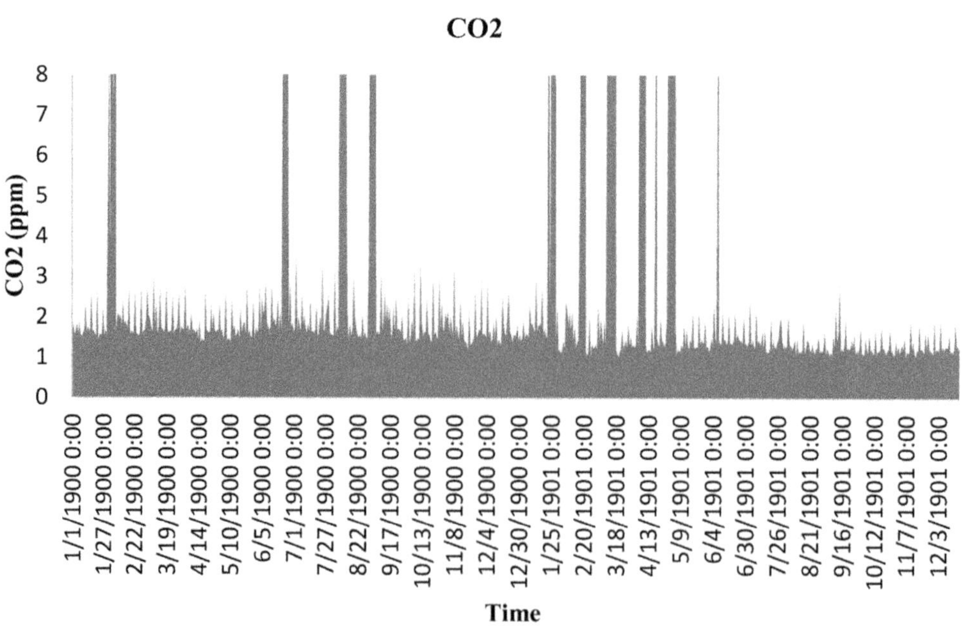

Figure 10. Plot of PM Emissions in Bahrain (July, 2016)

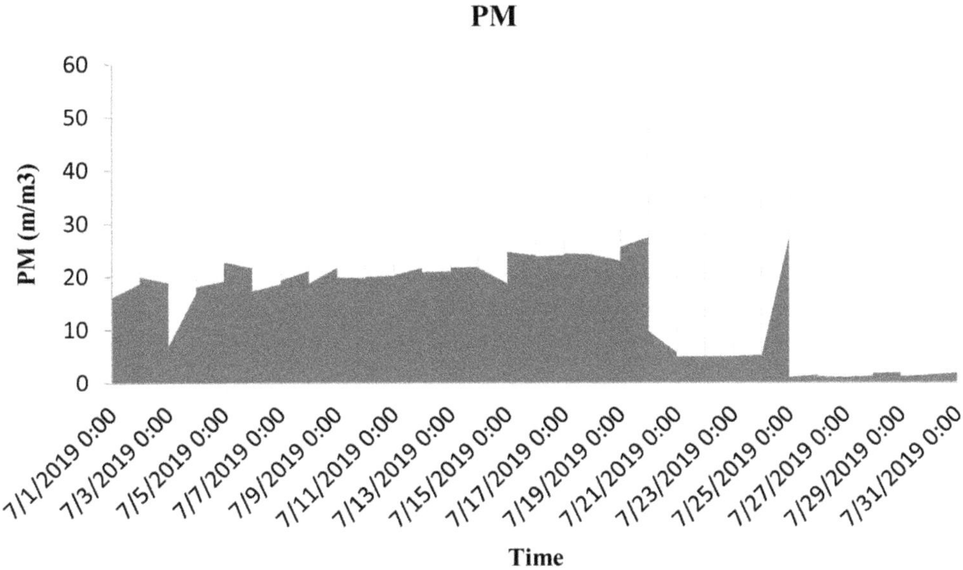

based on much lower energy consumption levels. And they should address climate change in ways that foster sustainable development-through job creation, cost savings, and the like-and reduce adverse impacts of climate change in developing countries. These provide a framework that national governments could employ to address energy consumption. Traditional ethics, by contrast, provides a more basic message: reduce unnecessary consumption; where this exactly what does ethical consumerism means.

The Convention's principles would apply to sub-national governments, corporations, individuals, and others, but only to the extent required by national governments. And they are likely to be less compelling, especially to individuals. The obligation from traditional ethics to reduce energy consumption, by contrast, applies to individuals and others regardless of the enactment of national legislation, and is more likely to be understood by individuals.

Although, the government of Bahrain has taken a number of critical steps to shift the country towards more efficient consumption of energy, there are still many other steps that may accelerate the actions of industry and individual households to act more ethical in consuming energy. For example, implementing electricity and transport subsidy reforms, and introducing important regulations, such as minimum energy performance standards for air conditioners and lighting products.

Paying more attention for the households in Bahrain may not only increase energy efficiency and conservation behavior but also frees households' money for spending on other goods and services, or for savings and investments. Therefore, a public program to raise awareness and disseminate information on energy efficiency complements the other initiatives proposed by increasing relevant knowledge and support amongst all stakeholders, including households and businesses. Information about the financial, environmental, and social benefits of energy efficiency can be communicated in various ways, such as via social media, mass media campaigns, pamphlets and stickers, and in-person interactions (including seminars, workshops, and presentations). The Awareness Raising initiative will focus on energy use, habits, and behaviors, and target energy-consuming equipment and appliances. Any efforts will not replace communication campaigns already under way, but instead complement them.

In more details, the households may be more ethical in consuming energy using efficient electrical devices for cooling, lightening, refrigerators, water heaters, water cooling systems, washing machines and electric ovens. This can done by understanding minimal helpful tips especially for cooling as Bahrain has a very hot weather:

1. Keeping the thermostat set of the air conditioner at 24 degrees celsius or higher, and on `auto', not `on'. Each degree can mean up to 9% savings on cooling costs.
2. Any central or room air conditioner more than 10 years old, can double the cooling costs.
3. Using ceiling fans to circulate air can make the feeling more comfortable at higher thermostat settings.
4. Cleaning or replacing the air conditioner filter monthly makes it more efficient.
5. Using drapes, shades, awnings and reflective materials can significantly reduce the heat entering through glass.
6. Applying weather stripping and caulking around all doors and windows help in keeping the chilled air inside your house.

In addition, pursuing energy efficiency, Bahrain's government should calls for implementing energy efficiency regulations and investment in technologies that reduce carbon emissions, minimize pollution and promote sustainable energy. In clear recognition of the benefits of energy efficiency, Bahrain should foster the development of low-carbon energy initiatives by unlocking the Kingdom's energy efficiency potential.

Under the `Environment and Urban Development' pillar, the government made commitments to improve the efficiency of electricity. To achieve this, it is recommended that the government seeks to:

1. Increase education and awareness to reduce the waste of electricity by promoting ethical green consumerism
2. Adjust the cost of services and encourage the take up of technologies geared towards rationalization
3. Work on the adoption of smart distribution mechanisms, where possible and appropriate, in order to improve the management of energy resources
4. Develop building regulations to contribute to the rationalization of electricity consumption in all new buildings.

REFERENCES

Ajzen, I. (1991). The theory of planned behavior. *Organizational Behavior and Human Decision Processes*, *50*(2), 179–211. doi:10.1016/0749-5978(91)90020-T

Armitage, C. J., & Conner, M. (2001). Efficacy of the theory of planned behaviour: A meta-analytic review. *British Journal of Social Psychology*, *40*(4), 471–499. doi:10.1348/014466601164939 PMID:11795063

Asafu-Adjaye, J. (2000). The relationship between energy consumption, energy prices and economic growth: Time series evidence from Asian developing countries. *Energy Economics*, *22*(6), 615–625. doi:10.1016/S0140-9883(00)00050-5

Auger, P., & Devinney, T. M. (2007). Do what consumers say matter? The misalignment of preferences with unconstrained ethical intentions. *Journal of Business Ethics*, *76*(4), 361–383. doi:10.100710551-006-9287-y

Azid, I. A., Ripin, Z. M., Aris, M. S., Ahmad, A. L., Seetharamu, K. N., & Yusoff, R. M. (2000, September). Predicting combined-cycle natural gas power plant emissions by using artificial neural networks. In *2000 TENCON Proceedings. Intelligent Systems and Technologies for the New Millennium (Cat. No. 00CH37119)* (Vol. 3, pp. 512-517). IEEE. 10.1109/TENCON.2000.892319

Boulstridge, E., & Carrigan, M. (2000). Do consumers really care about corporate responsibility? Highlighting the attitude—behaviour gap. *Journal of Communication Management, 4*(4), 355-368.

Bray, J., Johns, N., & Kilburn, D. (2011). An exploratory study into the factors impeding ethical consumption. *Journal of Business Ethics*, *98*(4), 597–608. doi:10.100710551-010-0640-9

Brown, D. (2007). Ethical Dimensions of Climate Change. *Proc Environmental Ethics Policy Conference*.

Carrigan, M., & Attalla, A. (2001). The myth of the ethical consumer–do ethics matter in purchase behaviour? *Journal of Consumer Marketing*, *18*(7), 560–578. doi:10.1108/07363760110410263

Carrigan, M., Moraes, C., & Leek, S. (2011). Fostering responsible communities: A community social marketing approach to sustainable living. *Journal of Business Ethics*, *100*(3), 515–534. doi:10.100710551-010-0694-8

Carrigan, M., Szmigin, I., & Wright, J. (2004). Shopping for a better world? An interpretive study of the potential for ethical consumption within the older market. *Journal of Consumer Marketing*, *21*(6), 401–417. doi:10.1108/07363760410558672

Carrington, M. J., Neville, B. A., & Whitwell, G. J. (2010). Why ethical consumers don't walk their talk: Towards a framework for understanding the gap between the ethical purchase intentions and actual buying behaviour of ethically minded consumers. *Journal of Business Ethics*, *97*(1), 139–158. doi:10.100710551-010-0501-6

Castells, M. (1997). An introduction to the information age. *City*, *2*(7), 6–16. doi:10.1080/13604819708900050

Chatzidakis, A., Hibbert, S., & Smith, A. P. (2007). Why people don't take their concerns about fair trade to the supermarket: The role of neutralisation. *Journal of Business Ethics*, *74*(1), 89–100. doi:10.100710551-006-9222-2

Cowe, R., & Williams, S. (2000). *Who are the ethical consumers? Ethical Consumerism Report*. Co-operative Bank.

d'Astous, A., & Legendre, A. (2009). Understanding consumers' ethical justifications: A scale for appraising consumers' reasons for not behaving ethically. *Journal of Business Ethics*, *87*(2), 255–268. doi:10.100710551-008-9883-0

Dernbach, J. C. (2007). Stabilizing and then reducing US energy consumption: legal and policy tools for efficiency and conservation. *Environmental Law Reporter*, *37*, 8-26.

Fishbein, M., Jaccard, J., Davidson, A. R., Ajzen, I., & Loken, B. (1980). Predicting and understanding family planning behaviors. In *Understanding attitudes and predicting social behavior*. Prentice Hall.

Griskevicius, V., Tybur, J. M., & Van den Bergh, B. (2010). Going green to be seen: Status, reputation, and conspicuous conservation. *Journal of Personality and Social Psychology*, *98*(3), 392–404. doi:10.1037/a0017346 PMID:20175620

Kapur & Graedel. (2002). Production and Consumption of Materials. *Stumbling Toward Sustainability, 63*(67).

Kok, M., Metz, B., Verhagen, J., & Van Rooijen, S. (2008). Integrating development and climate policies: National and international benefits. *Climate Policy, 8*(2), 103–118. doi:10.3763/cpol.2007.0436

Lee, C. C. (2005). Energy consumption and GDP in developing countries: A cointegrated panel analysis. *Energy Economics, 27*(3), 415–427. doi:10.1016/j.eneco.2005.03.003

Liverman, D. M., Hanson, M. E., Brown, B. J., & Merideth, R. W. Jr. (1988). Global sustainability: Toward measurement. *Environmental Management, 12*(2), 133–143. doi:10.1007/BF01873382

Low, W., & Davenport, E. (2007). To boldly go… exploring ethical spaces to re-politicise ethical consumption and fair trade. *Journal of Consumer Behaviour: An International Research Review, 6*(5), 336–348. doi:10.1002/cb.226

MacEachern, D. (2008). *Big green purse: use your spending power to create a cleaner, greener world.* Penguin.

Moser, S. C., & Dilling, L. (2007). Toward the social tipping point: Creating a climate for change. *Creating a climate for change: Communicating climate change and facilitating social change*, 491-516.

Naess, A. (1984). A defence of the deep ecology movement. *Environmental Ethics, 6*(3), 265–270. doi:10.5840/enviroethics19846330

Papaoikonomou, E., Valverde, M., & Ryan, G. (2012). Articulating the meanings of collective experiences of ethical consumption. *Journal of Business Ethics, 110*(1), 15–32. doi:10.100710551-011-1144-y

Poortinga, W., Steg, L., & Vlek, C. (2004). Values, environmental concern, and environmental behavior: A study into household energy use. *Environment and Behavior, 36*(1), 70–93. doi:10.1177/0013916503251466

Sachdeva, S., Jordan, J., & Mazar, N. (2015). Green consumerism: Moral motivations to a sustainable future. *Current Opinion in Psychology, 6*, 60–65. doi:10.1016/j.copsyc.2015.03.029

Shaw, D., Shiu, E., & Clarke, I. (2000). The contribution of ethical obligation and self-identity to the theory of planned behaviour: An exploration of ethical consumers. *Journal of Marketing Management, 16*(8), 879–894. doi:10.1362/026725700784683672

Strutton, D., Vitell, S. J., & Pelton, L. E. (1994). How consumers may justify inappropriate behavior in market settings: An application on the techniques of neutralization. *Journal of Business Research, 30*(3), 253–260. doi:10.1016/0148-2963(94)90055-8

Thøgersen, J., & Noblet, C. (2012). Does green consumerism increase the acceptance of wind power? *Energy Policy, 51*, 854–862. doi:10.1016/j.enpol.2012.09.044

Vitell, S. J., Singhapakdi, A., & Thomas, J. (2001). Consumer ethics: An application and empirical testing of the Hunt-Vitell theory of ethics. *Journal of Consumer Marketing, 18*(2), 153–178. doi:10.1108/07363760110386018

Wagner, S. A. (2002). *Understanding green consumer behaviour: A qualitative cognitive approach.* Routledge. doi:10.4324/9780203444030

Weizsäcker, E. U., Lovins, A. B., & Lovins, L. H. (1998). *Factor four: doubling wealth-halving resource use: the new report to the Club of Rome*. Earthscan.

ENDNOTES

1 For more information, read Kapur and Graedel (2002).

2 Available at: https://eurlex.europa.eu/LexUriServ/LexUriServ.do?uri=OJ:L:2009:140:0136:0148:EN:PDF

3 Intergovernmental Panel on Climate Change (IPCC), 1995, Second Assessment Report — Climate Change: http://www.ipcc.ch/pdf/climate-changes-1995/ipcc-2nd-assessment/2nd-assessment-en.pdf

4 More details are available at: https://unfccc.int/resource/docs/convkp/conveng.pdf

5 For more information, visit: http://www.ewa.bh/en/Network/Electricity/Statistics/2018/Pages/Yearly-Power-Generation-Per-Station.aspx

6 For more information visit: http://www.seu.gov.bh/wp-content/uploads/2018/04/02_NREAP-Full-Report.pdf

7 This would involve improving energy efficiency and enhancing international cooperation to facilitate more open access to clean energy technology and more investment in clean energy infrastructure. Plans call for particular attention to infrastructure support for the least developed countries, small islands and land-locked developing countries.

8 See https://www.ipcc.ch/site/assets/uploads/2018/07/WG1_TAR_FM.pdf

Chapter 7
Fair Trade and Ethical Consumerism:
A Complementary Perspective

Amal Nagah Elbeshbishi
United Nations Economic Commission for Africa, Morocco

Ebtihaj Ahmed Al A'ali
University of Bahrain, Bahrain

ABSTRACT

Fair trade is directed toward enhancing the satisfaction of stakeholders (i.e., producers, employees, consumers, environmental interest groups, and others). Ethical consumerism employs fair trade to fulfill different objectives related to consumers, environmental, and human resources issues. Fair trade can uphold ethical consumerism as well. This chapter attempts to highlight the interwoven relationship between fair trade and ethical consumerism. The chapter argues that ethical consumerism and fair trade are inseparable. Benefits and beneficiaries of ethical consumerism and fair-trade overlap. Gender issues reflecting women's work and employment are discussed as a reflection of fair trade. Policy recommendations on gender issues are stated at the end of the chapter.

INTRODUCTION

Trade is widely viewed as a catalyst for economic growth and sustainable development, it has been one of the key transformational forces of our time, often associated with creating major opportunities for poverty reduction.

DOI: 10.4018/978-1-7998-0272-3.ch007

Fair trade is a change agent, it promotes a new way of being, and it works because it is about involving people throughout the whole system in deciding on and making this change. It is a global movement made up of a diverse network of producers, companies, shoppers, advocates, and organizations putting people and planet first, its expansion often improves women's formal employment opportunities due to the increase in labour intensive exports from developing countries. Fair trade empowers people to make choices for the good of themselves and their community, regardless of gender, status, position in society, or position on the globe. Fair trade appears to offer a promising way for producers and consumers to challenge conventional market mechanisms.

The fair-trade symbol is displayed on the packaging, certifying that the production and marketing processes respect fair trade standards. The label is additional to other labelling information requirements, such as quality classification and origin, which are governed by the normal statutory rules. By buying products carrying a fair-trade label the customer can help improve the living and working conditions of producers in developing countries.

This chapter examines the issue of fair trade in relation to ethical consumerism, both issues are contemporary and relatively complex. Ethical culture leading to ethical consumerism can increase profit and trade is argued to induce economic growth and sustainable development. The purpose of this chapter is to illustrate the interwoven relationship between fair trade and ethical consumerism. The second section discusses the concepts of ethical consumerism and fair trade in an attempt to highlight similarities and differences. Benefits and barriers of ethical consumerism and fair trade are examined in section three. Section four discusses fair trade as a challenge to unfair global trading relations and investigates roles of Fair Trade Organization and World Fair Trade Organization. Women and fair trade are considered in section five. Finally, the chapter concludes and discusses the policy recommendations.

CONCEPTS OF FAIR TRADE AND ETHICAL CONSUMERISM

This section elaborates on the definitions of fair trade and ethical consumerism. The purpose of this elaboration is to highlight similarities and interwoven nature of fair trade and ethical consumerism.

Concepts of Fair Trade

The most commonly cited definition of fair trade comes from the European Fair-Trade Association (2006), which notes the following:

"Fair trade is a trading partnership, based on dialogue, transparency and respect that seeks greater equity in international trade. It contributes to sustainable development by offering better trading conditions to, and securing the rights of, marginalized producers and workers – especially in the South. Fair Trade organizations (backed by consumers) are engaged actively in supporting producers, awareness raising and in campaigning for changes in the rules and practice of conventional international trade".

Based on its definition, fair trade had three strategic intents to:

1. Work with marginalized producers and workers to help them move from a position of vulnerability to security and economic self-sufficiency;
2. Empower producers and workers as stakeholders in their own organizations; and
3. Actively play a wider role in the global arena to achieve greater equity in international trade.

Fair Trade is the most important and fastest growing market-based mechanism to improve the lives of producers in developing countries. It does so by offering small-scale producers in the global south fairer trade relations, including a guaranteed minimum price above world price and developmental support, hence it is a practical model for alleviating global poverty.

Fair trade, a key theme in the area of ethical consumption, has been subject to considerable research in marketing, as the debate evolved around its character as either a politically motivated anti-capitalist movement or a new market-driven consumption trend (Nicholls and Huybrechts, 2016). One of the pioneers of the fair-trade movement - Carol Wills - stated on a conference in the European Parliament in June 2005 that: "Fair Trade works! It works for poor people; it works for consumers. It works as a business model; it works as sustainable development; it works to protect the environment; it works as an idea!" (Fair Trade Advocacy Newsletter, 2005). By inspiring sustainable business practices, education, and fair prices while also providing measures to prevent child labor, the fair-trade movement is dramatically changing the lives of primary producers. As millions of hardworking farmers from all over the world sell more goods through fair trade, they will make a huge positive impact on the economic development of their countries.

A product with the Fair Trade Certified seal indicates that it was made according to rigorous social, environmental, and economic standards. Not all trade is fair! Farmers and workers at the beginning of the chain don't always get a fair share of the benefits of trade. Fair trade enables consumers to put this right. This emphasizes the role of consumerism in promoting ethics.

The objective of fair trade is to ensure that producers receive a price which reflects an adequate return on their input of skill, labour and resources, and a share of the total profit commensurate with their input.

Fair trade labels are awarded to goods imported from developing countries which have been produced according to social and environmental criteria based on international instruments such as the ILO (International Labour Organization) Conventions and the United Nations' Agenda 21 recommendations. The criteria cover for example, such things as employment conditions, controls to prevent pesticides from contaminating rivers and drinking water, and the protection of natural ecosystems. Appropriate criteria are established for each product by international organizations such as FLO (the Fair-Trade Labelling Organization), who are also responsible for monitoring and control of producers and traders applying to use fair trade labels to ensure that the conditions are strictly respected.

Concepts of Ethical Consumerism

Ethical consumerism refers to buyer behaviour that reflects a concern with the problems of developing countries, where producers are paid low wages and live in poor conditions simply to produce cheap products for developed countries' consumers and profits of multinational companies. Ethical consumers purchase products produced in the developing countries by people paid a fair wage, who work in good conditions and who benefit directly from the profits made. Ethical consumerism incorporates all the principles of environmental consumerism and more- taking on board the "people" element of ethical consumerism. "Fairly traded" products are those products purchased under equitable trading agreements, involving co-operative rather than competitive trading principles, ensuring a fair price and fair working conditions for the producers and suppliers.

The features contributing to the growth of fair trade and ethical consumerism form an integrated, self-perpetuating model. The themes behind the rise of ethical consumerism and the diffusion of fair trade values include increased levels of information available to help ethical consumers to make informed decisions; the existence of an increasing number of fair trade substitutes to traditional products and a shift in values towards concern for developing countries' sustainable development.

Weeden (2008) illustrates that there is no consistency in relation to the definition of ethical consumers, and there is a lack of studies examining the characteristics of ethical consumers. Ethical consumerism researches focus on intentions and attitudes. Weeden (2008) explains that fair trade and ethical consumerism have common concerns. Trade occurs when two participants agree to exchange goods and services on terms that each participant views as beneficial for himself. Trade has ethical value when it reflects and manifests these individuals' free choices to promote their mutual interests. For an increasing number of consumers in affluent societies, the social features of products- such as decent living and working conditions for producers in developing countries- are important ethical criteria in their shopping strategies. Researches on fair trade consumers historically are related to ethical consumerism. Weeden (2008) elaborated that some studies attribute the success of fair trade to ethical consumerism. She stated that consumers demand a say in all stages along the value chain from producing, processing and buying raw materials to final products sold. Motives for ethical purchasing can be categorized as religious, spiritual, social, environmental and political. These motives are concerned with the consequences of acts of purchasing.

Ethical consumerism is called ethical consumption as well. Crane and Matten (2016) argue that the phenomenon of ethical consumption has been around for centuries. This phenomenon however has received more attention and more focus since 1990s. The consumption is ethical as it is covering different activities including environmental concern, social values, fair trade products, recycling products, organic products, boycotting products produced by children, human resources and gender issues. Al A'ali and Al-Sarraf (2016) illustrate that "ethical consumerism is a decision-making process reflecting consumers' social values" (p. 138). Decision making process is characterized by considering other issues stated beyond self-interest. There are two influences affecting the ethical decision-making processes (Crane & Matten, 2016). The first group of influences is pertaining to individuals making decisions. The second group of influences is concerned with issues being examined and contextual or situational issues linked to ethical issues. Fair trade as stated earlier can be viewed as a strategy of ethical consumerism. There are three beliefs underpinning fair trade. Producers declare unity of consumers firstly. The present practices of the world trade leads to unjust distribution of wealth secondly. Thirdly, producers in developing countries receiving a fair price for their products can promote sustainable development (en.m.wikipedia.org). Ferrell, Fraedrich and Ferrell (2015) illustrate that ethical culture is a dimension of corporate culture standing for the unique norms and values for every organization individually. The values and norms underpin ethical reasoning. Ethical reasoning can support ethical decision-making processes. This leads to the promotion of ethical culture (Crane & Matten (2016), Ferrell, Fraedrich & Ferrell (2015)). Ethical culture through the positive reputation of a given business can contribute to three major benefits. The first promotes trust and commitment of employees. The second benefit nurtures trust and therefore loyalty of investors. The last develops consumers' trust and satisfaction leading to the enhancement of ethical consumerism. These benefits generate profits for businesses.

Ethical consumerism is an activity to influence the world. Fair trade is a tool of consumerism through which learning of the world issues are made. These issues are related to workers' rights, animal protection, sustainable development, fair trade in term of deals, farmers' rights, gender issues and child labor. This is to argue that people are more valuable than profit (Waterford One World Centre, 2018). Worcester (2000) illustrates factors shaping behavior of consumers. He said that such factors based on ranking as customer services as number one then outlets convenience and internet, image of brand, treatment of employees, environmental impacts, social and environmental policies and providing support to the community. He adds that the most important criteria used to judge companies' public i.e. consumers are employees' treatment firstly, social responsibility secondly, and thirdly environmental responsibilities. This is based on views of the public. Corporate responsibility consists of being trustworthy citizen, ethical consumerism, sourcing from overseas, community and employees' involvement. A summary of the different facets of ethical consumerism is summarized in table 1 below.

BENEFITS AND BARRIERS OF FAIR TRADE AND ETHICAL CONSUMERISM

Based on the above-mentioned concepts of fair trade and ethical consumerism it can be argued that different if not all stakeholders are served. Investors, employees, consumers, governments, communities and interest groups are all attempted to aid.

Benefits of Fair Trade and Ethical Consumerism

Both ethical consumerism and fair trade emphasize cooperation rather than competition in dealings at all stages of value chain from production to selling the final products. In this section, the overlap of benefits of ethical consumerism and fair trade reveals the interwoven nature of the relationship. A summary of benefits is discussed below.

Protecting the Environment

Fair trade as stated above is a tool of ethical consumerism that promotes environmentally friendly practices, such as improving soil and water quality, prohibiting harmful chemicals and encouraging biodiversity. Fair trade co-operatives provide training to farmers, and can support them to adapt to climate change and convert to organic production. In fact, over 50 per cent of all fair trade certified producers are also certified as organic.

Many co-operatives invest the fair-trade premium in environmental sustainability, such as providing more resilient crops to farmers struggling to cope with outbreaks of pests and diseases, or planting new trees to protect soils and indigenous wildlife.

Raising Living Standards

Consumers through environmental sustainability and green consumerism help farmers and producers receive fair payments for their effort. Consumers' movements started in the 19th and 20th centuries. The movement focused on treatment of labor by companies, food labeling requirements, drugs and cosmetics concerns. In USA in 1898 National Consumers League was formed. In UK Consumers Council was established in World War One for that time workers were not treated fairly (en.m.wikipedia.org).

Fair trade as an ethical consumerism tool, can improve economic sustainability and increase living standards for farmers and workers. The premium often goes towards living expenses that farmers and workers would otherwise have to pay themselves, such as school fees, that frees up money to use for other things, including food. Producers can also use the premium for projects to generate other food sources. For workers, subsidized food loans can offer a valuable lifeline during lean months.

Small scale farmers in the developing world suffer from poor market access and unfair international trade rules such as tariffs and rich countries' subsidies, they frequently do not share the benefits of global trade. Fair trade works with these disadvantaged farmers since it ensures that the price they get for their crop covers the cost of sustainable production and allows them to plan. Fair trade also aims to protect workers' rights to decent pay, a safe working environment as well as the right to join a trade union.

Improving Productivity and Quality

Ethical consumerism reflects positive acts and behavior of consumers. It is related to labor conditions. Organic products and green consumerism are choices to improve quality and productivity.

Farmers can earn more and protect the environment by improving the amount and quality of their crops, through technical support and better farming practices. Being part of fair trade means that co-operatives can learn more about their buyers and the importance of quality. They often use the premium to supply farmers with tools and equipment or shared facilities to improve quality and reduce wastage, resources often out of reach for individual farmers.

Stronger and Inclusive Businesses

Ethical consumerism as shown in table 1 above and based on the definition stated earlier attempts to develop win-win relationships. This includes producers and farmers. For this fair trade's endeavor can be said to be part of ethical consumerism's attempts.

Fair trade enables farming groups to become stronger businesses, with better leadership and governance. They can build strong relationships with different markets, reducing their dependency on just one buyer and boosting their confidence to negotiate. Making joint investments as a co-operative often improves their access to credit too.

Being part of the fair-trade network also means producers can share their knowledge and learn from others. Fair trade is 50 per cent owned by the farmers and workers themselves, which means they are part of the most important decisions about what fair trade does. Fair trade also works to strengthen the position of women in agriculture.

Making Life Better for Communities

Ecologically and socially concerned consumers look for products that do not affect the ecology negatively. Recycling can lead to the improvement of communities and assist to generate finance to use in different projects.

The premium means farmers and workers can invest in their communities – such as improving schools, paying teachers' salaries or providing bursaries for school fees. Other premium projects often include building roads and better healthcare, from new clinics and immunization programs to improving access to water.

Despite the benefits stated above, both ethical consumerism and fair trade may encounter barriers to implement. The barriers must be taken into consideration at the time of designing and implementing of ethical consumerism and fair trade.

Worcester (2000) stated that ethical consumerism encounters five barriers to implement. The barriers are seemed to relate to availability of information to consumers, ethics is not a corporate concern, education and age affecting perceptions of knowledge available, money issue in relation to size of family, other concerns related to reputation, brand and quality of products and services. Weeden (2008) expounds that consumers perceive dimensions of products purchased differently, many of products dimensions are not readily available to be grasped, which leads to confusion experienced in relation to ethical issues and motives for purchasing decisions. This can affect fair trade purchases.

FAIR TRADE AS A CHALLENGE TO UNFAIR GLOBAL TRADING RELATIONS

In the 1960s, there was an emerging theoretical argument that trade agreements were often crafted on terms unfavorable to countries in the Global South, which exacerbated inequality and poverty. Brown (2006) reported that those often perceived to be "left behind" were well integrated into global trade agreements. It was believed that the terms of trade, not the lack of trade, created the conditions for certain countries to be left behind and to share inequitably in the distribution of global wealth. The world had been divided into rich and poor, remarked Barratt Brown (1993) in his groundbreaking fair-trade text, and trade had driven the wedge between the two regions. Thus, an intellectual underpinning of fair trade stems from dependency theory, a body of literature that argues that resources are directed from the Global South to the Global North, thereby relegating the former to a persistent condition of so-called underdevelopment.

The deconstruction of free-trade theory and the assertion that it cannot deliver what it promises deepened the theoretical underpinning of fair trade. Michael Barratt Brown noted that rural producers do not benefit from free trade because several market failures are endemic to the free-trade system and that the neoliberal assumption of a level playing field is erroneous. These market failures are the norm rather than the exception. He blamed market failures on large transnational companies that dominate agricultural markets because they have access to finance, and they can easily switch from one supplier to another.

Two major organizations were established to protect producers, traders and consumers against unfair trading relations are discussed below.

Fair Trade Organization (FTO)

Consumers' movement started in 1891 in USA and in 1898 National Consumers League was formed. During First World War United Kingdom established Consumers Council. The ethical Consumer Research Association focuses on five areas of research. These five areas of focuses are environmental including pollution, climate change, nuclear power firstly. Secondly focuses on workers' rights, supple chain policy, unethical marketing and human rights. Thirdly the research is related to factory farming, and animals' rights. The fourth area of research in concerned with activities related to politics i.e boycotting, genetic engineering, ethos of companies. The last area of research is about sustainability of products. This is related to fair trade, features of environment and organic. (http://en.wikipedia.org/wiki/Ethical-consumerism).

A Fair-Trade Organization, also called an Alternative Trade Organization (ATO), has fair trade as part of its mission and at the core of its objectives and activities. Fair Trade Organizations follow the Fair-Trade principles. They are actively engaged in supporting producers, trading, raising awareness of fair trade issues and advocating the integration of fair trade principles into all international trade practices.

Examples of Alternative Trade Organizations are Asha Handicrafts Association (India), Undugu Fair Trade Limited (Kenya), Level Ground Trading Ltd (North America and Pacific Rim), CIAP Intercrafts Peru SAC, Pachacuti, Oxfam and Traidcraft (Europe).

World Fair Trade Organization (WFTO)

The World Fair Trade Organization is a global network of Fair Trade Organizations and WFTO associates representing the supply chain from producer to retailer.

WFTO prescribes ten principles that Fair Trade Organizations must follow in their day-to-day work and carries out monitoring to ensure these principles are upheld.

Principle One: Creating Opportunities for Economically Disadvantaged Producers

Poverty reduction through trade forms a key part of the organization's aims. The organization supports marginalized small producers, whether these are independent family businesses, or grouped in associations or co-operatives. It seeks to enable them to move from income insecurity and poverty to economic self-sufficiency and ownership. This is related to concern of ethical consumerism to value chain. It is stated earlier that consumers would like to have a say over every stage of the value chain.

Principle Two: Transparency and Accountability

The organization is transparent in its management and commercial relations. It is accountable to all its stakeholders and respects the sensitivity and confidentiality of commercial information supplied. The organization finds appropriate, participatory ways to involve employees, members and producers in its decision-making processes. It ensures that relevant information is provided to all its trading partners. For ethical consumerism, this is a requirement as stated above.

Principle Three: Fair Trading Practices

The organization trades with concern for the social, economic and environmental well-being of marginalized small producers and does not maximize profit at their expense. It is responsible and professional in meeting its commitments in a timely manner. Suppliers respect contracts and deliver products on time and to the desired quality and specifications.

Fair trade buyers, recognizing the financial disadvantages faced by producers and suppliers of fair trade products, ensure orders are paid on receipt of documents or as mutually agreed.

The organization maintains long term relationships based on solidarity, trust and mutual respect that contribute to the promotion and growth of fair trade. It maintains effective communication with its trading partners. Parties involved in a trading relationship seek to increase the volume of the trade between them and the value and diversity of their product offer as a means of growing fair trade for the producers to increase their incomes.

Fair trade recognizes, promotes and protects the cultural identity and traditional skills of small producers as reflected in their craft designs, food products and other related services. As mentioned above fair trade is a strategy of ethical consumerism. Weeden (2008) shows that some argue that the success of fair trade is attributed to ethical consumerism.

Principle Four: Fair Payment

A fair payment is one that has been mutually negotiated and agreed by all through on-going dialogue and participation, which provides fair pay to the producers and can also be sustained by the market, considering the principle of equal pay for equal work by women and men. The aim is always the payment of a local living wage. Fair payment is made up of fair prices, fair wages and local living wages. This is a concern of workers' rights in relation to ethical consumerism.

1. **Fair Prices:** A fair price is freely negotiated through dialogue between the buyer and the seller and is based on transparent price setting. It includes a fair wage and a fair profit. Fair prices represent an equitable share of the final price to each player in the supply chain.
2. **Fair Wages:** A fair wage is an equitable, freely negotiated and mutually agreed wage, and presumes the payment of at least a local living wage.
3. **Local Living Wages:** A local living wage is remuneration received for a standard working week (no more than 48 hours) by a worker in a particular place, sufficient to afford a decent standard of living for the worker and her

or his family. Elements of a decent standard of living include food, water, housing, education, health care, transport, clothing and other essential needs including provision for unexpected events.

Principle Five: Ensuring No Child Labour and Forced Labour

The organization adheres to the UN Convention on the Rights of the Child, and national/ local law on the employment of children. The organization ensures that there is no forced labour in its workforce and/ or members or homeworkers. Human rights in general is a priority of ethical consumerism. Besides workers' right is focus of human rights. Child labor is a concern of ethical consumerism which might lead to political acts explained above.

Organizations who buy fair trade products from producer groups either directly or through intermediaries ensure that no forced labour is used in production and the producer complies with the UN Convention on the Rights of the Child, and national/ local law on the employment of children. Any involvement of children in the production of fair trade products (including learning a traditional art or craft) is always disclosed and monitored and does not adversely affect the children's well-being, security, educational requirements and need for play.

Principle Six: Commitment to Non-Discrimination, Gender Equity, and Women's Economic Empowerment, and Freedom of Association

Ethical consumerism is about social responsibility, human rights and workers' rights. Human rights are about eliminating discrimination of all kinds especially in relation to rights of workers. This is seen in the effort of WFTO to promote fairness and equality.

The organization does not discriminate in hiring, remuneration, access to training, promotion, termination or retirement based on race, caste, national origin, religion, disability, gender, sexual orientation, union membership, political affiliation, HIV/ AIDS status or age.

The organization has a clear policy and plan to promote gender equality that ensures that women as well as men can gain access to the resources that they need to be productive and also the ability to influence the wider policy, regulatory, and institutional environment that shapes their livelihoods and lives. Organizational constitutions and by-laws allow for and enable women to become active members of the organization (where it is a membership based organization), and to take up leadership positions in the governance structure regardless of women's status in relation to ownership of assets such as land and property. Where women are employed within the organization, even where it is an informal employment situation, they receive equal pay for equal work. The organization recognizes women's full employment rights and is committed to ensuring that women receive their full statutory employment benefits. The organization considers the special health and safety needs of pregnant women and breast-feeding mothers.

The organization respects the right of all employees to form and join trade unions of their choice and to bargain collectively. Where the right to join trade unions and bargain collectively are restricted by law and/or political environment, the organization will enable means of independent and free association and bargaining for employees. The organization ensures that representatives of employees are not subject to discrimination in the workplace.

Principle Seven: Ensuring Good Working Conditions

Worcester (2000), stated that employees' treatment and environmental and social policies have a great impact on shaping consumerism. Supply chain from producers is a concern of ethical consumerism. Fair trade as a strategy focuses on the issues of producers and workers' rights.

The organization provides a safe and healthy working environment for employees and/ or members. It complies, at a minimum, with national and local laws and ILO conventions on health and safety.

Working hours and conditions for employees and/ or members (and any homeworkers) comply with conditions established by national and local laws and ILO conventions.

Fair Trade Organizations are aware of the health and safety conditions in the producer groups they buy from. They seek, on an ongoing basis, to raise awareness of health and safety issues and improve health and safety practices in producer groups.

Principle Eight: Providing Capacity Building

The organization seeks to increase positive developmental impacts for small, marginalized producers through fair trade. It develops the skills and capabilities of its own employees or members. Organizations working directly with small producers develop specific activities to help these producers improve their management skills, production capabilities and access to markets - local / regional / international / fair trade and mainstream as appropriate. Organizations which buy fair trade products through fair trade intermediaries in the South assist these organizations to develop their capacity to support the marginalized producer groups that they work with.

Principle Nine: Promoting Fair Trade

The organization raises awareness of the aim of fair trade and of the need for greater justice in world trade through fair trade. This is an objective of ethical consumerism as well. It advocates for the objectives and activities of fair trade according to the scope of the organization. The organization provides its customers with information about itself, the products it markets, and the producer organizations or members that make or harvest the products. Honest advertising and marketing techniques are always used.

Principle Ten: Respect for the Environment

It is shown that environment is a focus for ethical consumerism and its related research. Sustainability of resources are at the centre of attention of ethical consumers. Recycling of products, Organic and energy issues are at the heart of researches of ethical consumerism.

Organizations which produce fair trade products maximize the use of raw materials from sustainably managed sources in their ranges, buying locally when possible. They use production technologies that seek to reduce energy consumption and where possible use renewable energy technologies that minimize greenhouse gas emissions. They seek to minimize the impact of their waste stream on the environment. Fair trade agricultural commodity producers minimize their environmental impacts, by using organic or low pesticide use production methods wherever possible.

Buyers and importers of fair trade products give priority to buying products made from raw materials that originate from sustainably managed sources, and have the least overall impact on the environment.

WOMEN AND FAIR TRADE

The development of opportunities for women is one of the underlying principles for the fair-trade movement. Fair Trade organizations include respect for women in their criteria and aim to: recognize the work of women; secure their employment; improve income levels; and ensure access to technology, credit and the decision-making process (Redfern & Snedker, 2002). It is further suggested that empowering women means addressing the inequalities they experience in their own communities. Fair trade in this sense upholds the human rights of ethical consumerism since both are inseparable. As Redfern and Snedker (2002, p. 38) suggest:

Women work longer hours than men in every country in the world, yet their contributions at home and at the workplace are often invisible. Women are underrepresented and underpaid. Women comprise two thirds of the world's poor. As fair trade seeks to tackle poverty then it is necessary to identify and target women.

Many studies report on the impact that fair trade has had on the lives of women and gender relations in participating communities, identifying both direct and indirect effects on the livelihoods and experiences of women. These studies have examined gender relations in the context of fair trade and considered the extent to which these issues have been addressed. Women's involvement in fair trade is considerable. Oxfam have suggested that more than eighty per cent of the 100,000-people involved in the production of fair trade handicrafts in Bangladesh are women (Redfern and Snedker, 2002). Women are directly involved in coffee farming (Eshuis & Harmsen, 2003; Murray et al., 2003; Tallontire, 2000), shea butter production (Greig, 2006; Harsch, 2001) banana cultivation (Blowfield & Gallet, 2000), handicrafts (Mayoux & Williams, 2001), and horticulture (Tallontire et al., 2005). As more and more products are certified as fair trade the number of women involved is likely to increase, which enhance ethical consumerism since it is about social responsibility, human rights and workers' rights.

The most obvious economic benefit of women's involvement in fair trade is increased income through the payment of a "fair price" and other disbursements of the fair-trade premium. For women in India for example, craft production provides a route to paid employment when few such opportunities exist and this production can take place at home which allows the women involved to fit paid work around domestic work and any other agricultural work in which they are involved (Redfern & Snedker, 2002). For many women, this provides a valuable source of income, particularly when the fact that the women who are involved in such handicraft production are often single heads of households, with multiple responsibilities; this is in line with the first principle of the WFTO on creating opportunities for economically disadvantaged producers. Women often fulfill a productive role, but this is usually combined with the burden of other responsibilities such as domestic work and tasks within the community (Beneria & Sen, 1997; Moser, 1993). Increased income from fair trade can ease some of the burden of multiple responsibilities. Female peanut farmers in Malawi for example, have responsibility for caring for children and the elderly, domestic work, and fetching water when there is often not a safe supply. Fair trade has alleviated some of these pressures as fair prices provide greater security and the fair-trade premium has funded investment which frees women from some unpaid labour and enables them to be more productive. For example, the development of a clean water supply within communities has freed up time that would have been spent collecting water. The examples cited above prove that the success of fair trade is attributed to social responsibility and ethical consumerism.

Another example is shea butter (a product which is used in cosmetic production) that provides an income for women in Burkino Faso (Greig, 2006). Shea nut harvesting and butter production is unusual in that it is the sole preserve of women. The location and harvesting techniques are known by Burkinabe` women, who pass on the skills and knowledge regarding shea nut harvest through generations. Efforts to cultivate the trees have been unsuccessful so knowledge of the location of the trees is a valuable resource for women, and the production of the oil or butter from the nuts offers a unique opportunity for Burkinabe` women to generate income, and affords women respect, authority and control over resources that they would not otherwise enjoy (Greig, 2006; Harsch, 2001).

The above examples suggest that fair trade can offer economic resources to women, but there is also evidence that increased income can afford women more control in households as well as over their own future. In some instances, increased access to economic resources has the knock-on effect of increasing confidence and self-esteem among some women; this is in line with principle six of the WFTO on commitment to non-discrimination, gender equity and women's economic empowerment and freedom of association.

Shea nut production and handicraft production are areas in which women have traditionally been the main producers. To assess the general impact of fair trade on women we also need to consider those areas that have traditionally been controlled by men, such as banana and coffee farming (Blowfield & Gallet, 2000; Tallontire, 2000).

In the case of banana cultivation, plantation work is gender-specific, with men considering fieldwork such as harvesting, clearing and replanting, as an extension of farming responsibilities. While fair trade banana cultivation has increased livelihood opportunities, evidence suggests that women have been less likely to benefit in this context. Blowfield and Gallet (2000) found that only 16 per cent of workers in Volta River Estate banana production in Ghana were women, with the gender imbalance being blamed on the nature of the work.

Coffee farmers in the Kilimanjaro Native Co-operative Union (KNCU) which supplies coffee to Cafe´direct, the UK's biggest fair trade hot drinks company, are predominantly men which can be seen as a direct result of land ownership being a condition of membership. Although female labour is vital to coffee cultivation and harvest, their interests are not represented within the co-operative (Tallontire, 2000).

Tallontire goes on to argue that this gender imbalance has not been challenged by KNCU or Twin who are the partners in the fair-trade relationship. Women's involvement in commercial cocoa production is also circumscribed by issues to do with land ownership and gender stereotypes, even where affirmative measures have been put in place to encourage the active and effective participation of women in decision making. Madely (2000) review of the activities of the Kuapa Kokoo Farmer's Union (KKFU) in Ghana outlines some of the measures that have been put in place to encourage the involvement of women. These measures are centered around ensuring that there are many women representatives on committees such as the regional council, the National Executive Committee the KKFU Board and the Board of trustees.

Such affirmative measures would suggest that women are represented in the KKFU, however Mayoux's review indicates that access to these positions is highly dependent on access to land for cocoa production. As she suggests:

Women are involved in all aspects of cocoa production and primary processing: though cocoa as a cash crop is viewed as a man's crop largely because of the land ownership structure [which exists]. Even where women have access to their own land, their farm size is smaller because of a combination of factors: limited capital base, obligations to work on their husband's farm and more off farm workload. This lack of access to land, as well as gender stereotypes and divisions of labour also affects the types of other activities in which women can engage. In particular, it is difficult for them to plant permanent tree crops.

This is not an isolated case. In developing countries, women's access to land and credit is even more limited than that of men because of social, cultural and political factors (Datta & Kornberg, 2002; UNCTAD, 2004). Furthermore, within smallholder farming, family labour may not be factored into costs of production resulting in women not receiving direct remuneration for the work carried out. Fair trade encourages export crop cultivation where earnings are often controlled by men, despite the vital role that women play in production of commodities such as coffee and cocoa. The net result may be that women are not financially rewarded for the work that they do, while at the same time family farm obligations and land ownership restrictions prevent them from managing farms of their own, or having control over income (Redfern & Snedker, 2002). Even in the example of shea butter production, which is the preserve of women, such activity is confined to the informal sector. Traditional gender relations in which men control formal commodity production restrict women to small-scale subsistence production and the local market (Greig, 2006). Moreover, if a Burkinabe´ woman's husband does not approve of his wife's involvement in commercial activity he may prevent her from taking part (Saul, 1989 cited in Greig, 2006). Nicholls and Opal (2005) consider that women's participation in commercial agricultural production is a mixed blessing, in that women may be rewarded for their involvement, but this often leads to an overall increase in workload as productive activity does not exempt them from domestic responsibilities and other tasks within the local community.

The sexual division of labour highlighted in these examples is typical of gender relations in various parts of the developing world. Men are more likely to be employed in more highly skilled, core areas of production while women are often employed in lower paid, lower skilled jobs.

At Bahay, in the Philippines for example, men are usually working with machines but women are employed in the lower skilled manual jobs of sanding, finishing and assembly, which require careful attention to detail. There are equal wages for the same work but as only men run the machines, they receive higher wages (Mayoux & Williams, 2001).

The evidence seems to point towards involvement with fair trade having limited impact on traditional gender relations in developing countries. Research suggests that there is no challenge to gender segmentation, and that female stereotypes may have been reinforced (Das, 2009).

One of the most significant ways in which fair trade impacts upon the lives of women is through the payment of and the distribution of the fair trade social premium, that is often used for community projects. Women producers in receipt of this premium can decide who benefits from this, and to which projects the premium will contribute. Women cotton farmers in the Dougoroukoroni co-operative in Mali for example, spent their first fair trade premium on building a school. This prompted a jointly-funded project between the local government and the co-operative to increase the size of the original school which was overwhelmed by the number of pupils attending (Lamb, 2008a). Lamb's report also highlights the example of the UCIRI co-operative in Oaxaca in Mexico, which used the premium to create a training centre for women's literacy; this is in line with principle eight of the WFTO on providing capacity building.

CONCLUSION AND POLICY RECOMMENDATIONS

This chapter pointed out that ethical consumerism can improve organizational performance, this leads to enhance profit. The enhancement is caused by three factors: customers' trust and loyalty, investors' confidence, and employees' satisfaction. Organizations are to develop strategies to promote ethical strategies including inducing fair trade plans. Below are some recommendations to promote ethical consumerism and in turn fair trade in relation to human management in general and women's employment specifically. In addition, ecological and environmental concerns in relation to contexts of women employment are to consider. Social responsibility in relation to its four manifestations of economical, legal, ethical and philanthropic are reflected in fair trade attempts to improve the contexts of the underprivileged.

1. Developing and implementing strategies and policies that enable human resources, women as well as men, to benefit from opportunities associated with fair trade. Strategies should allocate resources for achievements of policies. In fact, policies must be accompanied by 'teeth'; they need to be backed by resources and commitment by senior staff, including incentives to put policies into effect. Policies are only as good as those in charged with implementing them.
2. It is critical that policy makers concerned with social equity improve their understanding of the intertwine between fair trade and ethical consumerism so that they can take the necessary steps to enhance the implementation of fair trade principles as well as develop complementary mechanisms to offset any negative effects and set in place policies, programmes and projects that will promote improvement in the lives of men and women in society.
3. Strategic alliances must be forced between gender equality and ethical consumerism advocates, fair trade activists and development actors working on policies and programs. This will ensure that workers' rights initiatives, market access programs, ethical and fair-trade schemes and human rights campaigns address gender equality and contribute to social and economic justice for all.
4. The participation of gender experts in fair trade discussions should be promoted at all levels, and multi- stakeholder mechanisms should be established to reorient the trade agenda in support of a pro- poor and gender- aware development framework. The participation of gender experts in different aspects of fair trade- related activities and transactions and their outcomes is crucial for determining whether fair trade is indeed acting as an engine of sustainable development.
5. Gender sensitive institutions, enabling legal systems and strong market- support systems are required to remove the structural barriers to improved women's participation in markets and to ensure their rights are upheld as workers, producers and consumers. Gender mainstreaming needs to be implemented in organizations working on fair trade related issues to ensure that women's gender- specific disadvantages are addressed. Support from trade unions and other employment institutions for labour rights that consider different gender roles and relations of unequal power are critical.

REFERENCES

Al A'ali, E. A., & Al-Sarrraf, A. R. (2016). Ethical consumerism: Contextual Issues of Ethical Decision-Making Processes: An Exploratory Study. In Ethical and Social perspectives on Global Business Interaction in Emerging Markets (pp.133-149). IGI Global

Aranda, J., & Morales, C. (2002). Poverty alleviation through participation in fair trade coffee: the case of CEPO, Oaxaca, Mexico. Colorado State University.

Ballet, J., & Carimentrand, A. (2010, April). Fair Trade and the Depersonalization of Ethics. *Journal of Business Ethics*, *92*(2Supplement), 317–330. doi:10.100710551-010-0576-0

Barratt Brown, M. (1993). *Fair trade: Reform and realities in the international trading system*. Zed.

Batliwala, S. (1994). The meaning of women's empowerment: new concepts for action. In G. Sen (Ed.), *Population Policies Reconsidered: Health Empowerment and Rights*. Cambridge, MA: Harvard University Press.

Beetham, G., & Demetriades, J. (2007). Feminist research methodologies and development: Overview and practical applications. *Gender and Development*, *15*(2), 199–216. doi:10.1080/13552070701391086

Beneria, L., & Sen, G. (1997). Accumulation, reproduction and women's role in economic development: Boserup revisited. In N. Visvanathan, L. Duggan, N. Nisonoff, & N. Wiegersma (Eds.), *The Women, Gender and Development Reader* (pp. 42–50). London: Zed Books.

Bhagwati, J. (1995). Trade Liberalisation and 'Fair Trade' Demands: Addressing the Environmental and Labour Standards Issues. *World Economy*, *18*(6), 745–759. doi:10.1111/j.1467-9701.1995.tb00329.x

Bliss, C. (2007). *Trade, Growth and Inequality*. Oxford, UK: Oxford University Press.

Blowfield, M., & Gallet, S. (2000). *Ethical Trade and Sustainable Rural Livelihoods – Case Studies: Volta River Estates Fairtrade Bananas Case Study*. London: Natural Resources Institute, University of Greenwich.

Booth, P., & Whetstone, L. (2007). Half a Cheer for Fair Trade. *Economic Affairs*, *27*(2), 29–36. doi:10.1111/j.1468-0270.2007.00727.x

Boserup, E. (1974). Women's Role in Economic Development. Gower in association with London School of Economics.

Bowes, J. (2010). *The Fair-Trade Revolution*. London: Pluto Press.

Brown, M. B. (2007). Fair Trade' with Africa. *Review of African Political Economy*, *34*(112), 267–277. doi:10.1080/03056240701449653

Brown, S. (2006). *Myths of free trade: Why American trade policy has failed*. New York: New Press.

ConsumerismE. (n.d.). Retrieved from http:// en.m.wikipedia.org/

Coote, B. (1992). The Trade Trap: Poverty and the Global Commodity Market. Oxfam/Alden Press.

Crane, A., & Matten, D. (2016). *Business Ethics: Managing corporate citizenship and sustainability in the age of globalization*. Oxford University Press.

Datta, R., & Kornberg, J. (2002). Introduction: empowerment and disempowerment. In R. Datta & J. Kornberg (Eds.), *Women in Developing Countries* (pp. 1–10). London: Lynne Rienner Publishers.

De Janvry, A., McIntosh, C., & Sadoulet, E. (2015, July). Fair Trade and Free Entry: Can a Disequilibrium Market Serve as a Development Tool? *The Review of Economics and Statistics*, *97*(3), 567–573. doi:10.1162/REST_a_00512

De Waal, A. (2006). Evaluating gender mainstreaming in development projects. *Development in Practice*, *16*(2), 209–214. doi:10.1080/09614520600562454

Eshuis, F., & Harmsen, J. (2003). *Making Trade Work for the Producers: 15 Years of Fairtrade Labelled Coffee in The Netherlands*. Utrecht: The Max Havelaar Foundation.

Fair Trade Fair. (2005). Retrieved from http://www.fairtradeexpo.org

Ferrell, O. C., Fraedrich, J., & Ferrell, L. (2015). *Business Ethics: Ethical Decision Making and Cases* (10th ed.). Stamford, CT: Cengage Learning.

Fisher, E. (2009). Introduction: The policy trajectory of fair trade. *Journal of International Development*, *21*(7), 985–1003. doi:10.1002/jid.1633

Fridell, G. (2003). *Fair trade and the international moral economy: within and against the market*. CERLAC Working Paper Series, York University.

Fridell, G. (2004). The fair-trade network in historical perspective. *Canadian Journal of Development Studies*, *25*(3), 411–428. doi:10.1080/02255189.2004.9668986

Goodman, M. K. (2004). Reading fair trade: Political ecological imagery and the moral economy of fair trade foods. *Political Geography*, *23*(7), 891–915. doi:10.1016/j.polgeo.2004.05.013

Greig, D. (2006). Shea butter: Connecting rural Burkinabe' women to international markets through fair trade. *Development in Practice*, *16*(5), 465–475. doi:10.1080/09614520600792440

Griffiths, P. (2010). Lack of rigour in defending fairtrade. *Economic Affairs*, *30*(2), 45–49. doi:10.1111/j.1468-0270.2010.02010.x

Groos, A. M. (1999). International trade and development: Exploring the impact of fair trade organizations in the global economy and the law. *Texas International Law Journal*, *34*(3), 379–411.

Harsch, E. (2001). Making trade work for poor women: Villagers in Burkino Faso discover an opening in the global market. *Africa Recovery*, *15*(4), 6–11.

Hartsock, N. (1985). *Money, Sex and Power: Towards a Feminist Historical Materialism*. Boston, MA: North Eastern University Press.

Hutchens, A. (2009). *Changing big business: The globalization of the fair-trade movement*. Northampton, MA: Edward Elgar Publishing. doi:10.4337/9781848447356

Jaffee, D. (2007). *Brewing Justice: Fair Trade Coffee, Sustainability, and Survival*. Los Angeles, CA: University of California Press.

Kabeer, N. (2005). Gender equality and women's empowerment. *Gender and Development*, *13*(1), 13–24. doi:10.1080/13552070512331332273

Kohler, P. (2006). *The economics of Fair Trade: for whose benefit? An investigation into the limits of Fair Trade as a development tool and the risk of clean-washing*. HEI Working Papers (6–2007). Geneva: Economics Section, Graduate Institute of International Studies.

Lamb, H. (2008a). *Fighting the Banana Wars and Other Fairtrade Battles*. Chatham: Random House.

Lamb, H. (2008b). *Fairtrade: working to make markets fair, Trade – What If? New Challenges in Export Development*. World Export Development Forum, International Trade Centre. Available at: http://s3.amazonaws.com/zanran_storage/www.intracen.org/ContentPages/12671071.pdf

Langen, N. (2012). *Ethics in Consumer Choice: An Empirical Analysis based on the Example of Coffee*. SpringerLink.

LeMare, A. (2008). The impact of fair trade on social and economic development: A review of the literature. *Geography Compass*, *2*(6), 1922–1942. doi:10.1111/j.1749-8198.2008.00171.x

Littrell, M. A., & Dickson, M. A. (1998). Fair Trade Performance in a Competitive Market. *Clothing & Textiles Research Journal, 16*(4), 176–189. doi:10.1177/0887302X9801600404

Lyon, S. (2002). *Evaluation of the actual and potential benefits for the alleviation of poverty through the participation in fair trade coffee networks: Guatemalan case study*. Academic Press.

Madely, J. (2000). *Hungry for Trade*. London: Zed Books.

Malone, S. (2012). *Understanding the role of emotion in ethical consumption: a tourism context* (PhD thesis). University of Nottingham.

Mayoux, L., & Williams, P. (2001). *Case study: Oxfam Fair Trade*. Available at: www.oxfam.org.uk

Mohan, S. (2010). *Fair Trade Without the Froth – a dispassionate economic analysis of 'Fair Trade*. London: Institute of Economic Affairs.

Moore, G. (2004). The Fairtrade movement: Parameters, issues and future research. *Journal of Business Ethics, 53*(1/2), 73–86. doi:10.1023/B:BUSI.0000039400.57827.c3

Moore, G. (2004). The Fair-Trade Movement: Parameters, Issues and Future Research. *Journal of Business Ethics, 53*(1/2), 73–86. doi:10.1023/B:BUSI.0000039400.57827.c3

Moore, G., Gibbon, J., & Slack, R. (2006). The mainstreaming of Fair Trade: A macro marketing perspective. *Journal of Strategic Marketing, 14*(4), 329–352. doi:10.1080/09652540600947961

Moser, C. O. N. (1993). *Gender Planning and Development: Theory, Practice and Training*. London: Routledge.

Murray, D., Raynolds, L. T., & Taylor, P. L. (2003). *One cup at a time: poverty alleviation and fair-trade coffee in Latin America, Fair Trade Research Group*. Fort Collins, CO: Colorado State University.

Murray, D.L., & Raynolds, L.T. (2007). *Globalization and its antinomies*. Academic Press.

Nelson, V., & Pound, B. (2009). *The last ten years: a comprehensive review of the literature on the impact of Fairtrade*. Academic Press.

Nicholls, A. (2005). *Thriving in a hostile environment: fairtrade's role as a positive market mechanism for disadvantaged producers*. Academic Press.

Nicholls, A., & Huybrechts, B. (2016). Sustaining Inter-organizational Relationships Across Institutional Logics and Power Asymmetries: The Case of Fair Trade. *Journal of Business Ethics, 135*(4), 699–714. doi:10.100710551-014-2495-y

Nicholls, A., & Opal, C. (2005). *Fair trade: Market-driven ethical consumption.* Thousand Oaks, CA: Sage.

Oxford Policy Management. (2000). *Fair trade: overview, impact, challenges: study to inform DFDI's support to fair trade.* Author.

Oxley, A. (1990). *The Challenge of Free Trade.* London: Harvester Wheatsheaf.

Pelsmacker, Driesen, & Rayp. (2005). Do Consumers Care about Ethics? Willingness to Pay for Fair-Trade Coffee. *Journal of Consumer Affairs, 39*(2), 363–385.

Poalisso, M., & Leslie, J. (1994). Meeting the changing health needs of women in developing countries. *Social Science & Medicine, 40*(1), 55–65. doi:10.1016/0277-9536(94)00127-F PMID:8146715

Porritt, J. (2007). *Capitalism as if the World Matters.* London: Earthscan.

Ransom, D. (2001). *The No-nonsense Guide to Fair Trade.* Oxford, UK: New Internationalist Publications.

Raynolds, L. T., Murray, D., & Wilkinson, J. (2007). *Fair Trade: The Challenges of Transforming Globalization.* London: Routledge. doi:10.4324/9780203933534

Raynolds, L. T., Murray, D. L., & Wilkinson, J. (2007). *Fair Trade: The Challenges of Transforming Globalization.* London: Routledge. doi:10.4324/9780203933534

Redfern, A., & Snedker, P. (2002). *Creating market opportunities for smaller enterprises: experiences of the fair-trade movement.* SEED Working Paper No. 30. International Labour Organization.

Reed, D. (2009). What do Corporations have to do with Fair Trade? Positive and normative analysis from a value chain perspective. *Journal of Business Ethics, 86*, 3–26.

Renard, M. C. (2003). Fair trade: Quality, market conventions. *Journal of Rural Studies, 19*(1), 87–96. doi:10.1016/S0743-0167(02)00051-7

Renard, M. C. (2005). Quality certification, regulation and power in fair trade. *Journal of Rural Studies, 21*(4), 419–431. doi:10.1016/j.jrurstud.2005.09.002

Riedel, C. P., Lopez, F. M., Widdows, A., Manji, A., & Schneider, M. (2005). Impacts of Fair Trade: trade and market linkages. In *Proceedings of the 18th International Farming Symposium*. Rome: Food and Agricultural Organization.

Ronchi, L. (2002). *The impact of fair trade on producers and their organisations: A case study with Coocafe´ in Costa Rica*. PRUS Working Paper No. 11. Poverty Research Unit.

Ruben, R., Fort, R., & Zuniga-Arias, G. (2009). Measuring the impact of fair trade on development. *Development in Practice*, *19*(6), 777–788.

Saul, M. (1989). Separateness and relation: autonomous income and negotiation among rural Bobo women. In R. Wilk (Ed.), *The Household Economy: Reconsidering the Domestic Mode of Production*. Boulder, CO: Westview Press.

Sen, G., & Baliwala, S. (2000). Empowering women for reproductive rights. In H. B. Presser & G. Sen (Eds.), *Women's Empowerment and Demographic Processes: Moving beyond Cairo* (pp. 16–36). Oxford University Press.

Smith, A. M. (2009). Fair trade, diversification and structural change: Towards a broader theoretical framework of analysis. *Oxford Development Studies*, *37*(4), 457–478. doi:10.1080/13600810903305208

Tallontire, A. (2000). Partnerships in fair trade: Reflections from a case study of Cafe'direct. *Development in Practice*, *10*(2), 166–177. doi:10.1080/09614520050010205

Tallontire, A., Dolan, C., Smith, S., & Barrintos, S. (2005). Reaching the marginalised? Gender value chains and ethical trade in African horticulture. *Development in Practice*, *15*(3/4), 559–571. doi:10.1080/09614520500075771

United Nations Conference on Trade and Development. (2004). *Trade and Gender: Opportunities and Challenges for Developing Countries*. United Nations.

Waterford One World Centre. (2018). *Going Beyond the Symbols: Ethical Consumerism and Fair Trade for Primary Education*. Author.

Weeden, C. (2008). *The values of ethical and responsible tourist* (Ph.D. thesis). University of Glasgow.

WorcesterR. M. (2000)*Ethical Consumerism Research*. Academic Press.

World Fair Trade Organization. (2010). *Fair Trade women's work for development and equity*. Author.

Chapter 8
The Effect of Demographic Factors of Consumers Online Shopping Behavior in a GCC University

Arpita Anshu Mehrotra
Royal University for Women, Bahrain

Hala Elias
Royal University for Women, Bahrain

Adel Ismail Al-Alawi
https://orcid.org/0000-0003-0775-4406
University of Bahrain, Bahrain

Sara Abdulrahman Al-Bassam
The Social Development Office of His Highness the Prime Minister's Diwan, Kuwait

ABSTRACT

This study aims to investigate the effect of certain demographic factors of Gulf Cooperation Council countries' (GCC) university students and staff in using online shopping. The study attempts to hypothesize and measure the features that affect the growth of the e-shopping trend in a GCC. The results indicate that education has a large influence on e-shopping use. Gender did not appear to be a significant factor, but consumer income significantly impacts the online shopping of consumers. The results also suggested a positive relationship between online trust and online purchase intention. Additionally, there is a relationship between the ability to use the internet and the online shopping of consumers. Therefore, the more consumers are capable of using the internet, the more online shopping users there will be. The study also suggests that online retailers need to provide competitive prices and user-friendly websites.

DOI: 10.4018/978-1-7998-0272-3.ch008

INTRODUCTION

Online shopping is one of the fastest growing technologies in the world as people from all over the world are engaging in online shopping (Monsuwe, Dellaert, & Ruyter, 2004). However, online shopping is considered as one component of any economy in any developed country since it might reinforce and enhance that economy in all circumstances (Bhattacherjee, 2001). The focus of businesses now revolve around cross-national and cross-cultural Internet marketing (Griffith, Davis, Myers, & Harvey, 2006). However, customers are always keen on receiving the goods or services on time with no delay. This applies to online shopping as customers prefer having different products and services from different brands to be able to have numerous alternatives to choose from (Al-Alawi & Al-Ali, 2015). The more options available, the more customer sales will exist. This study aims to determine the factors that may affect online shopping, such as gender, education level, and income.

This study also focuses on whether there is a positive or negative relationship between online trust and online purchase intention. In addition, the study attempts to identify the relationship between the consumer's ability to use the Internet and how that might affect online shopping.

Al-Alawi and Al-Ali (2015) stated that "Currently, the Internet has affected our day to day activities in a crucial way. It grows to be part of our routine due to the substantial yield." Online shopping is the act of purchasing products and services over the internet, online shopping has grown in popularity over the years. The communities must keep pace with this development. There are many factors affecting online shopping, therefore the statement of the problem can be represented in the following questions:

- What are the demographic factors that affect e-Shopping?
- What are the factors (in general) that affect e-Shopping?
- What encourages people to use e-Shopping?

The research significance due to the following:

- Millions of people are online on the Internet daily to search about products and purchase from thousands of different online merchants.
- Many literatures, such as Çelik and Yilmaz (2011), Al-Alawi and Al-Ali (2015), Rittiboончa, Kriwuttisom, and Ngo (2019) show that e-Business, which includes e-Shopping, has been expanding in the last few years. Due to various benefits of e-Shopping, more people today prefer this method over conventional shopping, as the consumer decision-making behavior has changed significantly toward e-Shopping. Many consumers from every age

are making more e-Shopping via their cell phone, hesitantly going to brick-and-mortar places.

Online shopping involves purchasing products or services over the Internet. E-Shopping is done through an online shop, e-shop, e-store, virtual store, or web-shop, and all the products in the online store are described through photographs and text. The objectives can be summarized as:

1. Identify the various demographic factors such as (age, education level, gender, income, salary, online trust) of Internet users who purchase online.
2. Study the effect of demographic factors on the online shopping behaviors of consumers.
3. Identify the main goods that consumers are interested using e-shopping to purchase.
4. Explore the advantages and disadvantages of e-shopping.
5. Shed light on the nature of e-Shopping and the importance.
6. Contribute to the development of electronic shopping through the final results of the search.
7. Review the identified consumer-perceived benefits obtained from online shopping.

Figure 1 represents the research model used to investigate the effect of demographic factors of consumers' online shopping behaviors.

Research Variables

The research variables are classified into independent and dependent variables.

- **Independent Variables**: Education level, Gender, Salary, Income, Trust, and the ability to use the Internet.
- **Dependent Variables**: e-Shopping

In order to achieve the objectives of this study, the following hypotheses were proposed from the research model. There are six hypotheses, as shown in Figure 1. The research hypotheses are:

Hypothesis One: There is a significant relationship between education level and online shopping.

Hypothesis Two: There is a significant relationship between gender and online shopping.

Figure 1. Research model, variables and hypotheses

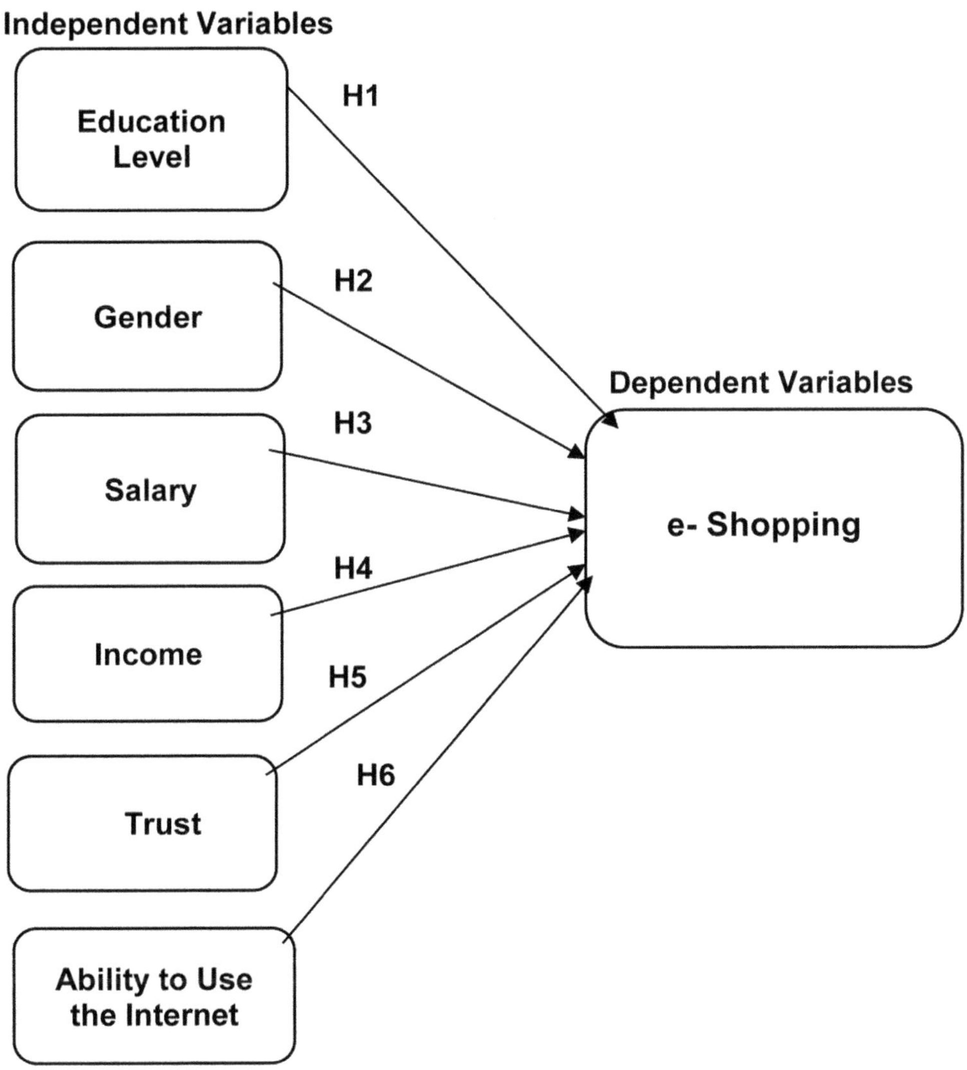

Hypothesis Three: There is a significant relationship between income and online shopping.

Hypothesis Four: Customers trust e-Shopping.

Hypothesis Five: There is a significant relationship between the ability to use the Internet and online shopping.

E-SHOPPING

The Internet is changing the way consumers shop for goods and services and has rapidly evolved globally. Online shopping is the process where consumers purchase products or services over the Internet. Electronic marketing (EM) is the transfer of goods or services from a seller to a buyer that involves one or more electronic methods or media. EM began with the use of telegraphs in the 19th century, with the advent and mass acceptance of the telephone, TV, radio, and then cable electronic media have become the dominant marketing force (Hong, 1993).

Bellman, Lohse, and Johnson (1999) proposed that demographic variables alone explain a very low percentage of variance in the purchase decision. Consumers' traits include their demographic factors (income, age, gender, and education), which would influence their intention to shop online. For the factor of age, consumers that are under age 25 have more potential to shop online because of their interest in using new technologies to search for products and also for information provided for comparing and evaluating alternatives. According to Burke (2002) and Wood (2002), four relevant demographic factors (age, gender, education, and income) have a significant moderating effect on consumers' attitudes toward online shopping. Based on several studies that were made on these variables, the studies have resulted in some contradictory results. As for age, it was found that younger people are more interested in using new technologies, such as the Internet to search for comparative information on products whereas older consumers avoid shopping online as the potential benefits from shopping online are offset by the perceived cost in skill needed to use the Internet. Ladhari, Gonthier & Lajante, (2019) studies sector of Generation Y female e-Shoppers attitude and found "four approaches to online shopping: trend shopping, pleasure shopping, price shopping, and brand shopping. Six shopping profiles have also been identified, each with different objectives: price shoppers, discovery shoppers, emotional shoppers, strategic shoppers, fashionistas, and shopping fans".

Monsuwe et al., (2004) suggested that there are five external factors that provide an insight into understanding the consumers' intentions when it comes to making purchases on the Internet. These factors are consumer personality, situational factors, product characteristics, previous online shopping experiences, and the consumers' trust in online shopping. Situational factors might also lead a consumer to have an intention shopping on the Internet, such as time pressure, lack of mobility, geographical distance, need for special items, and attractiveness of alternatives. A study by Shi, DeVos, Yang and Witlox (2019) suggested that "e-shopping and shopping travel behaviors are significantly determined by sociodemographic, Internet experience, car ownership, and location factors". Moreover, e-Shopping could be a solution for crowded area and in distant future the number of brick and mortar for clothes and shoes, electronics, food and drink, and cosmetics may shrink. Consumers' decisions whether or not to shop online are also influenced by the type of products or services under consideration. Lack of physical contact and assistance, as well as the need to "feel" the product influences the suitability and differentiates products according to their suitability for online shopping. Relying on product categories conceptualized by information economists, Gehrt and Yan (2004) said that search goods that are goods that can be evaluated easily before a consumer purchases them, i.e. (books), versus experienced goods that are more complex in terms of evaluation, i.e. (clothing). Studies of online shopping behaviors have focused mainly on demographic, psychographics, and personality characteristics. In their study, Xia, Monroe and Cox (2009) concluded that consumers with a shopping goal are more responsive towards promotional messages, such as "pay less" and "discount," while consumers without shopping goals are responsive towards promotional messages, such as "save more" and "free gift."

Gordon and Bhowan (2005) suggested that there are factors affecting consumer purchasing decisions and influencing consumers to purchase online. These factors include retailer, service, environment, purchasing motivation, culture, social, psychological, and personal factors. Lauden and Travel (2013) found that there are some demographic groups that have a much higher percentage to online businesses, such as (age, gender, ethnicity, community type, education, and income). Furthermore, 88% of users are shoppers, 72% are buyers. Moreover, Başev (2014) found in their study of Turkish consumers online that the demographic factors, satisfaction with computer, innovativeness in the previous experiences, and Internet usage were significant with age. Furthermore, a study by Baldevbhai (2015) stated there is no significance difference among gender and online shopping in India. Moreover, a Saudi study by Alqahtani, Goodwin, & de Vries (2018) found that "factors related to age, gender, and computer proficiency influenced the adoption and use of online shopping in the kingdom". Additionally, study by Bahaddad, Drew, Houghtoni, & Alfarraj. (2018), stated that the broad acceptance of e-Shopping among Saudi consumers enhances its growth and the main factors that possibly will affect the e-Shopping "can be divided into three main groups: the human and organizational factors, the environmental and technological factors and the cultural and traditional factors".

Table 1 shows factors that encourage and/or discourage online shopping.

RESEARCH METHODOLOGY

This study aims to identify the demographic factors affecting e-Shopping. In order to accomplish this, a literature review was conducted on the subject of e-Business

Table 1. Factors influencing consumers to purchase online

Factors Encouraging Online Purchases	Factors Discouraging Online Purchases
1. Buying online saves time. 2. Buying online is convenient (no traffic crowds/ no parking/24 hour's access). 3. Cheaper price. 4. Items purchased online are delivered. 5. There is a greater selection of products to choose from online. 6. Buying online is a fun and/or novel experience. 7. Buying online offers a greater variety of Stores to buy from. 8. Buying online allows one to rapidly survey a wide range of options.	1. There is a long time delay between placing in order and delivery of the item. 2. The item cannot be examined or sampled before purchase. 3. There is a risk of dealing with potentially unreliable or phantom merchants. 4. The atmosphere and ambience of the traditional shopping experience is lacking. 5. Web pages, not user- friendly (easy to use). 6. Slow loading web pages. 7. Computer and/ or technical malfunction. 8. Difficulty in finding shopping web sites and what products are for sale online. 9. Poor and/or lacking customer service. 10. Unable to communicate personally with a customer support representative.

and e-Shopping in general. Then, the authors conducted an Internet search of factors relating to online shopping attitudes. A questionnaire was created to obtain the data.

A questionnaire was prepared in English and the data for this study was gathered using questionnaires completed by 98 respondents. The sample consisted of students and the administrators at a GCC university. The questionnaires were distributed to 98 student respondents and administrators who were selected randomly. Respondents were asked to fill out the survey and return it immediately. They were asked many questions, such as gender, age, and education level, if they prefer shopping online or not, the preferred products that are purchased, and more. The questionnaire used the format of a typical five-level Likert scale: 1 Strongly Disagree, 2 Disagree, 3 Neutral, 4 Agree, and 5 Strongly Agree.

Research Population and Sample

The population of this study is from a GCC university. The sample for this study was collected from GCC students and administrators through the use of questionnaires. Questionnaires were distributed to randomly selected students and administrators who used e-shopping. The statements and questions were closed-ended. The questionnaires were distributed to a total of 98 respondents by hand in addition to permission letters. It consisted of students and administrators of different genders, different age groups, various backgrounds, and who were in different types of courses at the university. Confidentiality was assured by encouraging the respondents to return the questionnaires directly. The questionnaires were distributed to all categories of the respondents that were met in the classroom, library, office, mosque, and so on, at the main campus of the university. After the respondents completed the questionnaires, they were collected personally. The data was collected over a period of three weeks.

RESULTS AND DISCUSSION

The Demographic Data Analysis

Age

Figure 2 shows that there are mixed findings on the relationship between age and online shopping intention. People under 20 years old did the most online shopping by 67.3%.

Gender

Figure 3 illustrates that male consumers make more online purchases, with a percentage of 55.1%, and spend more money online than females. They are equally or more likely to shop online in the future and are equally or more favorable towards online shopping. Women have a higher-level of web apprehensiveness and are more skeptical of e-business than men.

Figure 2. Ages of respondents

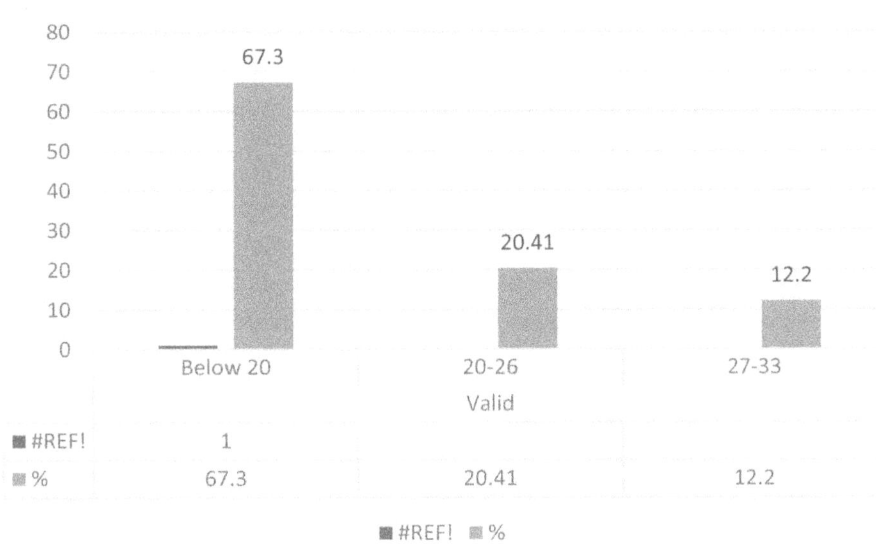

Figure 3. The classification of respondents' by gender

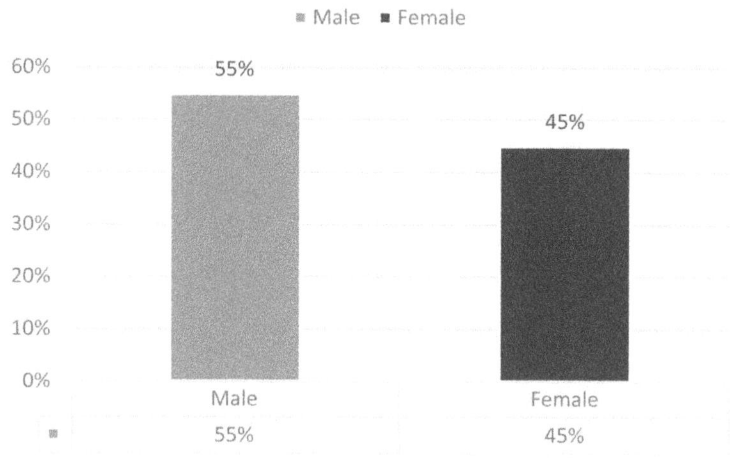

Marital Status

Figure 4 shows that marital status does influence online shopping and is an important factor. The result can be explained, because 64.3% of online shopping is done by bachelors, while divorced and widowed individuals who shop online percentages of 11.2% and 3.1%, respectively.

Main Languages

Figure 5 shows that consumers who speak Arabic are more likely to use the Internet for online shopping, with a percentage of 72.4%.

Nature of Work

Figure 6 shows that the nature of work affects the percentage of people who make online purchases. Respondents who spend the most amount of money and time on the Internet are students and administrators, with percentages of 35.7% and 32.7%, respectively. This result is compatible with the respondents by age because the majority of online shopping is done by individuals who are under 20 years of age.

Educational Level

Figure 7 shows that educational level produces mixed results ranging from no effect to a positive effect on online shopping. College students (two years after secondary

Figure 4. The marital status of respondents

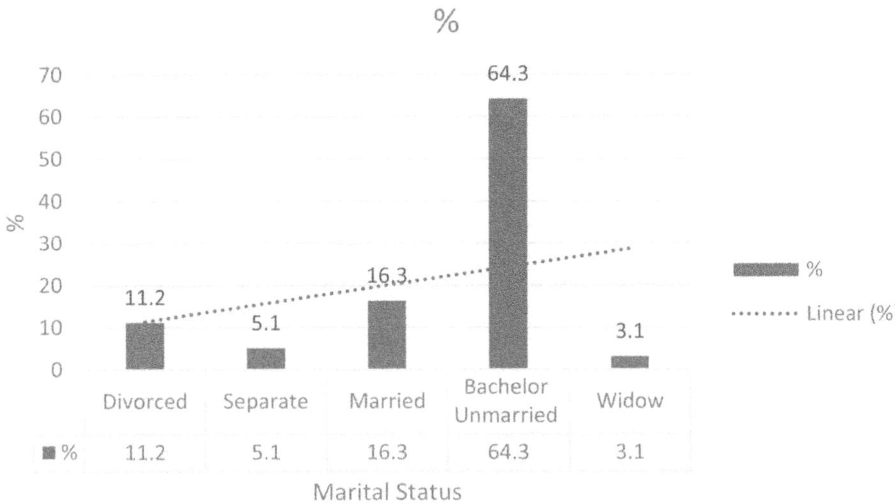

Figure 5. The main languages of respondents

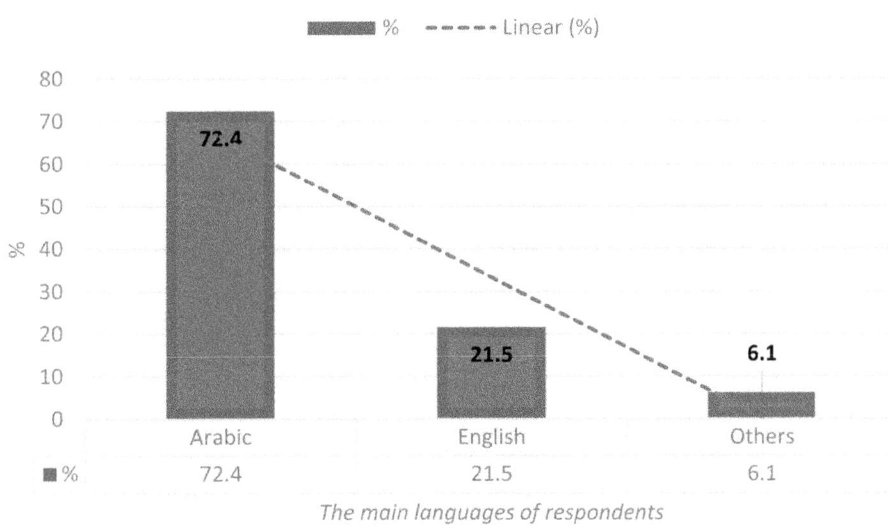

school) make more online purchases and spend more money online than other students, with a percentage of 41.8%.

Figure 6. How the nature of work affects the percentage of people who make online purchases

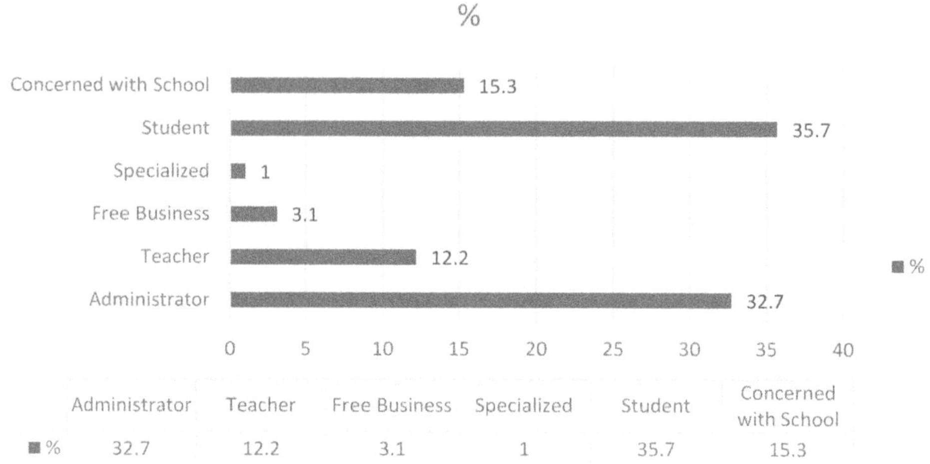

Monthly Income in B.D for the Family (Husband, Wife)

The results show that consumer income is positively related to online shopping tendencies. Figure 8 illustrates that people with income from BD260-BD775 (58.2%)

Figure 7. The educational level of respondents

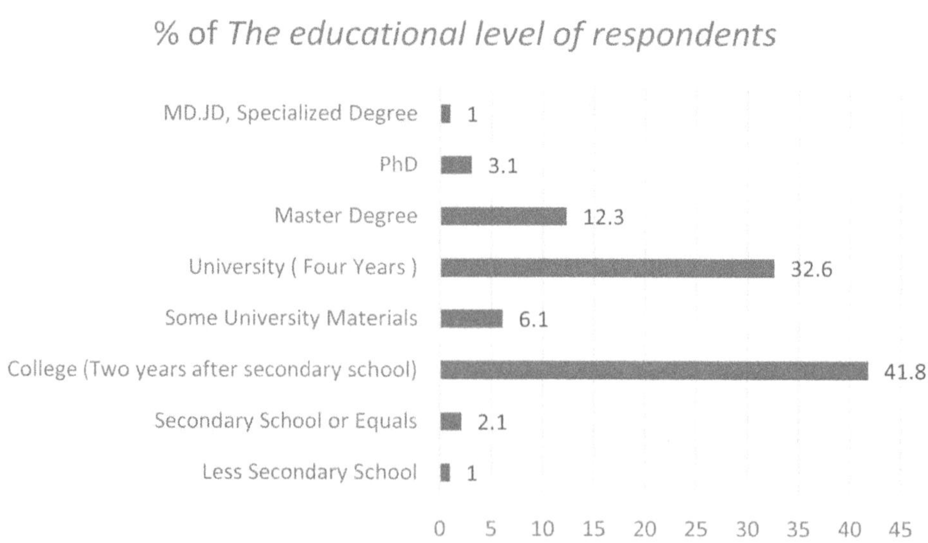

Figure 8. The monthly income of respondents

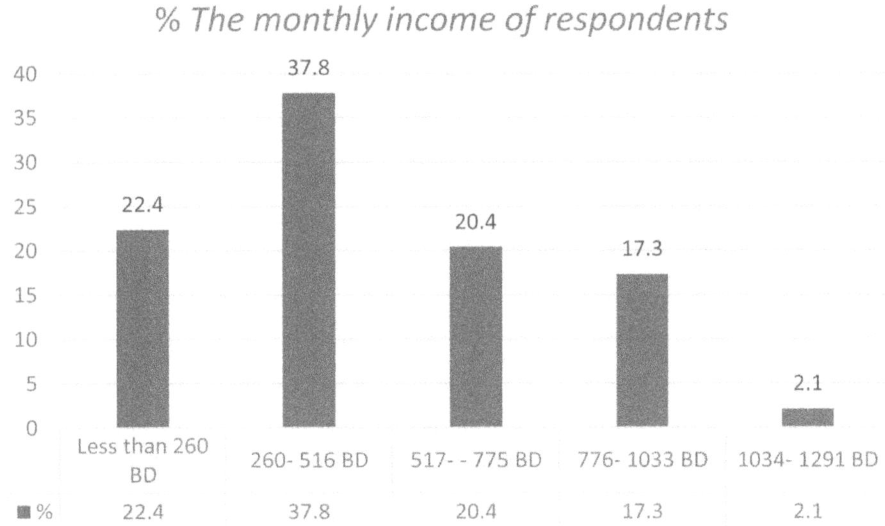

do more online shopping. Hence, 1BD = US$2.66. *(Note: the Bahraini currency used for this study).*

When Did You Use the Internet?

Figure 9 shows that there are mixed results for the effects of Internet usage on online shopping intention. Of the respondents, 43.9% had been using the Internet for six to seven years and are highly proficient at online shopping, while 2% of consumers had been using the Internet for less than six months to shop online.

Who Endures Subscription Expenses of Internet Services?

Figure 10 illustrates that 33.7% of workplaces paid the expenses for Internet services, which is the higher percentage, while 3.1% was paid for by a school or university.

How Many Hours on Average Do You Use the Internet Per Week?

The study found that most respondents use the Internet for about 21 hours per week. That means that they are using the Internet about four hours per day.

Figure 9. How long did respondents use the internet?

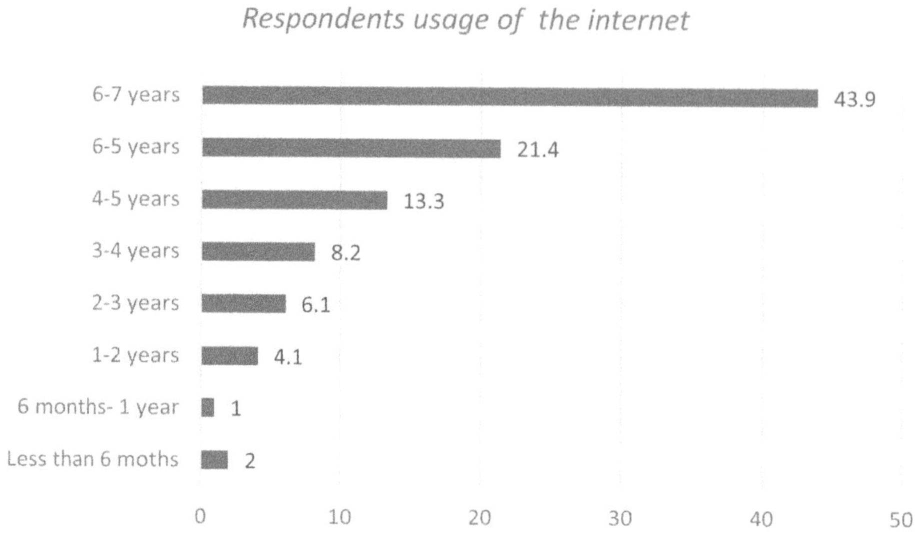

Goods That Reflect Rate of Using the Internet Uses in Surfing and Purchasing Process

Surfing

Table 2 shows that the respondents search for many goods on the Internet by using the surfing process. Concepts and plays are the goods most respondents surf for. The results show that 80% of respondents surfed the Internet for concepts and plays while only 33% of respondents surfed for newspapers and magazines once

Figure 10. Endure the subscription expenses of Internet services for respondents

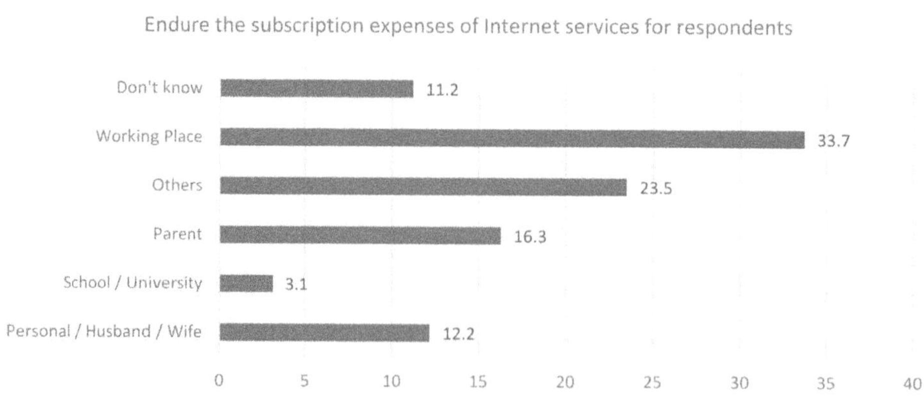

every week. Once every three months, 32% of the respondents surfed the Internet for consultations. The respondents rarely surfed the Internet for cars, motorcycles, tapes, movies, concepts, plays, roses, or flowers every week.

Purchasing

Table 3 illustrates that the Internet made shopping easier, faster, and it saved time and effort. The most purchased goods online are concepts and plays, with a percentage of 80% once every day.

As shown in Tables 2 and 3, the study found that respondents were very interested in purchasing and surfing for goods via the Internet. Respondents at surfed for concepts and plays, meaning that they usually used the Internet for fun and learning the same time. Respondents also used the Internet for tapes and movie shows as fun and enjoyment, and the results also revealed respondents interest in the field of real estate. The field of real estate in GCC is really prosperous and profitable, especially flats, shops, and villas, and it is easier to check online because the information is typically updated and will save them the hassle of calling and checking the market price condition.

Cars and motorcycles were also part of the respondents' interests. In addition, respondents used the Internet for computer programs or entertainment software, because most of them were already taking courses in computer and software, therefore they enjoyed identifying information about computer and entrainment software. Other concerns by the respondents was travel and transportation. Both staff and student respondents have two holidays every year. Therefore, they are interested in spending their holidays in cool and natural countries, particularly in Europe. Books are another area the respondents were interested in. No doubt they needed references to help them in completing assignments and research.

Selling Companies vs. Internet

The respondents were asked for their opinions about selling companies via Internet, compared to selling companies via other means of marketing. Table 4 illustrates the statistical description from respondents about selling companies vs. Internet. The online selling may be motivated by a personal or family crisis, a new business opportunity, or an unexpected change in business conditions.

Internet Marketing

Table 5 shows the statistical description of respondents about internet marketing. Internet marketing refers to advertising and marketing efforts that use the web and

Table 2. Goods that reflect respondent's rates of using the Internet in the surfing process

Goods	Never Happens %	Rarely Happens %	Once Every 3 Month %	Once Every 1 Month %	Once Every Week %	Once Everyday %
Newspapers & Magazines	0	2	4	19	33	42
Books	6	8	12	25	31	18
Computer Systems	1	35	28	31	3	2
Gems	64	13	23	0	0	0
Concepts & Plays	0	0	0	0	20	80
Tapes & Movies	0	0	0	10	15	75
Insurance Services	15	20	65	0	0	0
Consultations	5	5	32	54	2	2
Roses & Flowers	6	5	23	33	20	13
Computer Programs or Entertainment Software	3	10	13	22	27	25
Real Estates	4	7	8	19	24	38
Travel & Transportation	8	10	9	21	25	27
Songs Tapes	2	3	11	26	31	27
Entertainments Systems	33	24	22	10	5	6
Gold	7	10	23	22	18	20
Cars & Motorcycles	0	0	9	46	23	22
Electric Systems For Houses	60	20	20	0	0	0
Clothes or Shoes	20	20	21	24	10	5
Legal Services	18	20	37	22	3	0
Rates and Shares	3	5	12	51	24	5

email to drive direct sales via electronic commerce, in addition to sales leads from web sites or emails. Internet marketing and online advertising efforts are typically used in conjunction with traditional types of advertising like radio, television, newspapers and magazines.

Table 3. Goods that reflect respondent's rates of using the Internet in the purchase process

Goods	Never Happens %	Rarely Happens %	Once Every 3 Month %	Once Every 1 Month %	Once Every Week %	Once Everyday %
Newspapers & Magazines	0	2	4	19	33	42
Books	6	8	12	25	31	18
Computer Systems	1	35	28	31	3	2
Gems	64	13	23	0	0	0
Concepts & Plays	0	0	0	0	20	80
Tapes & Movies	0	0	0	10	15	75
Insurance Services	18	19	63	0	0	0
Consultations	6	6	30	50	4	4
Roses & Flowers	3	2	20	42	11	22
Computer Programs or Entertainment Software	3	13	10	22	27	25
Real Estates	8	3	5	22	22	40
Travel & Transportation	5	11	12	33	20	19
Songs Tapes	1	5	9	26	30	29
Entertainments Systems	21	21	22	20	10	6
Gold	5	8	31	18	18	20
Cars & Motorcycles	2	1	8	38	6	45
Electric Systems For Houses	55	18	18	2	5	2
Clothes or Shoes	17	16	22	27	12	6
Legal Services	13	17	35	23	7	5
Rates and Shares	5	7	15	44	21	8

Testing the Research Hypotheses

H1: There is a significant relationship between education level and online shopping.

To test this hypothesis, the study applied the test of One Way ANOVA that is concerned with testing the effect of demographic variables on the e-Shopping. Table 6 shows the results.

After applying the one-way ANOVA test, it was obvious that the significance was less than ($\alpha = 0.05$), meaning that education level is a factor that affects the

Table 4. The statistical description of respondents about selling companies vs. Internet

* I T ems	Don't Agree at All		Don't Agree		Neutral		Agree		Totally Agree		Mean	St. Deviation
	F	%	F	%	F	%	F	%	F	%		
1	12	12.2	26	26.5	22	22.4	21	21.4	17	17.3	2.95	1.295
2	0	0	12	12.2	51	52.0	21	21.4	14	14.3	2.62	0.880
3	25	25.5	20	20.4	27	27.6	16	16.3	10	10.2	3.35	1.301
4	0	0	52	53.1	25	25.5	13	13.3	8	8.2	3.23	0.972
5	5	5.1	8	8.2	47	48.0	22	22.4	16	16.3	2.63	1.019
6	19	19.4	29	29.6	27	27.6	12	12.2	11	11.2	3.34	1.243
7	4	4.1	44	44.9	24	24.5	26	26.5	0	0	3.27	.903
8	20	20.4	32	32.7	32	32.7	9	9.2	5	5.1	3.54	1.076
9	0	0	14	14.3	35	35.7	38	38.8	11	11.2	2.53	0.876
10	0	0	24	24.5	35	35.7	17	17.3	22	22.4	2.62	1.088
11	7	7.1	12	12.2	50	51.0	0	0	29	29.6	2.67	1.224
12	8	8.2	12	12.2	57	58.2	13	13.3	8	8.2	2.99	0.958
13	0	0	4	4.1	23	23.5	48	49.0	23	23.5	2.08	0.795
14	8	8.2	9	9.2	30	30.6	23	23.5	28	28.6	2.45	1.227
15	13	13.3	9	9.2	26	26.5	24	24.5	26	26.5	3.66	1.252
16	0	0	7	7.1	29	29.6	53	54.1	9	9.2	2.35	0.748

*Please refer to Appendix.

e-Shopping experience. This proves that the more educated an individual is, the better knowledge he/she has. Therefore, the first hypothesis is accepted.

H2: There is a significant relationship between gender and online shopping.

Table 7 illustrates the t-test to test the effect of gender on using e-Shopping. To test this hypothesis, the study applied the t-test with the results detailed in Table 7.

The t-test shows that gender is insignificant in using e-Shopping, since the significance equals 0.065, which is more than ($\alpha = 0.05$). Thus, both males and females are using e-Shopping without any distinction. Therefore, the second hypothesis is rejected.

H3: Respondents have information about monthly salary of a family.

Table 8 illustrates the results of the One Way ANOVA used to test whether respondents had information about monthly salary of their families. It is clear that

Table 5. The statistical description of respondents about Internet marketing

* ITEMS	Don't Agree at All		Don't Agree		Neutral		Agree		Totally Agree		Mean	St. Deviation
	F	%	F	%	F	%	F	%	F	%		
1	8	8.2	6	6.1	40	40.8	30	30.6	14	14.3	2.63	1.068
2	3	3.1	11	11.2	27	27.6	45	45.9	12	12.2	2.47	0.955
3	8	8.2	6	6.1	40	40.8	30	30.6	14	14.3	2.63	1.068
4	3	3.1	11	11.2	27	27.6	45	45.9	12	12.2	2.47	0.955
5	12	12.2	11	11.2	38	38.8	20	20.4	17	17.3	2.81	1.215
6	3	3.1	11	11.2	63	64.3	9	9.2	12	12.2	2.84	0.893
7	0	0	21	21.4	52	53.1	14	14.3	11	11.2	2.85	0.889
8	8	8.2	0	0	46	46.9	22	22.4	22	22.4	2.49	1.095
9	17	17.3	18	18.4	20	20.4	43	43.9	0	0	3.09	1.149
10	7	7.1	5	5.1	62	63.3	16	16.3	8	8.2	2.87	.904
11	0	0	0	0	44	44.9	54	55.1	0	0	2.45	0.500
12	12	12.2	26	26.5	22	22.4	21	21.4	17	17.3	2.95	1.295
13	0	0	12	12.2	51	52.0	21	21.4	14	14.3	2.62	0.880
14	5	5.1	8	8.2	47	48.0	22	22.4	16	16.3	2.63	1.019
15	0	0	30	30.6	49	50.0	19	19.4	0	0	3.11	0.702
16	0	0	14	14.3	35	35.7	38	38.8	11	11.2	2.53	0.876
17	0	0	24	24.5	35	35.7	17	17.3	22	22.4	2.62	1.088
18	7	7.1	12	12.2	50	51.0	0	0	29	29.6	2.67	1.224
19	8	8.2	12	12.2	57	58.2	13	13.3	8	8.2	2.99	0.958
20	24	24.5	9	9.2	42	42.9	17	17.3	6	6.1	3.29	1.192
21	0	0	4	4.1	23	23.5	48	49.0	23	23.5	2.08	0.795
22	12	12.2	26	26.5	22	22.4	21	21.4	17	17.3	2.95	1.295
23	0	0	12	12.2	51	52.0	21	21.4	14	14.3	2.62	0.880
24	25	25.5	20	20.4	27	27.6	16	16.3	10	10.2	3.35	1.301
25	0	0	52	53.1	25	25.5	13	13.3	8	8.2	3.23	0.972
26	5	5.1	8	8.2	47	48.0	22	22.4	16	16.3	2.63	1.019
27	19	19.4	29	29.6	27	27.6	12	12.2	11	11.2	3.34	1.243
28	4	4.1	44	44.9	24	24.5	26	26.5	0	0	3.27	.903

*Please refer to Appendix.

the significance equals 0.017, which is less than (α = 0.05), meaning that most respondents have information about the monthly salary of their families. **Therefore, this hypothesis is accepted.**

Table 6. One way ANOVA (test the effect of education on using e-shopping)

Dimension	Between Groups	SS	df	MS	F	Sig
Education Level	54.97	1	27.48	0.85	1.87	0.022*
	9555.2	96	32.17			
	9610.1	97				

* Significant at less than α =0.05.

Table 7. T-test (test the effect of gender on using e-shopping)

Sig	T	Females (N= 44)		Males (N=54)	
		S. Deviation	Mean	S. Deviation	Mean
0.065	3.755	0.232	3.99	0.339	4.00

* Significant at less than α =0.05

H4: There is a significant relationship between income and online shopping.

Table 9 shows the results of the One Way ANOVA test used to test the effect of income of consumers' online shopping. The test of the One Way ANOVA proves that the income of the consumer impacts online shopping. The significance equals 0.031, which is less than (α = 0.05). This simply means that the more income consumers have, the more online shopping the consumer will engaged in. Therefore, this hypothesis is accepted.

H5: Customers trust e-Shopping

Trust is a relatively old concept in the view of business practitioners. Table 10 shows the results of a simple regression test used to test the relationship between online trust and online purchase intention. In order to test this hypothesis, the study

Table 8. One-way ANOVA to test whether respondents have information about monthly salary of their families

Dimension	Between Groups	SS	Df	MS	F	Sig
Respondents Information About Family Salary	50.86	1	22.4868	0.73	1.982	0.017*
	89745.9	96	29.21			
	89796.76	97				

* Significant at less than α =0.05.

Table 9. One way ANOVA to test the effect of income of consumers on online shopping

Dimension	Between Groups	SS	Df	MS	F	Sig
Respondents Information About The Income	44.89	1	19.348	0.81	1.786	0.031*
	789.986	96	27.30			
	834.876	97				

* Significant at less than α =0.05.

had to apply a simple regression test that is concerned with measuring the impact of the independent variables on the dependent variables. There is a positive relationship between online trust and online purchase intention at a significance of 0.023, which is less than (α = 0.05). Therefore, the more online trust a consumer has, the higher that consumer's purchase intention will be. Therefore, this hypothesis is accepted.

H6: There is a significant relationship between the ability to use the Internet and online shopping.

Table 11 shows the results of a simple regression test used to test the relationship between a consumer's ability to use the Internet and the online shopping experience of consumers.

The results show that there is a positive relationship between the ability to use Internet and the online shopping behaviors of consumers at a significant of 0.041 (less than α = 0.05). The results clarify that the independent variable (the ability to use Internet) impact explains about 57% of the dependent variable (online shopping).

Therefore, the more ability to use the Internet by consumers, the more online consumers will utilize e-shopping. Therefore, this hypothesis is accepted.

Table 10. The simple regression test the relationship between online trust and online purchase intention

R^2	R	Sig	T Value	Squares Sum	Means of Squares	df	Sources	Dimension
0.40	0.63	0.023*	13.9	48.52543	48.52543	1	Regression	Online Trust
				74.88448	0.25045	96	The Standard	

* Significant at less than α =0.05.

Table 11. Results of the simple regression test used to test the relationship between the ability to use the Internet and the online shopping of consumers

R^2	R	Sig	T Value	Squares sum	Means of Squares	df	Sources	Dimension
0.33	0.57	0.041*	11.4	43.44367	43.56987	1	Regression	The Ability to Use Internet
				71.66712	0.22489	96	The Standard	

* Significant at less than α =0.05.

CONCLUSION AND RECOMMENDATIONS

This study concludes that online shopping is a process of purchasing goods, services, and products that might be available in any part of the world. Online shoppers can be affected by several factors. The more income consumers have, the more they will participate in online shopping and vice versa. Results suggest that customers trust online shopping when they are dealing with authorized companies and well-known websites such as e-Bay, Amazon, and so on. Gender, however, does not appear to be a main factor that effects online shopping as both males and females showed almost the same use in online shopping. The results also suggested that the more education customers or users have, the better knowledge they might have about online shopping, and the more likely it is that they will participate in online shopping.

All the hypotheses were accepted after applying the one-way ANOVA with significance less than ($\alpha = 0.05$) except H2 with significance equal 0.065 which is more than ($\alpha = 0.05$). The Education factor (H1) is positively correlated with the person's level of income, with indication that, there is a significant relationship between education level and e-Shopping behavior with significance less than ($\alpha = 0.05$). This factor affect the online shopping experience. The study found that there is no relationship between gender and e-Shopping (H2) as the t-test shows that gender is insignificant in using online shopping with significance equal 0.065. This indicate that both genders are using e-Shopping without any variation. H3 was accepted hypothesis because all the respondents are familiar with the their family income with significance less than ($\alpha = 0.05$). The study found that there is a significant relationships between income and e-Shopping (H4). This indicates that the more money they have, the more they spend online with significance equal 0.031 which is less than ($\alpha = 0.05$). Furthermore, for H5 'customers trust e-Shopping', this indicates that the more trust the consumer has the more purchase intention will be. Finally, for H6, the study found that there is a significant relationship between the ability to use the Internet and online shopping behavior of consumers at significant of 0.041. This indicate that the more capability to use the Internet, the more online consumers will utilize the online shopping.

The overall result indicates that the consumers have perceived e-Shopping in a confident approach. This noticeably justifies the growth of e-Shopping in Bahrain. Further research into online shopping of both users and countries may result in improving and enhancing the online shopping experience of consumers.

REFERENCES

Al-Alawi, A. I., & Al-Ali, F. M. (2015). Factors affecting e-commerce adoption in SMEs in the GCC: An empirical study of Kuwait. *Research Journal of Information Technology*, *7*(1), 1–21. doi:10.3923/rjit.2015.1.21

Alqahtani, A. S., Goodwin, R. D., & de Vries, D. B. (2018). Cultural factors influencing e-commerce usability in Saudi Arabia. *International Journal of Advanced and Applied Sciences*, *5*(6), 1–10. doi:10.21833/ijaas.2018.06.001

Bahaddad, A. A., Drew, S., Houghtoni, L., & Alfarraj, O. A. (2018). Factors attracting online consumers to choose e-Malls for e-procurement in Saudi Arabia. *Enterprise Information Systems*, *12*(7), 856–887. doi:10.1080/17517575.2015.1091952

Baldevbhai, P. (2015). A study on consumers demographic profile influence on online shopping behaviour. *Indian Journal of Applied Research*, *1*(3), 212–214.

Başev, E. S. (2014). Online buying behaviour of Turkish consumer: An Exploratory study on Hepsiburada.com. *Global Media Journal*, *5*(9), 97–132.

Bellman, S., Lohse, G., & Johnson, E. (1999). Predictors of online buying behavior. *Communications of the ACM*, *42*(12), 32–38. doi:10.1145/322796.322805

Bhattacherjee, A. (2001). An empirical analysis of the antecedents of electronic commerce service continuance. *Decision Support Systems*, *32*(2), 201–214. doi:10.1016/S0167-9236(01)00111-7

Burke, R. (2002). Technology and the customer interface: What Consumers Want in the Physical and Virtual Store. *Journal of the Academy of Marketing Science*, *30*(4), 411–432. doi:10.1177/009207002236914

Çelik, H. E., & Yilmaz, V. (2011). Extending the technology acceptance model for adoption of e-shopping by consumers in Turkey. *Journal of Electronic Commerce Research*, *12*(2), 15.

Gehrt, K., & Yan, R. (2004). Situational, consumer, and retail factors affecting internet, catalog, and store shopping. *International Journal of Retail & Distribution Management*, *32*(1), 5–18. doi:10.1108/09590550410515515

Gordon, A., & Bhowan, K. (2005). Factors that influence shopping behavior. *Alternation (Durban)*, *12*(1), 45–169.

Griffith, D. A., Matthew, M. B., & Harvey, M. G. (2006). An investigation of national culture's influence on relationship and knowledge resources in Brunel business school. *Proceeding of 2006 Conference Doctoral Symposium*.

Hong, C. (1993). *The electronic marketing manual*. New York, NY: McGraw-Hill.

Ladhari, R., Gonthier, J., & Lajante, M. (2019). Generation Y and online fashion shopping: Orientations and profiles. *Journal of Retailing and Consumer Services*, *48*, 113–121. doi:10.1016/j.jretconser.2019.02.003

Lauden, K., & Travel, C. (2013). *E-Commerce* (9th ed.). Business Technology Society.

Monsuwe, T., Dellaert, B., & Ruyter, K. (2004). What drives consumers to shop online? A literature review. *International Journal of Service Industry Management*, *15*(1), 102–121. doi:10.1108/09564230410523358

Rittiboonchai, W., Kriwuttisom, P., & Ngo, T. M. T. (2019). Factors affecting online shopping behavior of Thai and Vietnamese female students. *Rmutt Global Business Accounting and Finance Review*, *2*(2).

Shi, K., De Vos, J., Yang, Y., & Witlox, F. (2019). Does e-shopping replace shopping trips? Empirical evidence from Chengdu, China. *Transportation Research Part A, Policy and Practice*, *122*, 21–33. doi:10.1016/j.tra.2019.01.027

Wood, S. (2002). Future fantasies: A social change perspective of retailing in the 21st century. *Journal of Retailing*, *78*(1), 77–83. doi:10.1016/S0022-4359(01)00069-0

Xia, L., Monroe, K., & Cox, J. (2004). The price is unfair! A conceptual framework of price fairness perceptions. *Journal of Marketing*, *68*(4), 1–15. doi:10.1509/jmkg.68.4.1.42733

APPENDIX: QUESTIONNAIRE ABOUT INTERNET MARKETING

Table 12. 1-Our concern is to know your opinion about using Internet in marketing comparing to other means, Kindly express how you agree with opinions as follows:

Question Item	I Don't Agree at All	I Don't Agree	Undefined	I Agreed	I Totally Agree
1. Marketing via internet states the process of testing while marketing	O	O	O	O	O
2. It's easy to understand others while marketing via Internet	O	O	O	O	O
3. Marketing via Internet requires special systems, this is beyond my capacity.	O	O	O	O	O
4. I don't object to inform others about	O	O	O	O	O
5. Persons who are marketing via internet are considered VIP persons	O	O	O	O	O
6. I know lot about persons who are marketing via Internet	O	O	O	O	O
7. I can market via Internet when necessary	O	O	O	O	O
8. I trust companies which sell via Internet and consider marketing process via Internet is safe.	O	O	O	O	O
9. I know Internet Marketing is considered as an easy process for me.	O	O	O	O	O
10.Internet marketing is expensive for me, I will have to pay subscription amount at Internet network.	O	O	O	O	O
11.I got an opportunity of Internet marketing prior I decided to purchase.	O	O	O	O	O
12.Internet marketing is a risky process	O	O	O	O	O
13.Marketing via Internet gives me the opportunity to Select the best goods	O	O	O	O	O
14. I can provide necessary systems for Internet marketing	O	O	O	O	O
15. Marketing via Internet will improve my image in front of surrounding.	O	O	O	O	O
16. I can trust Internet Service providers in transforming necessary personal information to complete Internet marketing	O	O	O	O	O

continued on following page

Table 12. Continued

Question Item	I Don't Agree at All	I Don't Agree	Undefined	I Agreed	I Totally Agree
17.Internet marketing process is considered unpractical.	O	O	O	O	O
18.Internet Marketing gives me more control than purchasing process.	O	O	O	O	O
19.Internet Marketing is considered as safe purchasing and marketing process.	O	O	O	O	O
20. Internet Marketing needs mental effort.	O	O	O	O	O
21 I can market via internet quickly.	O	O	O	O	O
22.Internet Marketing is matching with marketing way.	O	O	O	O	O
23. I think I can show to others results of Internet marketing	O	O	O	O	O
24.In general, Internet marketing will improve my marketing process.	O	O	O	O	O
25. IN General, I think Internet Marketing can be done easily.	O	O	O	O	O
26. Internet Marketing gives a change for obtaining best prices.	O	O	O	O	O
27.Internet marketing is a clear and understanding process.	O	O	O	O	O
28. I got very good opportunity for Internet marketing	O	O	O	O	O

Table 13. 2-Our concern is to know your opinion about selling companies via Internet, comparing to selling companies via other means of marketing, in all sentences as follow, explain how you agree with both of them

Question Item	I Don't Agree at All	I Don't Agree	Undefined	I Agreed	I Totally Agree
1. It's easy to search about the seller on Internet who sells goods which I Want.	O	O	O	O	O
2. I can obtain information easily about products and services which I would like to purchase from Internet seller.	O	O	O	O	O
3. Internet Seller provides quick service	O	O	O	O	O
4. It's easy to ask about certain goods from Internet seller.	O	O	O	O	O
5. Internet seller provides best service to the consumer when purchasing, also he provides help after purchasing.	O	O	O	O	O
6. Submit order for obtaining certain goods, will take shorter time with Internet seller.	O	O	O	O	O
7. I can obtain more information about certain goods via internet seller.	O	O	O	O	O
8. Process of returning goods and recovering paid amounts is easier with internet selling.	O	O	O	O	O
9. Internet sellers provide easy way to obtain opinions of concerned about goods which I would like to purchase.	O	O	O	O	O
10.Payment process to purchase goods is easier with internet sellers.	O	O	O	O	O
11. Internet sellers provide better updated information about goods which I have purchased.	O	O	O	O	O
12.It's easy to compare similar goods between different internet sellers.	O	O	O	O	O
13. Internet sellers will provide easy way to identify opinion of other consumers about goods which I would like to purchase.	O	O	O	O	O
14. Payment process for sellers online on purchasing a more hazardous commodity.	O	O	O	O	O
15. I prefer to collect information related to purchase process via sellers online.	O	O	O	O	O
16. Process of delivery purchased goods via Internet takes long time.	O	O	O	O	O

Chapter 9
The Implications of Unethical and Illegal Behavior in the World of E-Commerce

Adel Ismail Al-Alawi
https://orcid.org/0000-0003-0775-4406
University of Bahrain, Bahrain

Arpita Anshu Mehrotra
Royal University for Women, Bahrain

Hala Elias
Royal University for Women, Bahrain

Hina S. M. Safdar
University of Bahrain, Bahrain

Sara Abdulrahman Al-Bassam
The Social Development Office of His Highness the Prime Minister's Diwan, Kuwait

ABSTRACT

The main focus of this chapter is to identify the behaviors of the consumers and sellers of e-commerce in Bahrain. It also seeks to understand the ethical and legal issues faced by the users of e-commerce and the various reasons for such behavior. The perception of the consumers regarding online retailers discussed through appropriate measures and research data. The chapter clearly explains the historical development of e-commerce in Bahrain and the processes and procedures of setting up an online business in the country. The common legal and ethical issues faced by the consumers discussed in detail and supported by different models to understand user behavior. The research onion method used to gather quantitative and qualitative data. The primary data collected through questionnaires and interviews whereas the secondary

DOI: 10.4018/978-1-7998-0272-3.ch009

data collected through literature. The data analysis shows the results of the mixed method supported by different graphs and models. The different recommendations provided to solve the most prevalent problems confronted by the buyers and the sellers of e-commerce.

INTRODUCTION

In this modern world of Globalization, the world is changing at a rapid speed and so is the technology around us. The factors affecting our daily life, along with the lives of the upcoming generation cannot be overseen. The modern advancement and developments have narrowed the space between human beings and machines (Al-Alawi, 2014). As has been stated by Cabell (2001),"around two years ago, the total amount of knowledge on e-Commerce could be collected in a small bucket of bits. But two years from now, we might float in a sea of information on digital technology alone". This is because technology keeps changing over time and it is hard to keep pace with the continuously changing digital environment. On one hand, human beings are using technology and compromising on their privacy and on the other hand, technology is satisfying the needs of the people. But we cannot overlook the fact that human beings are unpredictable, and it is not easy to control them. Due to this fact, there is a rise in the cybercrimes and a large number of people are misusing the technology to intentionally or unintentionally harm the other users around them. Despite the fact that there are many regulations and laws that protect the individuals, there has been a drastic increase in these crimes (Al-Alawi & Abdelgadir, 2006; Al-Alawi, 2014). These crimes are not just limited to using social media and internet, but they have also left a negative impact on the e-Commerce activities around us. The world of e-Commerce is so vast that it is almost impossible to measure the extent of this impact. In the modern world, e-Commerce has gained a widespread popularity and is one of the most useful platforms for businesses as well as individuals.

The emergence of e-Commerce has made the traditional business practices expand and reduced the limitations involved in the way people used to do business. For example, the appearance and forms of businesses have changed compared to the traditional systems and these changes are the basis of decisions in all economies. With the development of virtual systems in the markets and stores, it is possible for the consumers to shop at their convenience anytime and anywhere in the world without leaving their homes. They can choose and order products or services from a wide variety of virtual shops and pay on the spot. At the same time businesses can market their products and services through advertisements (Nanehkaran, 2013).

One of the most important characteristics of the Internet is its ever-changing and fluid characteristic. Web pages vanish in seconds and users pass through the electronic highway at a relatively fast speed. The ever-changing technology is also bringing along a vast number of unethical practices and actions and this issue has been widely discussed ever since the emergence of digital technology (Cabell, 2001).

On one hand, we can reasonably conclude that e-commerce has a large number of benefits which include faster buying and selling around the clock all over the world, low costs of operations and better quality of services, easy start-up and marketing, simple and fast business services and improved customer services. But on the other hand, we cannot overlook the threats posed by availing these benefits which include privacy and security issues, fraud, illegal access, initial costs of setting up web applications and websites, User resistance, technical software and hardware issues, unsolicited emails, false advertising, product warranty, cybersquatting and cyber security.

Statement of the Problem

The expanding growth of internet and e-Commerce activities have given rise to a number of legal and ethical issues being questioned. Most of the people want to get their tasks done as quickly as possible without much hassles and e-Commerce has provided them with a great medium where they can save time, money and efforts. In the past, mobile phones, faxes and telephones have opened vast opportunities for business processes. But we cannot deny the fact that every new business is born with some associated risks and same is the case with e-Commerce. Therefore, it is extremely important and beneficial to identify these issues and the different risks they carry for the users in order to try and create a safe environment for the buyers as well as the sellers.

It is fairly easy for businesses to get sidetracked in the hassle of keeping up with the technology and as a result lose track of the ethical implications. These implications would generally be easily addressed during face to face interactions with the customers, but it is a big challenge when it comes to e-Commerce. E-Businesses around the world are affected due to some of the most commonly prevailing issues which include web tracking, privacy issues, disintermediation and reinter mediation, fraud, copyright infringements, domain names and many more. These issues have to be resolved through the practical application of universally applicable ethical and legal laws, so people do not hesitate to reap the benefits of e-Commerce facilities.

The purpose of this report is to identify the behaviors of the buyers and sellers involved in online transactions in the Kingdom of Bahrain. It is directed towards providing appropriate solutions for some of the most common issues faced by the consumers and sellers in the country.

Research Significance

Ethics are usually formed through personal beliefs, thoughts, morals and behaviors of the individuals. The two main building blocks of any relationship are trust and communication. The framework for ethical web accessibility is a critical factor towards the success of the e-Commerce initiatives around the world. Studying the important factors which contribute to these issues, will help to provide suitable solutions to help the widespread issues related to e-Commerce. Managers can formulate different strategies and regulations to control the unethical actions which result in losing the trust of the customers. This research aims to understand the behavior and perceptions of the consumers of e-Commerce and provide suitable solutions so that they can reap the benefits of e-Commerce without any hindrance. It will also help to understand the viewpoints of different e-Commerce service providers, how they overcome some of the most common issues in e-Commerce and their suggestions or recommendations to improve the e-Commerce situations.

Research Objectives

The main objectives of this research are:

- To provide an insight into different practices and models of e-Commerce
- To identify the different kinds of unethical and illegal behaviors faced by the buyers and sellers in e-Commerce.
- To study the reasons for unethical consumer behavior and its impact.
- To provide recommendations and solutions to solve the most common types of unethical or illegal problems.
- To discuss suitable solutions to eliminate the risk of losing information security and prevent un- authorized accessing.
- To conduct a research on the development of e-Commerce in Bahrain.
- To study the factors influencing the e-Commerce behavior of the consumers in Bahrain.

Research Methodology

The secondary data in the literature review was collected through different websites, journal, articles and previous research studies. The research methodologies and the data collection techniques used in the literature review were reviewed properly and the most appropriate ones were used for this research. The first part of the methodology focuses on identifying the behavior of the consumers of e-Commerce. For this purpose, a quantitative method was adopted, and a survey was conducted which included a sample of 55 students from the University of Bahrain. This survey was conducted electronically through emails and other social media.

The data collected through the survey was then reviewed to focus on the main factors to be analyzed in the study. To analyze the data collected for this study, the study used the statistical packages of science (SPSS) software 22. In order to reach a more reasonable conclusion, the factors were further investigated by collecting the qualitative data. This was done by conducting interviews with the product and service providers of e-Commerce in the Kingdom of Bahrain. The interview was conducted with the owner of a UAE and Bahrain based online shop called MENA shoppers and with the IT project manager of the E-government authority in Bahrain. The research captured information from both the sources, which was analyzed to reach the appropriate conclusion.

Research Limitations

The research does not cover the social, technological and economic issues involved in e-Commerce and focuses only on the ethical and legal aspects. It focuses on the views, experiences and perceptions of some of the e-Commerce manufacturers in Bahrain. The sample consists of 2 manufacturers and around 55 consumers of e-Commerce. However, many consumers and manufacturers in Bahrain could not be interviewed and surveyed due to the access, time and cost limitations. In addition to this, one of the main obstacles was information access, since most of the organizations hesitate to provide confidential information about the issues they face with the customers and vice versa. This research provides suggestions and recommendations to improve the e-Commerce situations but does not help in implementing them.

Study Structure

The study consists of six sections. Section one provides a brief introduction about e-Commerce and the implications of different ethical and legal issues in the modern world of e-Commerce. Then it provides the research problem, significance, objectives, limitations and methodology.

Section two discusses the development of e-Commerce in Bahrain, while Section three consists of the literature review which discusses the history, definitions and types of e-Commerce and its objectives. It also illustrated the different factors affecting e-Commerce and the reasons for this behavior.

Section four provides an overview of the different methodologies used to conduct the research. It also discusses the research tools, procedures and the research design used in the report. The data collection method, instrument design and the sampling technique used in this research is also presented along with the procedures for data analysis.

Section five is devoted to providing the data analysis, presentation and discussion. The main results and findings from different methods are presented, compared and tested with the pre-existing theories of the literature review.

Section six concludes the research by giving a short review of the findings and the research in general. It also provides different recommendations for the buyers and providers of e-Commerce in order to help them overcome the issues in e-Commerce.

The Research Management Plan

A systematic approach was followed in this research and the research work was divided into three main phases and nine activities (Table 1). This study management plan was developed in order to help and develop a better understanding of the study structure and to facilitate the management of the study work.

E-Commerce in Bahrain

The Kingdom of Bahrain is a small island situated in the Gulf. Although the population of Bahrain is relatively less compared to other GCC countries, but the interconnectedness of organizations to the internet, makes it one of the most digitally connected regions in the Gulf. Bahrain was one of the first countries in the Gulf to install a mainframe computer in 1962 and digitalized its national and international telephone network in 1992. The internet service was launched in Bahrain in 1995 whereas the wireless internet connection 'WiMax' was launched in 2007. It also became the first country in the world to establish a Next Generation Network (NGN) in 2008 (Ms. Vivian Jamal, Bahrain Economic Development Board, 2013). Internet usage all around the world is increasing day by day and so is the use of e-Commerce in Bahrain (Alajmi, 2014). The importance of e-Commerce was realized in Bahrain in the early 1999 but a major boom in the e-Commerce activities was witnessed in 2004, when the Ministry of Industry and Commerce established the Directorate of e-Commerce and IT. This was a great initiative to support and strengthen the framework of Information technology and e-Commerce in the country, because it helped the individuals as well as the industrial and commercial sectors to reduce cost and save time through direct contact methods. The official website of the ministry has been developed throughout the years and a wide variety of online services have been included. Many programs have been administered as well in order to enrich the e-Commerce activities for all local businesses in the region. The latest technologies have been used for enhancing the website to successfully provide the e-government services to the customers. In order to encourage the citizens to avail

Table 1. The research management plan

	Phases	Activities	Outcome	Sections
Phase One	I. Research Project Definition.	1.Introduction of the research	1. Identifying the research problem, objectives, design, methodology and study structure.	Introduction
	II. Literature Review - General - Focused	2. Collect data based on pre-existing theories and previous studies through journals, articles, websites and previous research papers.	1.Understanding e-Commerce and its types. 2. Understanding the History and activities of e-Commerce in Bahrain. 3. Identifying the ethical and legal issues in e-Commerce	Literature Review
Phase Two	I. Quantitative Survey (Questionnaires).	1.Developing Questionnaire. 2. Selecting Sample population. 3. Distributing the Questionnaires.	1. Identifying the common issues faced by the consumers of e-Commerce and their importance. 2.Identifying the most common e-Commerce platforms. 3.Understanding the perceptions and reactions of the consumers. 4.Suggestions for improvement.	Methodology
	II. Qualitative Survey (Interviews).	1. Preparing Interview questions. 2.Conducting Interviews.	1. Understanding the reasons for unethical and illegal e-Commerce behaviors. 2. Identifying the issues. 3.Suggestions for improvement.	
Phase Three	I. Data Analysis	1.Entering data for analysis. 2.Findings Presentation	1. Testing the findings for research success factors. 2.Categorizing the responses.	Data Analysis
Phase Four	I. Conclusion and Recommendations. II. Write up and Submission.	1.Develop suggestions based on the findings. 2.Writing up the study	1. Concluding the research and providing solutions to solve the e-Commerce problems. 2. Final draft of the study.	Conclusion and Recommendations

the e-Commerce facilities rather than wasting their time by using the conventional methods, the ministry is taking many steps to promote awareness of the electronic services in the Kingdom and push it towards a digital society (moic.gov.bh).

According to Trade Arabia News Service (2011), the internet usage in Bahrain had increased from 1.2 million (2000) to 18.7 million (2010). As stated in the report by Visa and Interactive Media in Retail Group (IMRG) International, in 2011 the online sales in Bahrain had reached BD 66.15 million (an estimated $175 million), which implies that the internet usage has increased upto 800 percent compared to the year 2000, meaning 55 out of every 100 Bahrainis are using internet. This percentage is one of the highest in the GCC. The government of Bahrain has paved new ways to e-Commerce through the development of Central Informatics Organization (CIO). Stephen Leeds, the business leader of Visa Middle East e-Commerce stated in one of his interview that the youth of Bahrain is striving towards the development of the digital society since online shopping in Bahrain is still in its initial stages but just like all the countries of this world, the Bahraini consumers are also facing certain barriers in e-Commerce such as privacy concerns and lack of trust. Bahrain, being one of the world's largest retail electronic payment networks, provides a number of mediums to its consumers in Bahrain in order to encourage them and restore their trust in shopping online. The head of the IMRG, Aad Weening asserts that the aim of spreading e-Commerce awareness among the consumers is to attract foreign investors and initiatives to develop domestic websites (tradearabia.com).

Bahrain is being tested on by many companies for the new ICT technologies. Bahrain also received a special award by the United Nations in June 2010 for the improvement of e-services and for building up the delivery of its services through e-participation (Bahrain.com). Since 2010, Viva Bahrain has invested almost $300 million for the improvement and innovation of applications for using e-services and e-Commerce in Bahrain (Bahrain.com,2013). Some of the well-known electronic manufacturers in Bahrain are Ameeri Industries who deal in manufacturing and distributing electronic products under brands including AMETECH, AMELITE and AMGARD and Awal Gulf, which is one of the biggest manufacturers of air conditioners in the GCC, and their products are sold in more than 40 countries worldwide (Vivian Jamal, Bahrain Economic Development Board, 2013).

According to a report by Trade Arabia Business News Information (Manama, 2011), more than Bahrain's online sales hit 175 US$ during 2010 of the retail sales in Bahrain are generated through online businesses. The "Middle East B2C e-Commerce Report 2014" shows that 90% of Bahrain's population use internet and almost 5% of internet users prefer shopping online and this figure is expected to increase by 20% in the next five years. It was also found that despite the increasing popularity of e-Commerce in Bahrain, the users also face some barriers which include predominance of cash on delivery payments, low acceptance of online shopping by the consumers and low adoption of retail channels by the local businesses. However, there are still a few markets that lead the region in the adoption of e-Commerce. The highest revenue in the region is generated through online sale of products including jewelry, computers, clothing, watches and electronics (Avinash Saxena, GDN, 2014; Manama, 2011).

E-Government Services

E-government and its services were launched in Bahrain soon after the increase in internet users and the development of e-Commerce, but it was major step taken by the government to promote e-services and save the time and processes of paying utility bills, traffic fines and applying visas. The National E-government Strategy of Bahrain in 2016 is to increase the number of e-services used by the citizens and organizations by more than 90 percent. Companies in Bahrain can now process most of the registration works, visa applications, banking services and eTendering of government contracts online.

Bahrain ranked second in the GCC in a survey conducted by United Nations Government in January 2012. Another survey which was conducted by the UN Global eGovernment Readiness among 192 countries, placed Bahrain on the 36th position worldwide for the successful application of ICT technologies for the citizens. The government has also taken measures for simplifying the procedures of obtaining a commercial registration and other business licenses. The Business Licensing Integrated System (BLIS) was launched in 2010 which aimed to enhance Bahrain's position and improve its competitiveness among other countries. It also ensured transparency in all the procedures and business processes and simplified the streamlining of all licensing requirements. (Vivian Jamal, Bahrain Economic Development Board, 2013).

Entrepreneurs in Bahrain

The Northwestern University of Qatar conducted a study in 2014 to identify the trends of social media usage in the GCC. The study showed that Bahrain had the largest number of Instagram users compared to Qatar, UAE, KSA, Egypt, Jordan, Lebanon and Tunisia. It was clear from the study that it is a great opportunity for businesses to target their audience in Bahrain through Instagram. This application which was designed by Mike Kreiger and Kevin Systrom is a great platform for the developing SME businesses in Bahrain. Some well-known entrepreneurs from the cottage industry include Rocky by Rose, Canvas.bh, Baked by T and Acai Bahrain, who have realized the early benefits and opportunities offered through Instagram. The vendors are able to communicate with the consumers for taking orders, delivering and collecting payments through emails, SMS, WhatsApp or through Direct Messaging on Instagram and market their products through posting the pictures or videos along with the features of the product and its prices. The most popular product categories include clothes, accessories, cosmetics and electronics. The vendors deliver the products through shipping companies like Aramex or directly at the customer's address and in some cases the customers pick them up personally from the shops. The trend of 'Instapraneurs' has been recognized by both the government and the local franchises of international brands. Despite the growth and success of e-Commerce in Bahrain, the ability to make online payments has been a hassle in the process. Although Credimax and Benefit gateways do exist, but they can be difficult to use for businesses that are being run without any IT support, as it has to be integrated into the websites of the business. However, Paytab which has been launched recently allows the vendors to offer invoices and payments online without having a website (www.eastinnovations.com, 2014).

Setting Up an e-Commerce Based Business in Bahrain

In the past, setting up an e-business in Bahrain was a big hassle but now it takes less than 24 hours to develop an e-Commerce-based website. It requires less efforts due to the cheap hosting services, seamless application integration, plus and play e-Commerce utilities and custom-built web templates. One of the first ministries to provide electronic services in Bahrain is the Ministry of Industry and Commerce. A person who wishes to start an online business can apply for commercial registration with the Ministry of Industry and Commerce (Al-Alawi & Al-Ali, 2015). Tracking the status and approval of the application can also be done electronically through Business Licensing Investment System (BLIS) by visiting the website (www.business.gob.bh). The government of Bahrain established the Directorate of e-Commerce and Information Technology at the Ministry of Industry and Commerce, to provide an environment which is hassle free for the e-traders. For this purpose, the Directorate works in collaboration with the government entities, ministries and other directorates. According to the Ministry of Industry and Commerce, the steps to start an e-business in Bahrain are as shown in Figure 1.

Selecting an e-Commerce Activity

Investors do not have restrictions for investing in most of the business sectors in the Kingdom of Bahrain, but some activities are prohibited because of their impact on the society, economy and environment. 100% foreign ownership and investment is also allowed but there are certain business activities that are legally confined only to the GCC or Bahraini citizens or organizations. All the activities of e-Commerce like

Figure 1. Setting up an e-commerce based business in Bahrain
(Source: http://bahrain.smetoolkit.org)

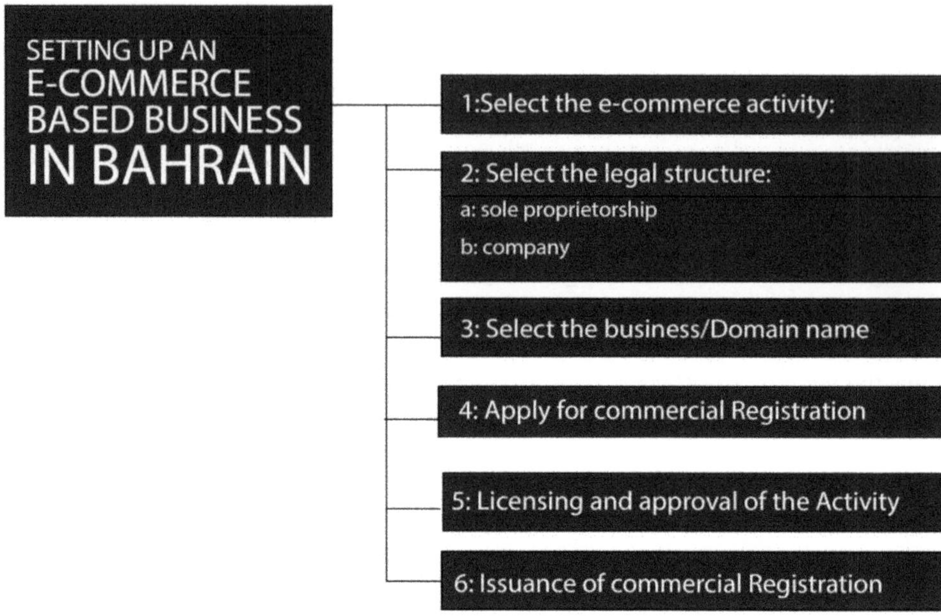

e-promotion of products and services, must be registered in the Ministry of Industry and Commerce. Individuals can start a new e-Commerce-based business, or they can add it to their existing Commercial Registration. Moreover, every applicant is entitled to have an eKey which includes the user ID and password for commencing the e-business. This eKey is provided either by the Ministry of Industry and Commerce or by the eGovernment Authority of Bahrain.

Selecting the Legal Structure

The next step for the investors is to select a legal structure for the e-business. There are certain rules and regulations for commercial companies which are imposed by the Kingdom of Bahrain for selecting the legal structures in order to establish a company. In some cases, the investor might be required to seek other government organizations or entities to choose the legal structure. For example, if the new online business is media based, the approval from the Ministry of Culture is required. Some of the most common forms of legal structures for IT and e-Commerce include:

1. **Sole Proprietorship:** This kind of legal structure is only allowed for Bahrainis or GCC citizens residing in Bahrain. It is owned only by a single person as a

non-incorporated entity and he is solely responsible for the debts and liabilities related to the business and his personal assets can be sold to cover the debts.

2. **Company**: A company may be owned by a single person or by multiple corporate persons and the liabilities of the company are only limited to the capital allocated by each person. The types of companies include Foreign branch company, Partnership, Single person company or a Holding company.

Selecting the Business/Domain Name

It is very important to select a unique and different name which does not match any of the existing business names. The following points should be considered while selecting a name:

- The business interest name should be unique.
- The name of the e-Commerce website should not match any of the registered businesses existing in Bahrain or anywhere else in the world.
- The Ministry of Industry and Commerce must not have the name already registered in its database.

It is important to keep in mind the terms and conditions stated by the Directorate of e-Commerce and IT and it is preferred to choose a name that ends with.bh.com.

Applying for Commercial Registration

There are two types of Commercial Registration that the investor can apply for. The first is the company commercial registration that can be applied to all types of company structures and the second is an individual commercial registration which can only be applied to a sole proprietorship. The applications for commercial registration of companies can be made at Bahrain's Investor Centre and the applications for individuals can be made at the Ministry of Industry and Commerce's Commercial Registration Directorates. The following are the required documents for the application process:

Documents required for an Individual establishment:

1. Application form
2. Registration form
3. Application form for the commercial name registration.
4. Copy of passport and CPR.
5. For employed applicants, a certificate from the applicant's employer is required stating that he has no objection on this matter and it should be signed and stamped by the employer.

6. For unemployed applicants, a proof is required that he is unemployed.

Documents required for a company:

1. Registration form
2. Single application form for the company registration.
3. Copy of CPR for Bahrainis and a copy of passport if the applicant is a GCC resident.
4. Draft of Memorandum of Association (for a single person company).
5. If the applicant is employed in the private sector and he is to hold a directorship or management post, he has to submit a no objection letter.
6. A copy of commercial agency, franchise or distribution agreement is required if the objectives of the company are related to such agreements.
7. If the company is one year old, a financial statement which is most recently audited is required.
8. A copy of the Commercial Registration of the company.
9. A license agreement for using a trademark (if applicable).
10. A resolution of the Board of Directors to join as partners.

Documents required for the single application form of company registration:

1. Copy of CPR and passport with visa pages (GCC residents).
2. Power of attorney for registration agent, if applicable.
3. A copy of commercial agency, franchise or distribution agreement is required if the objectives of the company are related to such agreements.
4. Copies of the CV, qualifications and a Draft of Memorandum of Association (for management and professional consultancy)
5. A reference letter either from a law firm, auditing firm or a licensed international bank (inside or outside Bahrain).

Documents required for an e-Commerce Activity:

If a company or an individual proprietor wishes to add a new activity, they need to apply at the Ministry of Commerce and Industry along with the following requirements:

1. Copy of CPR or passport.
2. Copy of related certificates or qualifications.
3. The applicant should have enough time to conduct the e-Commerce activity.
4. The applicant must create a website for conducting e-Commerce activities.
5. The applicant should provide a medium for payment.

6. The applicant to provide the delivery services (if required).
7. The address for the customer service shop must be provided (if required)

Licensing and Approval of the Activity

For starting an e-Commerce-based business in Bahrain, it is enough to have a commercial registration issued by the Ministry of Industry and Commerce but for some business activities, a license or approval is required by the government authorities, before obtaining the commercial registration. No license is required if the e-commerce is enabling an existing business which is already licensed and registered but in case the business is listed in the "license required" list of Ministry of Industry and Commerce then the business has to go through the licensing process. For example, if the business is health related then it has to seek approval from the Ministry of Health and some other authorities. The approval sheet for e-Commerce can be obtained from the Directorate of e-Commerce and IT. The investors need to provide the details of the domain name, business concept, education and payment gateway for the setup of the e-Commerce business. The document is processed by the Directorate within one to three working days and they have to present their recommendations about it. Once it is approved, the Commercial Registration is processed.

Issuance of Commercial Registration

After the issuance of the Commercial Registration by the Ministry of Industry and Commerce, it has to be published in the official gazette. The only document that is required at this point of stage is a letter of request by the ministry. The Ministry of Justice's Public Notary carries out the notarization at the Bahrain Investor's Center (BIC). All the documents related to the legal structure should be issued either in Arabic or in English and Arabic both.

LITERATURE REVIEW

This section explains the literature review using primary data, which was collected through previous research papers, websites, journals and articles on e-Commerce. The literature review is divided into two sections. The first section describes the general literature review on e-Commerce, its types, history and definitions. The second part of the literature review is focused on e-Commerce and its implementation in the Kingdom of Bahrain. The purpose of this section is to investigate and form a comparative study on the implications of e-Commerce and the factors affecting it. The main ethical and legal issues involved in e-Commerce will be highlighted in this section, which form the basis of the research. The impact of these issues on user behavior will be explained through appropriate research models. The research also aims to identify the adoption of e-Commerce and the process of setting up an e-Commerce-based business in the Kingdom of Bahrain.

Defining e-Commerce

e-Commerce is those activities which relate to the purchasing and selling of goods and services on the Internet 24/7. Riggins and Rhee (1998), stated according to a survey conducted among a few managers and practitioners, e-Commerce is the "buying and selling of products and services over the internet". However, according to a researcher, e-Commerce should include a wide variety of activities which should not be confined to the buying and selling of products, trading, services by using Information Communications Technology (ICT). e-Commerce can be divides into nine main different classes which include Business to Business (B2B), Business to Consumer (B2C), Consumer to Business (C2B), Consumer to Consumer (C2C), Government to Business (G2B), Business to Government (B2G), Government to Consumer (G2C), Government to Government (G2G) and Intra-organizational. The activities and the concept of e-Commerce has increased and acceptance globally (Goyal, et al. 2019, Al-Alawi & Al-Ali, 2015; Kant et al., 2015; Balasoui, 2015; Korper & Ellis, 2000).

Vladimir (1996, pp 3) defines e-Commerce as "conducting business transaction, sharing business information and maintaining business relationships by using telecommunications networks." He believes that "e-Commerce does not only include buying and selling of goods and services but the different individual business practices within the organization as well". Treese and Stewart (2003) assert that e-Commerce is, "using Internet for purchasing and selling goods and services along with customer support and service after the sale. Internet is a great tool for providing product information and advertising, but the main focus is on the complete transaction. In a broader sense. e-Commerce includes the use of communication technologies and computing in inventory management, order processing, financial business and online airline reservation. Historically, the best idea behind using e-Commerce has been the Electronic Data (EDI)."

According to Minoli and Minoli (1997), "E-Commerce is the integration of security capabilities, communications and data management in order to enable the business applications in various organization to successfully exchange information related to the selling of products and services with each other". The WTO (World Trade Organization) has defined e-Commerce as, "the distribution, production, sales and marketing of products and services through electronic means."

e-Commerce vs Traditional Commerce

The increased popularity of e-Commerce has induced many small and large businesses to adopt it as a medium for a highly profitable sales channel. It should be noted that there are many differences between traditional commerce and e-Commerce and it is important to understand these differences to save time, efforts and money. In this fast-paced world, a business may even choose to have a mixture of e-Commerce and traditional commerce which is not only profitable, but it will help the business to grow drastically. Many businesses are developing business models which are based on both the e-Commerce and traditional commerce practices. Table 2 shows the most important differences between both:

History of e-Commerce

Online shopping was introduced and invented by Michael Aldrich in 1979. With the emergence of internet technology, many businesses began to realize that it was great medium to share information for the consumers and also helped to create a unique brand image of the business in the consumer's mind. The advent of WWW (World Wide Web), opened doors of opportunities for businesses around the world and they found it a great source of reaching out to the customers and increase their sales by

Table 2. E-commerce vs traditional commerce

Key Elements	e-Commerce	Traditional Commerce
Value Creation	Information	Product or service
Strategy	Sense and respond Simple rules	Classical
Competitive Edge	High Speed	Quality and Cost
Competitive Force	Low barriers of entry Power of the customers	Product Substitution Power of the suppliers
Resource Focus	Demand Side	Supply Side
Customer Interface	Screen-to-face	Face-to-face
Communication	Technology-mediated channels	Personal
Accessibility	24x7	Limited time
Customer Interaction	Self service	Seller Influenced
Consumer Behavior	Personalization One-to-One market	Standardization Mass/One-way marketing
Promotion	Word of mouth	Merchandising
Product	Commodity	Perishables, feel & touch

(Source: Rahul Kavaiyya, Scope of e-Commerce, 2015)

putting the information for the customers on their Webpages. This also helped to create a unique brand identity for the businesses. In no time, big companies such as Amazon and E-bay were established.

According to Traver and Laudon (2008), e-Commerce history dates back to the innovation of selling and buying electrical equipment, and the internet. The e-Commerce become feasible during 1991 when Internet was initiated for business usage, then thousands of commerce taken place at the web sites. The history of e-Commerce is a "history of a new, virtual world which is evolving according to the customer advantage. It is a world which we are all building together brick by brick, laying a secure foundation for the future generations".

Early Use of Web

Businesses began availing the opportunity of e-commerce in the early 1990's, even though the use of internet among common people was not much popular back then. Most of the websites only provided basic information about the company such as their products and services or contact numbers. Due to the evolution of the technology, the use of internet became common and when the marketing departments realized that the worldwide usage of websites have increased, they decided to introduce the idea of selling products and services online. These online sales started in 1994, increasing the popularity of credit cards.

Early Online Sales

In 1994, a company called Netscape introduced SSL (Secured Socket Layer), through which the websites were able to encrypt data, and this made the use of credit cards much safer. Due to the increased security measures, many vendors and businesses shifted their focus to selling their products electronically.

Birth of Modern Web Sales

The evolution of technology soon resulted in developing websites, solely for the purpose of online buying and selling. Some examples of these websites include Amazon and eBay. Prior to the development of the modern websites, each product was manually added into the webpage, but with the invention of websites, up to 10,000 products could be added at a time which saved a lot of time. When the number of products displayed on the website increased, the online traffic and sales volume increased as well, which proved to be really beneficial for the businesses.

Advances in the Payment System

The SSL system was good, but it also had a few drawbacks. Firstly, people still did not fully trust the online transactions through credit cards. Secondly, it proved to be expensive for them while making small payments. The solution to this problem was provided by PayPal, which allowed safe and secure online payments and money transfer from bank accounts and credit cards without compromising on the users' privacy. Even today, PayPal is one of the most common and secured form of payment all around the globe.

Dot Com Boom of 2001

In the late 1990's the customer's trust began to deteriorate, and they started to hesitate using credit cards. Investments gained through Initial Public Openings (IPO) helped people to raise large amount of capital, which in turn proved to be quite profitable for companies, as it raised the value of the company. Even though many companies had good ideas, but their business plans were weak. The results were soon visible when many companies started to shut down their operations during 2001 and 2002 due to huge losses. A large number of investors started to sell their stocks below their actual values and companies like eToys were forced to shut down. Many other companies with poor business plans were also shut down during the period.

e-Commerce in Today's World

In the modern world, e-Commerce has not only revolutionized the way companies make profit, but it has also proved to be equally beneficial for the consumers. A wide variety of services including the exchange of information between the customers or other businesses, order processing through electronic means, supply chain management, electronic purchasing, and handling customer services, is effectively and efficiently carried out through e-Commerce. It cannot be denied that soon enough, e-Commerce will be the vital element of the global business marketplace. But at the same time, we cannot ignore some of the ethical issues involved in the world of e-Commerce which include "privacy and security issues, fraud, illegal access, unsolicited email, trustfulness, targeting children, false advertising, pornography, product warranty, plagiarism, intellectual property and cyber-squatting" (Jie, 2012).

The Evolution of e-Commerce

The three stages in the evolution of e-Commerce are Innovation (1995-200), Consolidation (2001-2006) and Reinvention (2006-future). Innovation was characterized by excitement and idealistic visions of market in which both the buyers and the merchants could easily avail quality information. However, these visions were not fulfilled by e-Commerce in the early years of its development. e-Commerce entered its second stage called Consolidation, after 2000. The use of e-Commerce became more popular among traditional firms and they started using Web to grow and enhance their existing businesses, but they gave less importance to creating new brands. In 2006, e-Commerce entered the present stage also known as the Reinvention Stage. e-Commerce was reinvigorated with new Web 2.0 applications and social networking which helped to create new business models (D'Andrea, Ferri & Grifoni, 2014). Table 3 shows the evolution of e-Commerce and its three stages.

The Types of e-Commerce

Most of the people make the mistake of thinking that the idea of e-Commerce is limited to buying and selling of products and services online but that is not true. We can divide e-Commerce into six broad groups according to their functions. As seen in the model displayed in Figure 2 there are six different types of e-Commerce. The figure shows the different processes of e-Commerce and how they are linked with each other through mutual connections.

Table 3. The evolution of e-commerce

1995-2000 **Innovation**	**2001-2006** **Consolidation**	**2006 - Future** **Reinvention**
First mover advantages	Strategic followers	New market (1st mover)
Pure play	Bricks & Clicks	Retail (bricks & clicks) New market (pure play);
Perfect markets	Imperfect markets, brands, network effects	Online market imperfections
Disintermediation	strengthening intermediaries	Propagation of small online intermediaries
Entrepreneurial	Traditional / old economy	Large pure web-based firms
Obtaining Finance through Venture Capital	Obtaining Finance through Traditional methods	Merger & Acquisition
Focus on the Revenue Growth	Focus on Profits and Earnings	Focus on the growth of Social network and Audience
Driven by Technology	Driven by Business	Driven by Community, Customer and Audience

(Source: Rahul Kavaiya, Scope of e-Commerce, 2015)

Figure 2. The types of e-commerce
(Source: Wall J.E, Types of e-Commerce, 2014)

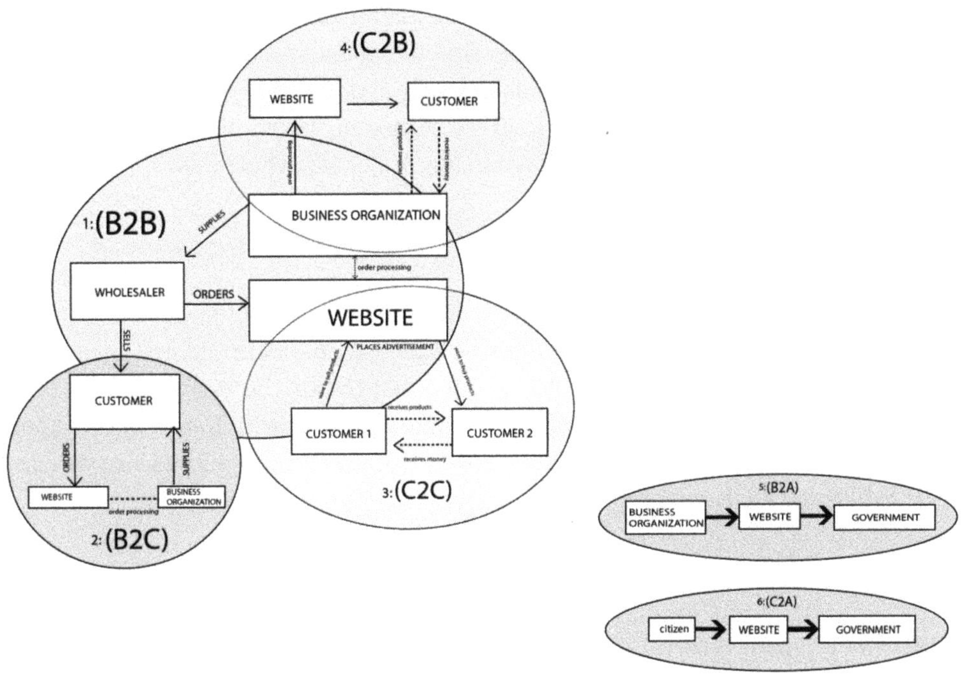

Business-to-Business (B2B)

This type of business is also known as B2B and it includes the exchange of products and services or commercial transactions between two businesses rather than business to customers. Manufacturers or wholesalers generally indulge in this kind of e-Commerce. Alibaba, Staples, Quill, Office max, Medline are all some of the well-known companies dealing with B2B (Wall J. E, 2014).

Business-to-Consumer (B2C)

A business that sells the products and services directly to the customers is known as B2C business. This form of e-Commerce gained wide popularity during the Dot Com boom in the late 1990's. During that period, B2C was mainly referred to address the online retailers who sold products directly to the customers through internet (Nemat, 2011). This type of e-Commerce has been greatly developed and is one of the most common type of e-business, due to its popularity since the late 1990's. There are a large number of virtual stores and markets around the globe which sell books, cosmetics, medicines, software, electronics items, stationeries, cars, food, clothing etc. Compared to the traditional retail methods, B2C is much more convenient as it provides the customers with the necessary information of the product without leaving their homes. Most of the customers also find much cheaper products compared to other methods of purchasing with quick delivery and processing of their orders and an enhanced customer service (Wall, 2014). Amazon, Tesco, Starbucks, Taco bell and TOMS are some of the well-known examples of B2C business.

Consumer-to-Consumer (C2C)

This type of e-business involves the transactions of a variety of goods and services between one consumer and another. Individuals use an electronic platform which acts as a third party, to advertise their products or to buy the products from other consumers. There are a large number of electronic platforms which are dedicated only to carry out the C2C transactions (Wall, 2014). Some examples include expatriates.com, E-bay and OLX.

Consumer-to-Business (C2B)

C2B is a complete reversal of the business to consumer e-business and involves the selling of products or services from the consumer to the business. Groups of individuals work together to provide a variety of goods or services that are being sought by the companies. There are a number of websites where graphic designers present some samples for company logos and the companies choose the best one amongst them to purchase it. IStockPhoto is a well-known market that sell images, royalty photographs, media and design elements (Wall, 2014).

Business-to-Administration (B2A)

This form of e-business mainly deals with all kind of online transactions between companies and public administrations. B2A involves a large number of services including employment, fiscal, legal documents, social security and registers etc. It has gained worldwide recognition in the form of e-government services with a lot of investments from the government. It is a form of facility provided by the government for the ease of the citizens, with the support of information technology (Wall, 2014). Example includes the University of Bahrain using the e-government portal for the payment of fees.

Consumer-to-Administration (C2A)

C2A e-Commerce involves all kinds of online transactions between consumers and public administration. It is mainly used for the purpose of the payments of taxes, distance learning in education, making payments for social security and fixing appointments or collecting information from health centers. This is also a facility provided by the government for the support and ease of the citizens (Wall, 2014). Table 4 shows the different types of e-Commerce and their examples.

The Objectives of e-Commerce

Many small and medium businesses are not financed enough, so they cannot afford to spend a large amount of money on expanding their market through expensive advertising. They are also unable to spend money on opening stores or hiring people for sales. e-Commerce allows such businesses to reap all these benefits without much investment. Some of the main objectives of e-Commerce are listed below:

- To reduce administrative and other costs
- Increase customers
- Enter global marketplaces
- To offer customizable products

Galant (2005) has described the following in her article "Blending E-Commerce theory and application".

Advantages to the Organization

1. By using e-Commerce, organizations can expand their businesses on a national and international level without much investment in the capital. They can also

Table 4. Examples of e-commerce

Type of e-Commerce	Example
Business to Business (B2B)	Alibaba, Staples, Quill, Medline
Business to Consumers (B2C)	Amazon, TESCO, Starbucks
Consumer to Consumer (C2C)	Expatriates.com, e-bay, OLX
Consumer to Business (C2B)	Istockphoto
Business to Administration (B2A)	LMRA, EWA, e-government
Consumer to Administration (C2A)	E-government

easily locate the potential suppliers, customers, competitors and business partners anywhere around the world.

2. Organizations can save a lot of money and paper work by providing the information on their websites instead of printing booklets or fliers for advertising and marketing.
3. e-Commerce helps the organization to create a strong brand image and identity.
4. It helps to provide a quick and better customer service.
5. It also helps to speed up the processes of the business and increase efficiency.
6. e-Commerce has facilitated the manufacturing process by using the just-in-time method, where the business process is started only after the customer places a request for the product or service (Galant, 2005).

Advantages to the Customers

1. Customers can buy or sell products and services around the clock from anywhere around the world without any time or geographical limitations. They can also avail the quick customer service in case of any enquiries.
2. Customers can use different applications and have a wide variety of choices. They can also track their orders and receive quick delivery of products.
3. They can compare the prices among the different products and sources and select the cheapest option available to save money.
4. Customers can provide feedback of their products and also read the reviews and comments from other users before buying the product.
5. Customers can have virtual auctions of their products.
6. Customers can have easy access to information in a short period of time without having to wait for days and weeks.
7. Due to the increased competition as a result of e-Commerce, many organizations provide discounts in order to win the customers over the competitors (Galant, 2005).

Advantages to the Society

1. Since the customers do not need to travel to the physical stores in order to purchase the products, the traffic on the roads and air pollution is prevented.
2. e-Commerce helps to provide the products at a lower cost, so the less privileged people can easily afford them too.
3. People living in the urban and rural areas can have easy access to the products and services which were not available in their cities before.

4. The government uses e-Commerce to deliver public service messages and awareness campaigns to serve the society and educate them (Galant, 2005).

Factors Affecting e-Commerce

Since 1990's e-Commerce has not only become a fundamental part of people's life but it has also introduced a new way of conducting business (Al-Alawi & Al-Ali, 2015; Lee et al, 2007). A research in 2011 shows that 96% of the organizations of the sample population had used internet, while 69% used their own website (Chen &Holsapple, 2013). The e-Commerce has opened vast opportunities for employment for people all around the world and have also revolutionized the relationships between organizations and individuals (Lee & Lin, 2005). According to Harridge and March (2004), e-Commerce reduces the cost of the consumers since it eliminates the use of distribution channels by transferring the goods directly from the manufacturer to the consumer.

There are many classical ethical theories which were developed during the early days but most of those theories are inapplicable in today's business world since "e-Commerce is a new paradigm in business which was only developed back in 1993" (Greblikaite, Pervazaite, 2014). e-Commerce has been made possible because of the internet and this new digital technology has surely transformed the business environment, activities and processes (Judson and Kelly, 1999). Kracher and Corritore (2004) have written that "the ethical dimensions are very critical to examine in the world of e-Commerce due to the degree and speed at which its developing around the world". Big names, organizations and small or medium enterprises use e-Commerce as a basic necessity and it is one of the most appropriate method for conducting business. e-Commerce also has a positive impact on the environment protection factor, as it reduces some costs and processes (Tiwari, Singh, 2011). It provides a medium for sustainable development in digital technology and environment. Nevertheless, it should be mentioned that e-Commerce is also a way of conducting business and just like the traditional business practices, e-Commerce carries the risk of unethical and illegal behaviors and actions as well. As Freestone Mitchell (2004) states that e-Commerce is a "new environment for unethical behavior".

Kracher and Corritore (2004) state that "one of the most prominent differences in the application of ethics in the traditional business practices and e-Commerce is the *question of ethical lag,* which occurs when the speed of technology overtakes the ethical development". According to Marshall, there are several reasons for this lag. Firstly, the complexity and expense of the development of technology in today's world makes the technology developers draw more towards extremely focused and controlled business structures. And secondly, in a highly competitive environment, there are great economic returns offered by new technologies. Researches show that business ethics are quite slow in development as compared to technological developments and cultural environment which keeps on changing continuously. Krachure and Corritore (2004) also consider the "lack of exploration of e-Commerce ethics" as a main factor for the unawareness among individuals and corporations. They have also stated that e-Commerce consists of immoral and unacceptable problems that occur while confronting the e-Commerce websites. According to them, some of the main issues in e-Commerce include security of information, protection of children, access, trust, privacy and informed consent and intellectual property (Kracher & Corritore 2004).

The ability of people to stay connected on the internet at all times and to get an easy access to information can be one of the limitations for e-Commerce. Despite the fact that internet is available easily in most of the public places, the factors which determine the access to information is the time and the amount of information available. The issues related to intellectual property have actually become a source for development for the internet network. It is fairly easy to violate the personal rights of an individual, but it is extremely difficult to identify the person or organization responsible for it (Kracher & Corritore, 2004). Privacy and personal information is one of the most important issue in e-Commerce (Milne, Rohm, 2000). Copyrights, patents and trademarks give rise to a number of ethical and legal issues to be questioned (Maury & Kleiner, 2002). Niranjanamurthy and Chahar (2013) state that if the consumers fear a breach of their privacy and feel that their information on the website is not secure, they will hesitate to visit such e-Commerce websites. Paddison and Englefield (2003) assert that "making e-Commerce websites, web-site accessible is a way of assisting disabled users in achieving their freedom". However, research by Leitner and Strauss, (2008) and Lightner and Eastman (2002) shows that there are a lot of e-Commerce websites which fail to provide web accessibility. Many companies collect the usernames, address, contact numbers and emails of the users who visit their website, but the use of this personal information is often vague and such issues call for customer awareness. Privacy is mostly considered as a critical and central factor in the development of ethics in e-Commerce (Whysall, 2000).

When users give their personal information on websites, it gives birth to insecurity problems and invoke more distrust and difficulties compared to brick-and-mortar businesses (Kracher & Corritore 2004). The cookies on the browser store the personal information without the knowledge of the users and these cookies can be used in any way since there is no legal restriction to prevent it. Cookies are similar to small diaries where the data of the users' website history is stored and every time a user re-enters a website, a cookie is opened by the website. This is also called "data-mining" or "profiling" (Stead, Gilbert, 2001). Most of the customers are unaware of the fact that their private information can be used in an insecure and inappropriate way. According to Bart et al (2005) credit cards and financial security is the main base of security issues. In contrast to their statement, Venkatesh (1998) have argued that the development and extension of commerce in cyberspace gives everyone the right, freedom and place to establish their identity.

Internet and the possibilities of actions on the internet give rise to children pornography issues and special measures should be taken to protect the children. Unless the child is very young, webpage blocking might not be very effective as the information on the internet is easily available worldwide (Spencer, 2002). Customer trust is the basis of a buyer-seller relationship and in this technological environment, trust is often intangible (Hwang, Kim, 2006). Teo, Thompson and Jing (2007) conducted a research in U.S, Singapore and China to find out the cultural aspect and peculiarities of e-trust and they found out that the cultural environment does have an impact on e-trust. Social trust is beneficial for e-Commerce because it helps to decrease the transactional costs of interacting with other individuals. But when it comes to economic transactions, the need for monitoring the employee's behavior is being eliminated due to this trust and the transactions become economically affordable.

However, we cannot overlook the fact that in e-Commerce the distance between the buyer and seller is long, so unethical or illegal actions and behaviors are hard to notice due to their intangible nature. The entrepreneurs of e-Commerce are often young at age and therefore the moral quality of e-Commerce alone is not necessarily sufficient to maintain. At the same time the e-traders should also bear in mind that the customers do perceive ethics as something really valuable and expect to be treated fairly and ethically (McMurrian & Matulich, 2006). The traders can easily minimize the trust of the customers through unethical actions in the company or business or they can benefit profitably by being ethical and winning the trust of the customers (Donaldson, 2003, Kurt & Hocioglu, 2010).

This report focuses on the laws and ethics surrounding the e-Commerce world. According to Lyu (2012), "ethics and laws are similar to some extent but they are not same". Laws are formulated and approved by the government of the state or country whereas ethics are generally known as the rules and are in most cases unwritten. A couple of traditional theories provide some solutions for situations that are ethically questionable. "Just like the traditional business practices, ethical decision making can be incorporated in e-Commerce as well and values that are based on traditional ethics will be the basis for a strong and successful relationship between the customer and the seller" (Williams & Premchaiswadi, 2016).

Ethical Issues

Ethics can be defined as the knowledge between what is right and what is wrong. There are certain rules to follow when we interact with other people around us and our actions affect them on a great level. These rules are universal and applicable to everyone in certain situations. Business ethics are those ethical questions that the managers have to confront in their everyday decision-making. Similar to this, e-Commerce also has some ethical rules and regulation that have to be followed by e-businesses and by the consumers who avail the e-Commerce facilities (Shivani, 2012; Dozier, 2013)

The digital technology is really vast and is no doubt a great platform for e-Commerce. The e-Commerce has the ability to provide products and services at the convenience of the consumers in a fast and efficient manner, save time and money and secure the transactions through the use of credit cards. Furthermore, e-Commerce is not only a technology but a business availing the technology. Nonetheless, it is also surrounded by some rules and regulations that have to be followed while making use of the technology. This new form of technology has unrestrained advantages, but it also carries a few risks, which will now be discussed in detail (Babu, 2011; Nardal & Sahin, 2011). Table 5 shows the most common ethical issues and their definitions.

Web Tracking

Most of the businesses can track how the online visitors use their websites with the help of log files. When the log files are analyzed, the data is converted into application service or in some cases a software can be used to store the data. This is how companies track their users through cookie analysis and tracking software's, which raises an issue of privacy concerns. The tracking history is also stored in the hard disk of the Pc or laptop and this is how the computer already knows which websites have been visited by the user before. To prevent this, many users often install programs like Spam Butters, Cookie cutters etc. (Babu, 2011; Agag, 2019).

Privacy Invasion

This problem is basically related to the consumers and is one of the most major issues faced by the consumers. Privacy invasion occurs when the personal information of the user is accessed or used by an unauthorized party. This can be done in four ways:

1. Many e-Commerce businesses may buy the personal information of the users like their webpage visits, shopping preferences or their personal details, with or without the user's consent. Websites which ask the users to fill in their

Table 5. Ethical issues in e-commerce

Ethical Issues in e-Commerce	
Problem	**Definition**
1. Web Tracking	Website tracking is the act of storing the existing websites, in order to track the changes made to it overtime. (Wikipedia).
2. Privacy Invasion	Using the private information of someone without his/her knowledge or permission (Business Dictionary).
3.Disintermediation & Reintermediation	Disintermediation is known as the elimination of intermediaries like distributors and brokers that provided a link between the company and its customers and Reintermediation is known as the creation of new intermediaries between suppliers and customers in order to provide different services (Chaffey, 2009).
4.Counterfeit goods	The selling of high quality and branded products, under a different brand's name without the knowledge of the brand owner (Wikipedia).
5.False Advertising	The act of providing false information about a product or service in order to attract the consumers (Wikipedia).
6.Hacking	"Hacking is the process of accessing a computer or website in order to view, copy, or create data without destroying or harming the data or the computer (Urban Dictionary).
7.Email Spamming	Email spam involves sending identical messages via email to a large number of recipients at a time (Wikipedia).
8.Web Spoofing	Web spoofing means creating website identical to an existing website in order to lure the users and mislead them into thinking that it has been created by another source (Wikipedia).
9.Cyber Squatting	The process of registering names of famous companies or brands in order to resell them at a profit. (Wikipedia).

(Source: Wikipedia, Urban Dictionary, Business Dictionary)

personal information often sell this user data to other companies who use it for marketing purposes.

2. The personal data of the users can often be intercepted by a person other than the person to whom it is intended. The privacy of communication cannot be easily protected and in a vast pool of digital technology it is often impossible to avoid the interference of such intruders.
3. Since the internet cannot remember the history of a user or his frequently visited web pages, passwords or usernames, this information is stored in the cookies as a reminder. Due to this, when the user visits a webpage, malicious programs can automatically be delivered to reveal the confidential credit card information, passwords and usernames. Most of the electronic payment systems are aware of the identity of the users (Shivani, 2012).
4. Many companies track their employees' online activities through monitoring systems, in order to find out the amount of time they spend on business activities and the amount of time spent on non-business activities. This might put the

employees at a risk of losing their jobs and this treatment may lead to raise many ethical questions (Babu, 2011).

Disintermediation and Reinter Mediation

One of the most common issue is related to the employees losing their jobs which is known as intermediation. The intermediaries help in providing information and value-added services like consultations. Matching and providing information can be done through portals or e-marketplaces which provide free services and are fully automated. On the other hand, the value-added services are partially automated, and they require some level of expertise. The circumstances which eliminate the intermediaries who offer matching and providing information is called disintermediation and this has a negative impact on the traditional sales channels. Whereas the brokers and agents who are providing value added services may not only grow but also survive this intermediation. This process is known as reinter mediation. The internet provides many opportunities for reinter mediation through the support of e-Commerce. Therefore, an expert computer mediator is required to predict the number of participants, and the processing of large information etc. (Babu, 2011; Nardal & Sahin, 2011; Agag, 2019, and Al-Alawi & Al-Bassam, 2019)

Counterfeit Customer Goods

Alibaba is one of the most widely used online source for purchasing products and it has about 8 million small sellers who sell about 8 million different products. According to BBC news, the website has spent $160m on fake goods. Many famous luxury brands like Armani, Gucci, Yves Saint Laurent and Balenciaga filed a case against Alibaba for selling fake products of their brands and earning millions through it.

Every business is based on winning the trust of the customers to gain customer loyalty and retention. When a company displays fake goods, it loses the trust of the customers and its reputation is negatively affected. One of the basic principle of ethics is to act true to the customers and to be honest with them and displaying fake goods is an unethical act. In order to remove the fake goods and replace them with the authentic ones, a huge amount of money and time is wasted.

False Advertising and Information

Many e-Commerce websites provide wrong information to the customers regarding the price and quality of the products. Many advertisements promote feature and prices which are not actually present in the products when they are delivered. In some cases, the customers also receive damaged products or something which they did not pay for to purchase. Many websites also sell outdated products. For instance, in 2013, the Walmart's website displayed computers and other electronic items at a price of $8.85 only. However, Walmart later claimed that this was a technical error, but this received a lot of attention from the customers (Kelly & Williams, 2016).

Firstpost.com featured an article about a well-known website in India called Snap Deal which hit the news when a customer ordered a Samsung phone from their website and received a brick and half a soap bar inside the delivery box. The soap company later had to send him a Samsung phone as a compensation. Such incidents shatter the trust of the customers and they hesitate to order products online. This act is not only unethical but also a huge loss for companies (Kelly & Williams, 2016).

Hacking

Hacking is referred to as the act of bypassing the computers or its network system. e-Commerce websites are more prone to hacking due to the ability of online payments and the use of credit cards. Therefore, they are more attractive to the hackers. All the transactions occur at the server level as it is known as the "e-Commerce place of Business". The main website for the products and services as well as the customer's database is stored at the server and if the server is attacked, all the information can be lost in seconds.

Websites like E-bay have faced a hacking attack in 2014, where all the users' information and passwords were hacked. The hackers can use this information for wrong purposes and it is quite risky for the users. Therefore, E-bay warned its users to change their private information in order to avoid any inconvenience (Orji, et al. 2016). Around 13,000 credit card numbers and passwords were hacked by a hacking group from well-known websites like Wal-Mart and Amazon. All the information was posted on a site called Ghostbin which is a data sharing site (Methmali, 2015). The bank called HSBC was also a victim of hacking and 2.7 million credit cards were exposed (Paganini, 2014).

Email Spamming

Email Spamming occurs when companies send unwanted advertisements through emails for marketing purposes. A person who sends these emails is usually referred to as a spammer. A lot of spammers also send emails with their personal information to defraud people and use their credit card or account information. Many times, the spammers send emails with links that direct the users to a fake website that looks almost the same as an authorized one and lure them to enter their personal data like credit card details or their account numbers on that webpage. This is known as phishing and is one of the most widely faced ethical issue in the e-Commerce world (Shivani, (2012).

Web Spoofing

Attackers often set up a fake website which is similar to the original one in order to lure the users to provide their credit cards and accounts details. This is called web spoofing. An example of web spoofing is when the attacker sets up a website called www.micros0ft.com, where he uses the number zero instead of an "O". Many users can sometimes mistype alphabets, but it leads them to a similar website and they pass on their personal information by trusting the website. According to the Signal magazine, a web spoofing incident involving the U.S Air Force was on the rise in 2011. Many users were fooled when they entered their passwords and usernames on a fake website which was accessed by an unauthorized party. Only the most attentive users were able to spot the difference while the others fell victims to the incident (Rita Boland, The Signal Magazine, 2011).

Cyber Squatting

When a person uses the domain name of a well-known company in order to infringe its own trademark, it is known as cybersquatting. This is done mainly for the purpose of obtaining the payments and money from the original owner of the trademark. They offer the organization domain names at a far higher price than the purchasing price. Many cyber-squatters use derogatory remarks against the company which the domain is meant to represent, in order to force it to re-buy its own domain from them (e.g.www.amazonsucks.com).

In 2007 Belgium Domains, Domain Doorman and Capitol Domains were charged by Dell for cyber-squatting and selling a domain called dellfinancialservices.com. Similarly, BBC claimed back their rights to the domain bbcnews.com from a cyber-squatter (Faisal Alani, 2009).

Legal Issues

Companies involved in e-commerce must also consider the legal side of the e-Commerce and be aware of the potential risks involved in the process. When the buyers and the sellers involved in e-Commerce transactions do not know each other, the risk of crimes increase. However, the authorities who want to apply legal control and policies on e-Commerce may face many hurdles due to the global nature of internet. Similar to the traditional way of doing business, there are certain behaviors which require a legal action (Nasir, 2004). Table 6 highlights some of the major legal issues in the world of e-Commerce and their definitions:

Fraud on the Internet

Due to the popularity of the websites and their usage, the cases of fraud in e-Commerce have increased over the years. It is a major issue for click-and-mortar as well as cyber merchants. Swindlers are the people who try to con the users to rob them off their money and they are mostly present in the area of stocks. Stock promoters try to lure the investors by promising them false profits. Auctions also induce fraud either by the buyer or the seller. The presence of pop-up ads and unsolicited emails have created a clear path for the financial criminals to gain an easy access to the personal information of the users. Phantom business opportunities and fake investments are also considered as a part of fraud on the internet (Babu, 2011; Agag, 2019). Websites like expatriates.com are widely used in Bahrain but it is also a main hub for scammers who try to lure people by promising them jobs and other incentives in order hack their systems and personal information or to rob them off their money.

Infringement of Intellectual Property

Intellectual properties include copyrights, patents and trademarks and they cannot easily be used by anyone. The copyright laws generally protect the intellectual properties, but it cannot easily be protected in e-Commerce. When a person buys a software, he is authorized to use it but not distribute it because the distribution rights

Table 6. Legal issues in e-commerce

Legal Issues in e-Commerce	
Problem	**Definition**
1.Internet Fraud	It is known as the use of internet to take advantage of the victims and defraud them.
2.Intellectual Property infringement	It refers to the act of violating the rights of an intellectual property which include trademarks, patents and copyrights.
3.Freedom of Speech	It is known as the right to express one's opinions or beliefs without any restrictions or limitations.
4.Electronic Contracts	It is a kind of contract made between two parties, using electronic means.
5.Taxation	It is referred to as a process used by the government to bear its expenditures by charging the normal citizens or corporate entities

(Source: Wikipedia)

only lie with the person who owns the copyrights. Plagiarism and copying contents of websites is also considered against the copyright laws (Babu, 2011, Agag, 2019).

Freedom of Speech vs Censorship

Censorship can be defined as the attempt of the government to restrict the content displayed on the internet. If the users find the material offensive, they might report or present it for censorship, and this can also have an impact on e-Commerce. Some child protection laws are present in every country which protect the children from viewing inappropriate content. But this censorship is only useful if the children are at a very young age and do not have the proper skills to use internet. These facts have to be kept in mind while conducting an e-business (Udo, (2001).

Electronic Contracts

All contracts are based on an offer, acceptance and consideration between two parties. When these contracts are made and presented electronically, the human element is eliminated and therefore it loses its authenticity and the three basic elements (offer, acceptance and consideration) are difficult to establish. However, according to McDonald (2001), the Uniform Computer Information Transactions Act (2000) states that contracts can be made even without the physical presence or direct involvement of the human beings.

Taxations

This issue is related to the fairness in competition and has a huge impact on e-Commerce when it competes with off-line marketing channels that require the payment of taxes. The borderless nature of the internet and the globalization in e-Commerce makes it extremely hard for taxation. It is also quite tricky to predict the future of the e-business and therefore the government still cannot figure out how they can tax the e-Commerce activities. e-Commerce allows an individual to participate in multiple foreign marketplaces at a time, and deal with customers all around the world without having to enter any market in particular. This idea is not much welcomed according to the rules and regulation of the government of most countries and creates a big hurdle in taxation (Srivastava, 2018).

The Theory of Planned Behavior

Early attempts to understand the behaviors and issues of the consumers and merchants on e-Commerce led to the theory of Planned Behavior (Figure 3), which

Figure 3. The theory of planned behavior
(Source: Ajzen, 2009)

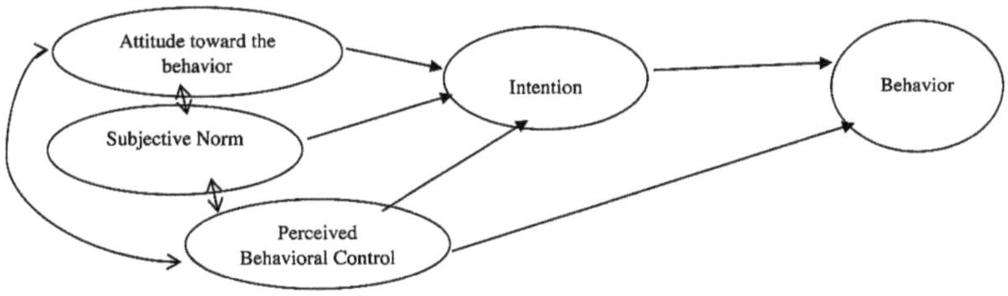

was formulated by Ajzen (1985,1991) as an extension to the Theory of Reasoned Action (TRA) (Ajzen and Fishbien, 1980). This theory will attempt to explain the impact of unethical and illegal behavior on the attitudes of the users. According to the TBP, "the attitudes of the users of e-Commerce, towards the target behavior and subjective norms of engaging in the behavior, greatly influence their intentions". It also stated that "the perceived behavioral control of indulging in the behavior also directly influences the intention". TBP has been used many times in the past for different studies on the behavior of users while purchasing online. TBP explains that the performance of an individual's behavior is determined by his intention to perform the particular behavior. The attitudes and subjective norms of the behavior and the perceptions on the success of the individual's behavior are responsible for informing the intent. Ajzen (1991) describes attitude either as "a positive or a negative evaluation of performing the behavior. The beliefs are responsible for informing the norms, the normative beliefs and motivation to comply are responsible for informing the norms and the beliefs about the individual's possession of the opportunities and the resources required to indulge in a particular behavior are responsible for informing the perceived behavioral control". TBP has not specified the particular beliefs, related to a particular behavior, so it is left up to the choice of the researcher to determine them (George, 2004).

This study is based on the unethical and illegal behavior of the users of e-Commerce and TBP provides a strong framework for testing whether attitudes lead to indulge in a specific behavior or behavior lead to the formation of an attitude. Based on TBP, beliefs of the users about the safety and security of e-Commerce should also influence their intention to use e-Commerce which in turn will influence their behavior.

As mentioned earlier, privacy is one of the main concerns of the consumers while making purchases online and many users refrain from using e-Commerce websites due to privacy concerns. A poll of the internet users in March 2000, showed that 94% of the individuals had not purchased anything online due to privacy concerns, as they feel that the companies might use their personal information to send them irrelevant information (Business Week, 2000). In other words, this is known as

Email Spamming. Byford (1998) has mentioned two aspects of privacy, "a social relationship view and a property view". "The social relationship view assumes privacy as a balance for social relationship development. On the other hand, in the property view, the individuals view privacy as the extent to which they can control their information online". Although both these views are equally important in order to understand the individual online behavior, but the property view is more specific and related to the individual's concern for privacy. For instance, the GVU internet survey conducted in 1997, showed that 53% of the online users know that their personal information is being collected by the Web sites, while 66% said that they do not make online purchases because they fear that their information might be used in an inappropriate way. Culnan and Smith (1993) conducted a research on "direct marketing and attitudes towards secondary information use". According to them, "there are two scales for measuring two different aspects of the user's attitudes towards using e-Commerce. The first one is the loss of control, and the second is the unauthorized secondary use. Loss of control scale refers to the loss of control of the users over their personal information and losing their privacy while using credit cards. Secondary use means that the information is being used for some other purpose rather than for what it was collected". Culnan reached a conclusion and found out that the people who are less concerned about their privacy, are more positive about using e-Commerce, and can easily cope with receiving unwanted information as compared to the users who are more concerned about their privacy. The findings of this study by Culnan can be used for studying internet privacy and the concerns of the users, which is directly related to their behaviors (George, 2004).

A similar instrument was developed by Smith et al. (1996) to measure the dimensions of the practices of information privacy by the organizations. They mentioned four different dimensions in their work, which include unauthorized secondary use, improper access, errors and collections. Although the focus of their study was on the user's attitude about how the organizations used their personal information, it can easily be used to measure the attitudes towards how different websites and online businesses deal with them or use their personal data (George, 2004; Al-Alawi & Hafedh, 2006).

An individual's attitude towards using e-Commerce for online purchasing, is influenced by their trust. Most of the users do not trust the websites enough with their personal data, to indulge in online transactions with them (Hoffman et al., 1999). A laboratory experiment conducted recently, showed that consumers perceived "online shopping as more risky as compared to print catalog shopping" (Jones and Vijayasarathy, 1998). This shows that the views of the consumers on the trustworthiness of internet, is expected to influence their willingness to make online purchases. Another study by George (2002) evaluated the trustworthiness of the users of e-Commerce by using three items which were taken from the GVU survey instruments. According to his findings, the positive attitudes toward online purchasing were developed only because of the "positive beliefs about the trustworthiness of the users". Pavlou (2002) used the TPB to prove that "the trust of the user on the online retailer was directly correlated with their attitudes towards online purchases and with perceived behavioral control" (George, 2004).

Mukherjee and Nath (2003), found out that the trust of the users is directly related to the commitment of the relationship to an online retailer. Although they did not clarify the instruments used by them for measuring the trust, but it presents a global measure for trust in the internet. In their study based on the Internet Banking, they mentioned that "the customer's orientation toward the technology of electronic communication and the Internet is frequently a proxy for their trust in Internet banking" (George, 2004).

SUMMARY

The purpose of this section was to explain the concept of e-Commerce in the modern world and its evolution since its existence. The material presented in this section also threw light on the different models of e-Commerce and its objectives, which helped to understand why e-Commerce exists and how it has facilitated our day to day lives in a positive or a negative way. Since the basis of this research is to identify the consumer behavior while using e-Commerce in the Kingdom of Bahrain, it highlighted the presence of e-Commerce and its development in the country along with the procedures of opening an e-Commerce-based business in Bahrain. The most important part refers to the factors which affect e-Commerce, aiming to explain some of the most common ethical and legal issues prevailing in the modern e-Commerce world. These behaviors of the consumers were supported and explained further on by using The Theory of Planned Behavior by Ajzen (1991). Therefore, it can be summed up that the literature review presented in this section revealed some pre-existing theories and concepts based on the subject of the research which provided a basis and will help to formulate the research methodology in next section.

METHODOLOGY

This section will focus on the different methodologies used to conduct the research for testing the study. There are different methods used by the researchers for collecting data for their research. The research can either be qualitative or quantitative or both depending on the preference of the researcher. This research will use a combination of quantitative and qualitative methods which include questionnaires and interviews to depict the viewpoints of the buyers and sellers. The research outcome will help to gain a better understanding of the major problems of e-Commerce, the behaviors of the individuals and the reactions of the consumers towards the unethical issues.

The concept of e-business is so vast that it definitely requires a philosophical research into the behaviors and actions which provoke the unethical problems. For the purpose of collecting qualitative and quantitative data, the research onion method will be adopted to undermine the issues and provide appropriate solutions to the problem. This research will help to develop an understanding of why people tend to engage in unethical behavior when dealing with online transactions and how we can help to prevent such behaviors.

Identifying e-Commerce Focus Area

The e-Commerce literature suggests that there are a number of ethical and legal issues prevailing in the e-Commerce activities which affect the attitude and behavior of the consumers and raises some important concerns for the e-Commerce users. Therefore, the research will focus on what are the most common e-Commerce issues of the consumers and how they affect their behavior. The influence of each factor will be tested using various techniques.

Research Tool

The research Onion method will be used in this research to collect the qualitative and quantitative data.

The Research Onion Method

The Research Onion method was developed by Saunders *et. al.,* (2007). In this method, he has explained the stages that should be covered to develop a research strategy. Each layer of the onion presents a different stage of the process (Saunders et. al., 2007). The core or inner most layer of the onion consists of the final elements of the research and they are closely related to the outer layers, which depict the design elements. It is a very useful model to design a research methodology which is adaptable for almost any type of research in any context (Bryman, 2012).

There are different stages that a researcher has to pass in order to design a methodology which is effective and useful. The six different layers of the onion have a different and specific role in formulating the methodology. The first layer consists of the philosophies and this acts as a starting point to reach the appropriate research approach, which is the second layer. The third layer focuses on the different strategies or methods which can be approached for the research. The fourth layer consists of the choices that can be used for collecting the data. The fifth layer identifies the time horizon of the research to decide whether it is going to be a long term or a short-term research. Finally, the sixth layer represents the techniques and procedures which help to identify the method for data collection.

Figure 4 shows the research onion method formulated by Mark Saunders and the six different layers of the research. Each of the layers will be discussed in detail to link them to the steps used in this research and to provide a clear vision for the adopted methodology.

Research Philosophies

Research Philosophies are related to the beliefs of the researcher on the method through which the data is analyzed, used or gathered (Bryman, 2012). Saunders et al. (2009) has defined it as the "the development of the knowledge and the nature of that knowledge." These philosophies are different for achieving different types of goals and also for how those goals are going to be achieved (Goddard & Melville, 2004). They exemplify the importance of understanding the aim of the researcher and what methods he will adopt to develop knowledge on the particular topic in

Figure 4. The research onion
(Source: Saunders et al, 2007)

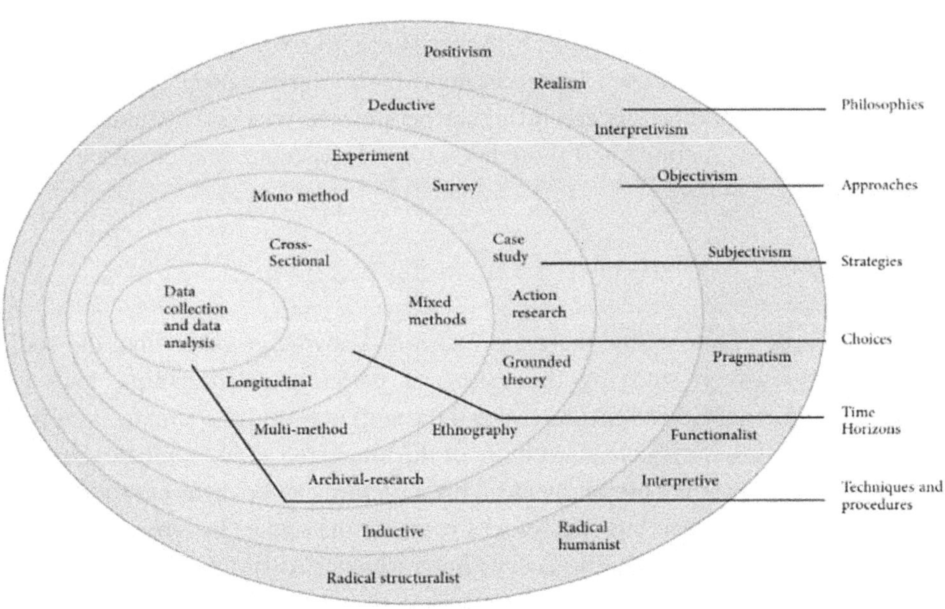

order to provide clarification for the assumptions used in the process of the research and how they relate to the methodology.

Positivism

In order to generate questions for testing the hypothesis, positivism is used. The research questions can be tested, and they help us to measure the world's accepted knowledge. Positivism is generally concerned with adopting the philosophical stance where the researcher would like to observe and then predict the results of a particular situation. This phenomenon is quite similar to the situation of a scientist in a laboratory. Researchers who use this philosophy usually base their hypothesis on an existing theory. The existing hypothesis is properly tested before making any further developments which could be used by researchers in the future. This layer is based on the quantitative data and it needs a statistical analysis, in order to reach a conclusion. Therefore, it is known as a continuous process where the previous theories are tested and confirmed by the researchers (Saunders et al. 2009).

Interpretivism

Interpretivism is known as the study of a subject that the researcher wants to identify in the natural environment. The researcher should begin by understanding the different roles of the social actors which include human beings rather than any other sources. Saunders et al (2009) clarified the term social actors by saying that "the metaphor of the theatre suggests that being humans we are responsible for playing a different part on the stage of human life cycle. Similar to the actors who play different roles in theatrical productions and then act according to their interpretation". Interpretivism implicates that cultural factors can influence people's actions and by understanding the people's beliefs, actions and thoughts, cultural existence and change can also be understood.

Objectivism

According to this philosophy, there are forms of knowledge other than the social factors. It focuses on studying the nature of patterns, relationships, laws and regularities among the different situations measured in terms of social facts. A good example of this is to have a clear structure of the interested sample, job descriptions and duties, organizational hierarchy etc. This structure can be different for different organizations and places, but the content remains the same. In other words, true and fair information is available everywhere which is distinct from the feelings or interpretations of an individual (Saunders et al. 2009). Another example of the phenomenon is heavy rain where the people who want to go outside for the picnic are the social actors. In this case the rain exists and is real and it is acknowledged by everyone except the people who had their plan ruined due to the social phenomenon.

Subjectivism

Unlike objectivism, subjectivism in emotionally driven and refers to the judgments and decisions based on an individual's personal beliefs and opinions instead of being based on facts. Remenyi et al. (1998) states that it is important to understand and study the phenomenon in detail and try to identify the reasons behind such beliefs or perceptions in order to gain a better understanding of the situation. Decisions based solely and separately other than the social factors are based on objectivism, while subjectivism revolves around emotional values.

Philosophies Used

The philosophies used in this research are a combination of positivism and objectivism. Using positivism, the pre-existing theories on e-Commerce and its issues are revised and tested to check if the new theories are in line with the previous ones or if they are opposing them. This was done by providing proofs and evidences. Objectivism provides a scientific information which will refrain from providing personal judgments and opinions and their interference in the results presented by this study.

Research Approaches

The second layer of the research onion consists of the research approaches. After selecting the appropriate philosophies in the first layer, we then move to the second step and that is to choose the research approaches. There are three different approaches namely, Deductive, Inductive and Abductive. If the researchers properly and clearly understand the theory they are taking, it would be easy for them to identify the type of approaches they can use, and this is why this step relies strongly on the previous step because the deductive method is related to positivism, while the inductive approach is more related to interpretivism philosophy. However, such theories are deceptive not considered to be practical in real life (Saunders et al., 2009).

Deductive

This approach is similar to a scientific research, where a researcher develops a theory and then tests it. In the deductive approach, the questions or statements developed can be answered through the research. The target would be to respond to the questions either as a yes or as a no. The questions which the researcher believes can be answered, could be in the form of informed speculations or statements. The hypothesis is developed on a theory which is pre-existing and then it is tested through the formulated research approaches. Therefore, the steps of deduction include moving from the theory to the research questions, to the collection of data, from findings to the confirmation or rejection of the research question. This leads to the theory being revised and repeated by starting the process over and over again. "The deductive approach is best suited to the positivist approach because it allows the formation of the hypothesis and the statistical testing of the results to a certain level of probability" (Snieder & Larner, 2009). Having concluded that, this approach can also be used for qualitative research but the expectations formed by the pre-existing research may vary slightly (Saunders et al, 2007).

Inductive

In this approach, the theory is formulated after the research questions are answered. The process of the inductive approach is the opposite of the deductive approach and rather than taking its focus from the existing theory, it takes its focus from the researcher's working title. In other words, the researcher moves from the research questions to the observation and description to analysis and then to the theory. Therefore, the inductive approach is the best approach for the researcher if little or no information exists on the topic or subject of research. This method is most beneficial for qualitative research because it does not contain a theory and reduces the researcher preference during the data collection (Bryman & Bell, 2011). "Interviews are conducted regarding the particular phenomenon for collecting the data and then the data is tested for patterns between the respondents of the interview" (Flick, 2011). However, this approach can also be used in combination with the positivist approach where the first step is to do the data analysis and then the patterns are used to find the results.

Approaches Used

The deductive approach was used to conduct this research. Since it was quite difficult to build a new theory in a limited period of time, so the pre-existing theories were studied. The approach will be both qualitative and quantitative in nature. Curran, J & Blackburn (2001) state that "a single research study may use a combination of both qualitative and quantitative techniques as well as primary and secondary data."

Research Data

There are two types of data that can be collected by the researchers for business and management researches and they are qualitative and quantitative data (Saunders et al, 2009). The type of data selected will determine the choices of the research methods which will be elaborated later in this section.

- **Quantitative Data:**Quantitative data is based on researches which rely on numbers and is used in a lot of data collection methods which include surveys, or data analysis techniques like graphs and statistics (Saunders et al, 2009).
- **Qualitative Data:**The Qualitative approach is based on the data which is non-numerical in nature and the researchers use interviews as a method to collect data and then analyze it accordingly. It represents information as pictures, videos and words (Saunders et al, 2009).

Research Data Used

The research will be based on both qualitative and quantitative data to provide more accurate and detailed results for the research.

Research Strategies

The third layer of the research onion present the research strategies and they are critical in answering the questions of the researchers as well as for data collection and data analysis. There are seven different types of strategies, out of which some belong to the deductive approach while the others clearly belong to the inductive approach. All strategies hold equal importance and the best strategy should be chosen according to the objectives and questions of the research (Saunders et al, 2009).

Survey

Surveys are used to answer questions concerning "what", "why", "how much" and "how many". The researchers are able to obtain data from large samples and enables different possibilities between the variables and the reasons for their existence. They are commonly used to collect quantitative data through questionnaires. They are commonly used in the deductive approach and helps the researcher to control the research process. Furthermore, it is simple and easy to understand (Saunders et al, 2009).

Case Study

Case studies are used for investigation or examination of certain situations by using real life evidences from a number of sources. They are able to answer questions such as "why", "what" and "how" and are most commonly used in exploratory or explanatory researches. The researchers who use case studies as the research strategy have to follow a technique known as "triangular Technique". Triangular "refers to the use a combination of techniques for data collection within a study for ensuring that the data is telling you what you think it is telling you." (Saunders et al, 2009). Case studies are basically divided into four categories which are the "holistic case study, the multiple case study, the single case study and the embedded case study". Each type is different from each other because the number of cases, the unit of analysis and the location is different for each. Survey is a very helpful tool for researchers because it allows them to explore theories which already exist and opens doors to develop new research questions (Saunders et al, 2009).

Experiment

This strategy is basically related to natural sciences and it allows the researcher to identify the links between two different variables (Hakim, 2000). It is used for identifying "the size of change existing between two independent variables" and answers questions like "why" and "how". Furthermore, it contains two kinds of groups known as experimental group and the control group. In the experimental group, the researcher attempts to study the particular group by manipulating or interfering factors that affect the behavior, whereas in the control group, the researcher does not use any such factors. This strategy is not commonly used in the field of education or business because it is perceived to be unfair or unethical (Saunders et al, 2009).

Ethnography

Ethnography means "to describe and explain the social world the research subjects inhabit in the way in which they would describe and explain it" (Saunders et al, 2009). It is closely related to the inductive approach and it helps the researcher to study the situation within the context of which it is appearing. In order to collect data in ethnography, participant observation is used as a technique and is used only if the researcher wishes to understand the phenomenon from the participant's perspectives or points of view. However, it requires a lot of patience and time from the researcher as many unpredictable changes may occur (Saunders et al, 2009).

Grounded Theory

This strategy is a very helpful tool for research as it helps to forecast and analyze behavioral patterns and emphasizes its role in building theories (Goulding 2002). Grounded theory is mostly used in an Abductive approach. This strategy does not need a theoretical framework as the data is collected through different observations. According to Suddaby (2006), this theory is not perfect because it is unorganized. He also stated that "the seamless craft of a well-executed grounded theory study, however, is the product of considerable experience, hard work, and creativity and occasionally, a healthy dose of good luck".

Strategies Used in This Research

Since the research is based on the deductive approach, a combination of surveys and interviews will be used in this research. Surveys are used for collecting the quantitative data and is one of the most affordable and easy ways to find answers to the research questions in a short period of time. For qualitative data, the interviews will be conducted in order to reach the ultimate conclusion of the research.

Research Choices

The fourth layer of the research onion is that of the research choices and it provides the researcher with more flexibility in cases where both the quantitative and qualitative data are needed along with the secondary and primary data (Teddlie & Tashakkori, 2003).

Mono Method

In this method the researcher chooses a single procedure for collecting data and analysis instead of choosing both the quantitative or qualitative methods. This method does not allow to collect information though the combination of both the methods because of the demands or choices of the philosophy and the employed strategies. It can also be used to research an opposing view to the existing mono - method. (Saunders et al., 2009).

Multi Method

If the researcher chooses a combination of procedures and techniques for collecting data, it is referred to as the multi method. It consists of two subdivisions known as the multi-method quantitative study or a multi method qualitative study. However, it is preferred not to mix the quantitative and qualitative techniques while pursuing multi method (Saunders et al, 2009).

Mixed Methods

In this method the researcher can choose both the qualitative and the quantitative data and this can be done in two ways. The researcher can either use them together in a parallel way or separately in a sequential manner. In other words, the qualitative data can be used with the quantitative data or vice versa (Saunders et al., 2009; Feilzer, 2010)

Research Choices Used

This research will adopt the mixed method since both qualitative and quantitative data will be used as a procedure for the data collection and analysis.

Time Horizons

This is the fifth layer of the research onion and it operates separately from the research choice and the research study itself. The time horizon is largely dependent on the research questions to determine if it will be conducted in a limited or a long time period (Saunders et al., 2009).

1. **Cross-Sectional Studies:** Cross sectional studies focus on pondering at one phenomenon at a time and due to time constraints, it is used widely in academic researches. They are often used with quantitative data and help to identify the reasons behind certain incidents. However cross-sectional studies can also be used with qualitative data because a lot of interviews can be conducted in a short period of time (Saunders et al, 2009).
2. **Longitudinal Studies:** Longitudinal studies are able to clarify the developments that have occurred over time. According to Schvaneveldt & Adams (1991), when the researchers have enough time to observe the people or events, they will have the capability to evaluate the undertaken variables in the research as long as the research itself does not affect them. However, if the researcher is properly aware that there has been a change overtime, longitudinal studies can also be carried out in a limited period of time (Bouma & Atkinson, 1995).

Time Horizon Used

This research will use the cross-sectional studies due to limited time. Moreover, since the deductive approach is used in the research, it will be more extracted better using the cross-sectional study rather than the longitudinal study.

Data Collection and Data Analysis

This is the final and the sixth layer of the research onion and is "dependent on the methodological approach used" (Bryman, 2012). At this stage, the reliability and validity of the research depends mainly on the process used for the research (Saunders et al., 2009). Regardless of the used research approach, two types of data can be collected, namely primary data and the secondary data.

Secondary Data

Secondary data is a very useful tool for research as it can help to gather information from the existing or new theories. Cowton, C.J (1998) states that secondary data provides information that is of great value and can answer a wide range of questions with the least cost. It includes literature publications, journals, articles, and other forms of archival data. The use of secondary data has significantly increased in the last ten years (Nicholson & Bennett, 2009).

Primary Data

Primary data is collected after the researcher spends a reasonable amount of time to collect the secondary data. The actions that the researcher takes to study his understanding of the primary or research data which was previously collected is known as primary data. It can be collected through questionnaires, survey, observations and interviews (Nicholson & Bennett, 2009).

Data Collection Technique Used

This research will use both primary and secondary data. Secondary data was collected in the literature review and the introduction, in order to find the different theories for testing, while the primary data was collected through the survey and interviews.

THE RESEARCH DESIGN

The research design depicts the processes and the description of the way the research will be completed. It determines the different factors that led to the selection of the chosen methodology, the method for selecting the respondents and the method of data analysis (Flick, 2011). There are three different types of research designs which are the explanatory, the exploratory and the descriptive.

The explanatory research design is used to explain the nature of a specific social phenomenon or population (Saunders et al., 2007). This can be quite useful for quantitative framework where one variable has an influence on the other (Kothari, 2004). The exploratory study design is used for exploring a certain phenomenon or issue which has taken place without much information known for the research process and it is usually used for collecting further information about the subject in order to conduct the research (Neuman, 2003).The descriptive research design reflects the respondents' experiences and is most closely related to the ethnographic studies but it can also use a quantitative framework (Bryman, 2012).

Figure 5 shows the research design used for this research. Two kinds of research designs were adopted, which were Qualitative and Quantitative. First, the quantitative data was collected through a survey and analyzed. Based on the findings of the survey,

Figure 5. The research design

the qualitative data was collected through interviews. The data from the interviews was then collected and captured and then analyzed to reach the final conclusions.

Data Analysis Procedures

Survey

Survey was used as a research method for collecting the quantitative data and it aims to understand the consumer's behavior while using e-Commerce. The quantitative method helps to collect data from a large number of individuals in a short period. This method generally relies on numerical data to provide an understanding of the problem so appropriate measures can be taken to solve the problem (Cohen, 2000).

The Purpose

The purpose of the quantitative research was to develop an understanding of the consumers who use e-Commerce services in Bahrain. It provided an understanding of what are the main problems faced by the consumers, their reaction, perceptions and beliefs. In order to reach a conclusion and provide suitable recommendations to the problem, it is very important to gather important facts from the consumer's point of view and this was basically done through a quantitative research. Data collected from the questionnaire will be used to evaluate different e-Commerce behaviors and issues and will help us to reach the ultimate solution to e-Commerce problems.

Data Collection

The method used to collect the quantitative data was through distributing questionnaires to the consumers of e-Commerce. Questionnaires are one of the most used research methods for quantitative research and it helps to collect specific information as a response to highly directed questions. The questionnaire was distributed electronically through social media and via emails. The response rate was much better compared to the interviews, as the respondents had to answer simple and straight forward questions which were quite basic and easy to understand.

The Questionnaire Design and Structure

The questionnaire was designed after a thorough study and research conducted in the introduction and literature review of this report. Based on the data collected in section 1 and section 2, the questions were designed in a quantitatively measurable method by using multiple choice questions, Likert scale, checkboxes and open-ended questions and it was created using survey monkey. The questionnaire had 10 questions which were direct and simple and aimed to understand the preferences and perceptions of the consumers to develop a better understanding of their behavior. The collection and data analysis of the questionnaire was done through charts and graphs created by the survey monkey website.

Validity

The questionnaire was analyzed to check the consistency. The data was organized for statistical measurement of the sample population. The validity of the study was assured through different sources of evidence, questionnaires and interviews. The layout of the questions was based on the understanding of the ethical issues prevailing in the world of e-Commerce and the individual behaviors. The questions were direct and easily interpreted and were based on the facts and information gathered in section 1 and 2 of this report.

Reliability

To ensure the reliability of the study, the questionnaire was distributed and presented to the participants in the same manner to assure uniformity of the study.

The Interviews

The interviews were used to gather qualitative data for the research. According to Yin (2017), a qualitative research refers to the gathering of data which is not numerical in nature and it helps to provide an insight into the underlying problem, generate ideas and helps to understand the hypothesis which will later support the quantitative research method. It includes an interpretive approach and helps to study the subject within its context and understand the subjective meanings that people bring to the situation. There are many e-Commerce businesses in Bahrain. However, it was impossible to conduct interviews with most of them due to limited time and limited access. The interviews were conducted with the owner of an online Instagram shop called Mena Shoppers based in UAE and Bahrain and with the IT project manager of the e-government authority in Bahrain.

The Purpose

This study was conducted because the background and introduction of e-Commerce in Bahrain (Section 2) did not provide enough information about the e-Commerce behavior in the country. This study was conducted to explore the facts and provide reasoning for the data collected through the survey. The purpose of this study was to gather qualitative data from the products and service providers of e-Commerce in Bahrain and to understand their perceptions and ideas on the subject. The different problems encountered by the e-traders were discussed based on the results of the survey, along with the suggestions and recommendations to improve the situations concerning unethical and illegal activities of the consumers of e-Commerce and how it affects the e-Commerce business.

The Methods

The data collected for the qualitative research was through semi-structured, face to face interviews through email and telephone, with 2 service providers of e-Commerce products and services in Bahrain. The interview focused on collecting the necessary information required to investigate and study the different unethical and illegal issues in the organizations of Bahrain.

Research Population and Sampling

A research population is known as the collection of individuals who have the same characteristics and common traits (Saunders, 2011). The questionnaire was designed to target those individuals who use e-Commerce in their day to day life. For this purpose, the questionnaire was mainly submitted to young, university students and fresh graduates because according to a survey conducted by the European Union in 2015 on ICT (Information and communication), young people between the age of 25-34 are more active e-shoppers compared to other age groups. To achieve the objectives of the study, the questionnaires were distributed to 55 consumers of e-Commerce. Since it is quite difficult to distribute the questionnaires to all the e-Commerce consumers in Bahrain, so the most convenient method was to distribute it among the most active consumers. Therefore, the sample can be used to generalize the results and make recommendations for the study, for the rest of the population.

SUMMARY

This section has explained the research approaches used in this project. After identifying the research variables and the focus area, the research onion method was selected as a tool to conduct the research. The different layers of the research onion were explained, and the most appropriate methods were selected. It also reported the research design which consisted of the interviews and questionnaires and the data analysis procedures followed by the sampling technique of the questionnaire. The next section will focus on the findings of the research methodology developed in this section.

Figure 6. Frequency of usage

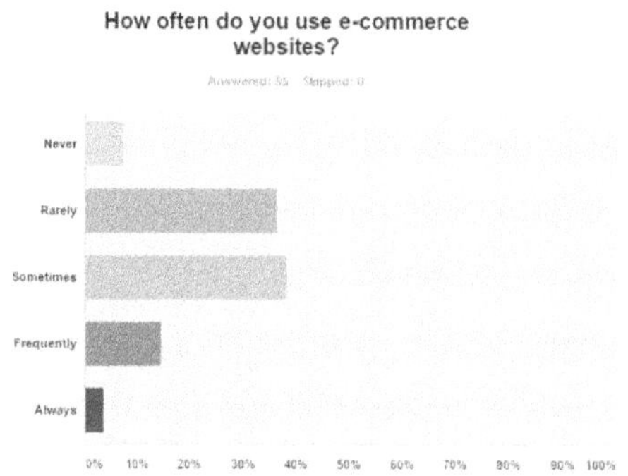

Answer Choices	Responses	
Never	7.27%	4
Rarely	36.36%	20
Sometimes	38.18%	21
Frequently	14.55%	8
Always	3.64%	2
Total		55

DATA ANALYSIS

This section focuses on explaining the results and findings which were collected through the interviews and the questionnaires distributed among the consumers. It will link the responses to the literature review in order to throw light on the issues highlighted in the first section. The data analysis is divided into two parts. The first part focuses on the findings of the survey, while the second part focuses on the findings of the interviews. It will also link the responses of the interview with that of the questionnaires to reach the ultimate solutions to the problems.

Findings of the Questionnaire

The questionnaire was distributed to a sample of55 students of University of Bahrain, who used e-Commerce websites. The response was collected from 55 students in a period of three days.

Frequency of Usage

It is important to know the frequency of e-Commerce usage among the university students in order to find out how many individuals from the sample population indulge in e-Commerce most frequently. Figure 6 shows that 38.18% of the students use e-Commerce sometimes, while with a slightly lower percentage 36.36% of the consumers use it rarely. The lowest percentage was that of the students who always (3.64%) or never (7.27%) use e-Commerce. However, the target of this research were the students who frequently, sometimes or always used it.

Figure 7. Safety

Answer Choices	Responses	
Yes	70.91%	39
No	29.09%	16
Total		55

Safety

The next question focused on finding out the number of consumers who find it safe to order products and services online. According to Figure 7, a majority of 70.91% of the students answered that it is safe to buy products and services online. Opposing to this, 29.09% of the students do not think that is a safe method of purchasing goods and services. Even though there was a positive response from the consumers, we cannot overlook the fact that a percentage as high as 29.09 consider it unsafe to indulge in online shopping activities.

Satisfaction

From Figure 8 we can see that 45.15% of the students surveyed were neither satisfied nor dissatisfied with the online shopping experience, while 38.18% of the students were satisfied. On the other hand, 7.27% of them were dissatisfied and only 5.45%

Figure 8. Satisfaction

	Extremely dissatisfied	Dissatisfied	Neither satisfied nor dissatisfied	Satisfied	Extremely Satisfied	Total	Weighted Average
Rating	3.64% 2	7.27% 4	45.45% 25	38.18% 21	5.45% 3	55	3.35

Figure 9. Most common platforms

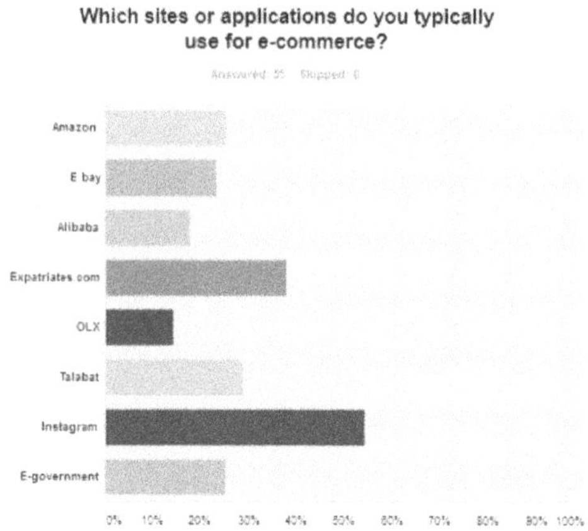

Answer Choices	Responses	
Amazon	25.45%	14
E bay	23.64%	13
Alibaba	18.18%	10
Expatriates.com	38.18%	21
OLX	14.55%	8
Talabat	29.09%	16
Instagram	54.55%	30
E-government	25.45%	14
Total Respondents: 55		

were extremely satisfied. This implies that there is a positive response as the majority of them are either neutral or satisfied with the e-Commerce websites.

Most Used e-Commerce Platforms

The consumers of e-Commerce use a variety of applications or websites, out of which, some of the most common were listed for the consumers to choose from. We can see from Figure 9 that almost 54.55% of the students use Instagram as a source for buying products and services online. As mentioned earlier Bahrain stands at the first place with the greatest number of Instagram users as compared to other GCC countries. The survey proves the fact of the rising trend of Instapreneurs and Instagram users in Bahrain. Another widely used website known as expatriates.com provides the users with the facility of buying or selling products and services online. This website is widely used all around GCC and figure 4.4 shows that almost 38.18% of the students use the website. Talabat ranked at the third place with almost 29.09% users who order food through the application. Other famous websites like amazon, e-government and e-bay were ranked next with nearly 25% users with the minority of 18.18% using Alibaba and 14.55% using OLX.

Reasons for Using e-Commerce

It was necessary to find out the reasons why the consumers prefer to order products and services and online in order to link it to the pre-existing theories mentioned in the literature review. As shown in Figure 10, a majority of 63.64% of the users ordered products or services from websites because it is easy to place an order

Figure 10. Reasons for using e-commerce

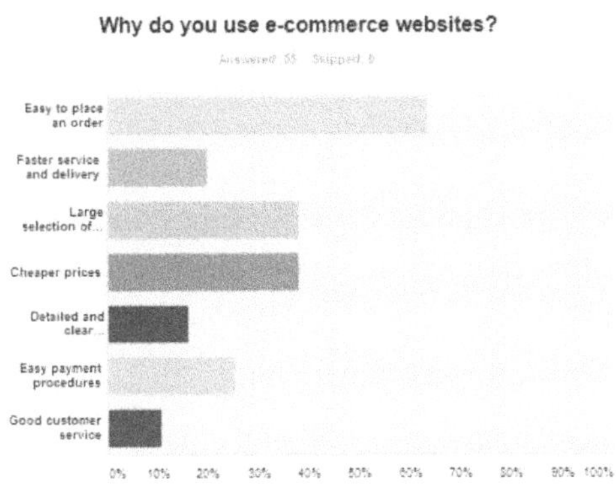

Answer Choices	Responses	
Easy to place an order	63.64%	35
Faster service and delivery	20.00%	11
Large selection of products	38.18%	21
Cheaper prices	38.18%	21
Detailed and clear information about the product and service	16.36%	9
Easy payment procedures	25.45%	14
Good customer service	10.91%	6
Total Respondents: [illegible]		

electronically instead of going to the physical location. Furthermore 38.18% of the consumers use it due to a large variety of products and cheaper prices. As far as cheap prices are concerned, they could also be due to unauthentic products which sometimes the consumers are unable to recognize. The ease of online payment was one of the reasons as stated by 25.45% of the consumers. On the other hand, 20% of the consumers order due to fast service and delivery, 16.26% order due to detailed information about the products or service and only 10.91% order due to good customer service.

Most Concerning Factors

The consumers were asked to rate some of the important factors on a scale of 1 to 4, on the basis of their importance to them and the results were as follows (as shown in Figure 5):

Information Security

A majority of 58.18% of the consumers considered the information security to be very important and 32.17% said it was important. On the other hand, 7.27% consider it to be less important and 1.82% say it is not important at all.

Privacy

According to Figure 5, a majority of 69.09% consider privacy to be a very important factor and 25.45% think it is important. While a minority of 1.82% say it is not much important and 3.64% say it is not important. This shows that while the majority is really concerned about the privacy, but there are people who do not give much importance to it.

Guarantee

The guarantee of the product or service is very important for 65.45% of the consumers whereas it is important for 27.27%. On the other hand, 5.45% consider it to be less important while 1.82% say it is not important.

Product Authenticity

Figure 5 shows that 63.64% of the consumers consider the product authenticity to be very important, whereas 30.91% think it is important. 3.64% say it is less important and 1.82% consider it as not important.

Customer Service

Good customer service plays a major role for any kind of business and it implies on e-Commerce as well. The survey results show that 43.64% of the consumers think it is very important to have a good customer service, 38.18% say it is important. A minority of 12.73% say it is less important and 5.45% do not think that it is important.

Product Quality

A majority of 72.22% of the respondents consider it to be very important for the product to be of good quality. This is higher than any other factor which were mentioned in the question. 25.93% of the respondents think it is important, whereas a 1.85% think it is less important. However, it should be noted that none of the respondents think that product quality holds no importance.

Price

As per Figure 11, 45.45% of the respondents think that the price of the product is very important or important. 7.27% said that is less important while a minority of 1.82% consider it as not important.

Figure 11. Most concerning factors

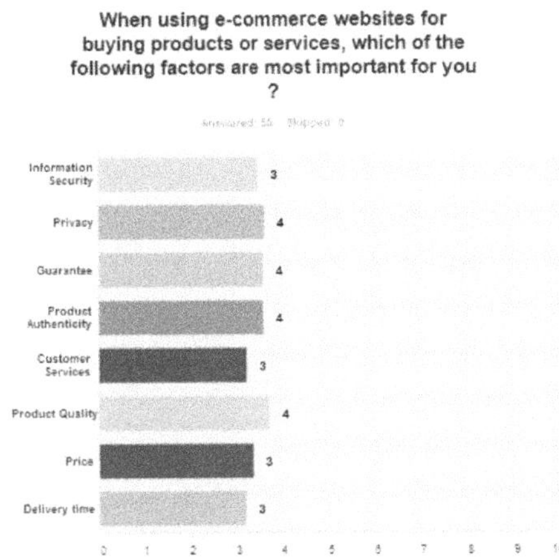

	Not important	less important	Important	Very important	Total	Weighted Average
Information Security	1.82% 1	7.27% 4	32.73% 18	58.18% 32	55	3.47
Privacy	3.64% 2	1.82% 1	25.45% 14	69.09% 38	55	3.60
Guarantee	1.82% 1	5.45% 3	27.27% 15	65.45% 36	55	3.56
Product Authenticity	1.82% 1	3.64% 2	30.91% 17	63.64% 35	55	3.56
Customer Services	5.45% 3	12.72% 7	38.18% 21	43.64% 24	55	3.20
Product Quality	0.00% 0	1.85% 1	25.93% 14	72.22% 39	54	3.70
Price	1.82% 1	7.27% 4	45.45% 25	45.45% 25	55	3.35
Delivery time	1.82% 1	20.00% 11	36.36% 20	41.82% 23	55	3.18

Delivery Time

A majority of 41.82% of the respondents said that the delivery time of the product is very important, 36.36% of them said that it is important, while 20% said that it is less important and 1.82% said that it is not important.

Common Issues

The respondents were asked to choose some of the most concerning issues faced by them while shopping online through a checklist which contained the most common issues discussed in the introduction. 54.55% of the respondents chose late delivery of products as the most common issue, while 43.64% said that false advertising and information is a big issue. The percentage of respondents who chose fake products was 38.18%, whereas poor customer service ranked next with 32.73%. About 27.27% chose damaged products as a commonly faced issue, while 21.82% chose fraud. Email spamming and privacy issues got an equal percentage of 20% from the respondents. On the other hand, 10.91% selected multiple payments as a common problem followed by 9.09% for hacking. Web spoofing received 7.27% while 7.27% of the respondents selected "none" as an option. Figure 12 shows the percentage and the selection of the respondents.

Reactions to the Problems

As seen in Figure 13, a majority of 44.44% of the respondents said that they contact the customer service, while 42.59% choose another website for buying the product or

Figure 12. Common issues

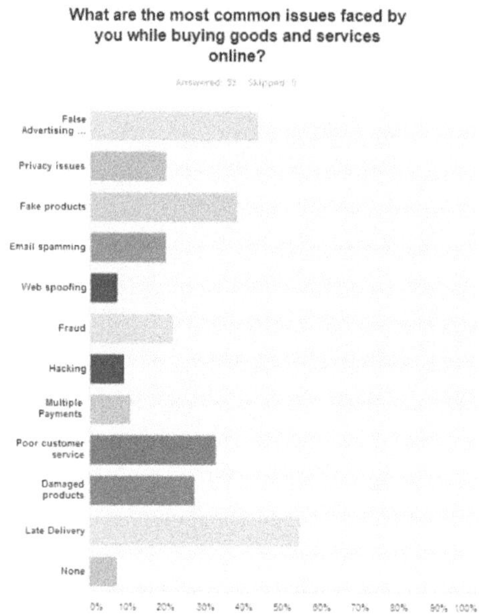

Answer Choices	Responses	
False Advertising and information	43.64%	24
Privacy issues	20.00%	11
Fake products	38.18%	21
Email spamming	20.00%	11
Web spoofing	7.27%	4
Fraud	21.82%	12
Hacking	9.09%	5
Multiple Payments	10.91%	6
Poor customer service	32.73%	18
Damaged products	27.27%	15
Late Delivery	54.55%	30
None	7.27%	4
Total Respondents: 55		

service. 33.33% of the respondents ask the supplier for a refund as a compensation for the issue faced by them, while 27.78% stop using e-Commerce websites and start purchasing things manually. However, only 16.67% of the respondents said that they do not take any action.

Online Payments

Figure 14 shows that when the respondents were asked for their opinion about online payments, 70.91% said that they found it safe, while 20% said that it was not safe. Among the people answered that online payments are unsafe, some of mentioned

Figure 13. Reactions to the problems

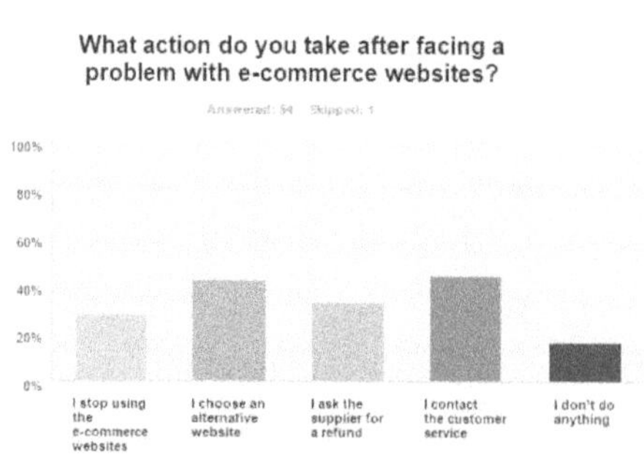

Answer Choices	Responses	
I stop using the e-commerce websites	27.78%	15
I choose an alternative website	42.59%	23
I ask the supplier for a refund	33.33%	18
I contact the customer service	44.44%	24
I don't do anything	16.67%	9
Total Respondents: 54		

Figure 14. Safety of online payments

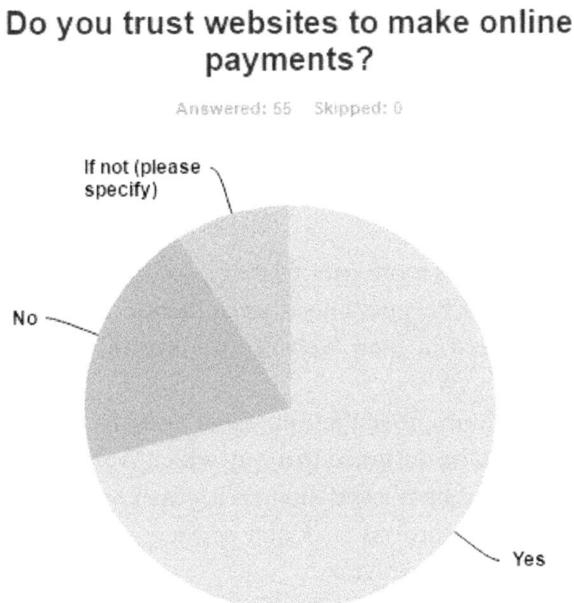

Answer Choices		Responses	
Yes		70.91%	39
No		20.00%	11
If not (please specify)	Responses	9.09%	5
Total			55

different reasons for their beliefs. According to one of the respondents the payment should be made on delivery and in cash terms, while another said he/she is concerned about online payments as their credit card information can be misused over the internet. Some respondents also mentioned that their main concern is privacy and they do not know if they can trust the website as their information might be at risk.

Suggestions for Improvement

Out of 55 respondents, only 26 of them provided some suggestions to further improve the e-Commerce transactions because it was optional to answer. According to the respondents:

- The websites should provide more variations and cheap prices because the delivery prices are high.
- More security measures should be taken, and the websites should be certified by inspection teams.
- The personal contact number of the suppliers should be provided as a safety measure.
- The delay in delivery should be reduced and the product quality should be guaranteed.
- The websites should be more user friendly, so it is easy to use.
- The products should be guaranteed as authentic and in case they are not, it should be specified in their websites to save the time and efforts of the consumers.
- The websites should improve their payment systems.
- The websites should be designed in a way which is attractive to the customers and the orders should be tracked along with cash on delivery options.
- There should be an improved customer service, so in case of any issue they can report it directly to resolve it.
- Financial and information security measures should be taken along with faster shipping.
- The information of the product should be genuine and true because the idea of buying a product without seeing is very risky for the customers and the e-Commerce websites should also be accountable for the delivery of the product.
- The websites should have more ways to secure customers' details and information and guarantee the customer that the product being sold is authentic and approved by the brand.
- The government websites also need improvement to secure information.
- Email spamming should be reduced.

The majority of the respondents emphasized on faster delivery of products, product authenticity, information security and privacy.

Findings of the Interviews

As mentioned earlier, the interviews were conducted in order to develop an insight into the problems faced by the buyers of e-Commerce services and products. Based on the findings of the survey, the interview was conducted with one product and one service provider of e-Commerce in Bahrain.

MENA Shoppers (Products)

As mentioned earlier, the trend of instapreneurs in Bahrain is increasing day by day. The owner is a marketing student at the University of Bahrain and the owner of an online shop on Instagram called Mena shoppers which is a retail shop for the latest fashion trends and is based in Bahrain and UAE. The manufacturers are based in Dubai, so whenever there is an order for a product, it is shipped directly from UAE to customer. The owner explained that her fiancé is responsible for managing the orders in the UAE and she manages the orders in Bahrain.

Q.1: Why Did You Choose to Have an Online Shop Rather Than a Physical Store?

The owner explained that her business is not located in Bahrain, but it is based in the UAE. E-Commerce is good way to reach the customers not only in Bahrain but in the UAE as well, as a lot of people now prefer online shopping compared to the traditional shopping methods. Instagram is an upcoming trend in the Middle East, so she decided to choose it as a medium to reach the target customers. She also explained that her target customers are mainly the women as they are more into online shopping compared to men.

Q.2: What are Some of the Ethical Issues Faced by You From the Customers Side?

Most of the customers expect on-time delivery and since the products are shipped from UAE, sometimes they get delayed from the courier company, so the owners are blamed for the delay which causes a problem. Many customers are also reluctant to provide their personal information like their house address or their contact number for the delivery of the products which creates a lot of problems in delivering the product on time. And lastly, sometimes the customers travel after placing an order which creates a problem for the owners as the product has to be returned back.

Q.3: How Can You Prevent the Issue of Late Delivery?

The owner explained that the courier agents that she dealt with before mostly delayed the delivery and due to a large number of complaints from the customers, she changed the courier agents to professional ones which are expensive, but they are really good and fast in delivering the product. But most of the late deliveries are due to the suppliers and not due to the owners.

Q.4: How Do You Convince the Customers to Provide Their Personal Information?

The wonder stated that she tries to gain the confidence of the customers by convincing them that their information will be highly confidential, and it will be used solely for the purpose of delivering the product. But on the other hand, if they do not wish to provide the information, they have the option of directly contacting the courier agents or the shipping company and explain them the address.

Q.5: Do You Face Any Technical Issues or Any Other Problems Due to the Customers Lack of Knowledge About Using the Application?

According to owner, there are usually no technical issues but sometimes the customers do not know how to place an order, so they are instructed on the procedures and payment policies which makes it easy to solve such problems.

Q.6: According to You, Does e-Commerce Create Employment or Unemployment in the Economy?

The owner explained that e-Commerce is a great platform for young students who wish to start their own business and earn as a part time worker, since it can easily be managed and is highly profitable, so it creates more employment.

Q.7: There Are A Lot of Online Shops Similar to Yours. How Do You Provide the Competitive Edge to the Customers, So They Choose to buy From You?

Compared to the competitors, Mena shoppers provides a wide range of varieties to the customers along with seasonal offers and promotions on Eid, Christmas and other festivities. The delivery charge is also comparatively less than the other competitors.

Q.8: Do You Think the Customer Can Sometimes Lie About the Quality or Quantity of the Product? How Can This Be Solved?

The owner explained that she has never experienced any such situations, but the quality of the product is always checked before sending it to the customer to ensure that there are no such cases.

Q.9: Did You Ever Send a Wrong Order Due to Wrong Address Information?

Mena shoppers have never faced such situations because the courier agents always do a background check of the customers to ensure that the address is correct. The products are only sent after ensuring and double checking the address with the customer.

Q.10: What are Your Suggestions to Improve e-Commerce in the Future?

There should be more security measures taken by the e-Commerce sellers to ensure that the products being sold are genuine because the customers cannot see them before buying.

Q.11: Do You Provide Cash on Delivery or Online Payments?

Mena Shoppers provide cash on delivery and it is one of the reasons the customers choose them among the competitors. The payment is done after the product reaches the customer, so they can pay for what they get and if they do not like it, they can return the product. Companies like Amazon and E-bay are well-known, and the customers would not hesitate to pay online but on the other hand, they would be reluctant to make online payments for companies that are small and not well-known.

E-Government (Services)

The IT project manager at the e-government authority in Bahrain is currently working on a project which is directed towards helping the business community, particularly the individuals who wish to start online activities for their businesses in Bahrain. Any person who wants to register for an online business activity in Bahrain can do so by applying on the e-government portal and then seeking an approval to commence their online business activities. The following data was captured and collected through the interview.

Q1: Why do you think the government has taken this initiative of providing online services to the citizens?

The manager responded by saying that e-government is different from e-Commerce in the sense that it is directed towards providing online services to the customers, while e-Commerce focuses on providing products. As far as online services are concerned people use it for their ease, so they can avail the services sitting at their homes.

Q.2: Does e-Commerce create employment or unemployment in the economy?

e-Commerce creates more employment according to the manager because there are a lot of direct things in e-Commerce which include delivering the products to the customer. So, a driver has to be hired or an alliance has to be made with another company which can provide the service. When there is more demand, more people will be hired for the service. At the same time when it comes to the logistics, there is no need for a physical store or a salesperson and since we cannot pay cash online, credit cards have to be used so there is no need for a cashier, but more technicians and website developer are required along with online agents to provide customer services around the clock. On one hand there will be no need for employees but at the same time other employees are hired for these things which definitely creates employment.

Q.3: According to a survey, the majority of the consumers are concerned about their information security and privacy. Do you think it is safe for the customers to rely on e-Commerce websites? How can the websites ensure security?

The customers can rely on e-government services because there are certain procedures and policies that are implemented by the e-government authorities for the security of the consumers but not all e-Commerce websites can be trusted. There are a lot of websites that ensure security and the users can know if the website has been secured or not, but many websites also capture the information of the users. So, the users should be aware about which of them are safe and which are not.

Q.4: What are Some of the Ethical Issues Faced by You From the Customers Side?

The manger stated that one of the main issues faced by e-government is that the users provide wrong information which results in them receiving wrong service and this creates a lot of problems because sometimes there are some requirements which not everyone wants to provide. Whereas in e-Commerce websites, when the customer's order a product, they need to provide their credit card information, and if the website is not secured, this information can be used unethically. There are a lot of security measures which are being implemented to ensure the customers that the website does not save the credit card information and it is only used for payment purposes.

Q.5: Sometimes There are Cases of Multiple Payments. Is it Due to the Technical Reasons or Due to the Customers Lack of Knowledge in Using the Website?

The manager asserts that multiple payments are due to technical errors and cannot be avoided most of the time. When the users send their information to the gateway, sometimes due to network issues there is a delay, but the user keeps pushing which results in another request being sent to the server and so there are cases of multiple payments. Many times, during the payment process, the bank sends a notification to the user that the payment has been done and the user closes the window which makes it difficult for the provider to find the source or destination of the payment. In these cases, the payment is made but not updated in the system. For this reason, the payment gateways display messages asking the users not to close the window while the payment process is going on. The users have to read these messages and follow the instructions carefully. Another reason for this is the infrastructure or bandwidth as not all of them has the same speed. Some may be faster than the others and vice versa. But all these technical issues can be solved if the users disclaim against them and after it has been proved, the user can be refunded.

Q.6: What Steps Can be Taken to Educate People About Using e-Commerce?

The manager explained that in the Middle East, people are not well educated in dealing with online websites or e-government services and educating people takes time and effort. This can be done through television, social media and websites which should provide clear instructions and steps to the users. There should be a lot of campaigns and brochures to educate the people on the subject. The banks should educate people on how to use credit cards for online shopping.

Q.7: When You Update Your Website, Are the Users Still Able to Use It?

It depends on the type of update in process. If it is a normal update, they put on a notice for the people but for major updates either the website is shut down or it is running but people cannot use it for a while. But the priority is to inform people about it.

Q.8: Many Websites Provide False Information to the Customers, Which Raises Trust Issues. How Can This Be Solved?

The manger asserted that people should never believe what they see, and the customers need to be educated properly. Many people recommend websites, but it should be taken into consideration that not all can be trusted. When people use a new website, they should read about it before doing any transactions.

Q.9: Websites or Online Portals Like E-Government are More Prone to Hacking Due to Online Payment Procedures. Have You Ever Faced Any Such Issues?

The manger stated that as far as e-government is concerned, people are forced to use it because sometimes they do not have another channel for making payments. But since there are a lot of services combined in one portal, e-government is usually targeted for hacking. However, there are a lot of security measures taken so it is rarely hacked. On the other hand, the e-Commerce websites are optional, and people have another source to provide them the products, so sometimes the e-Commerce sellers compromise on the security of the customers in order to ensure fast service without losing the customer. So, they are easily hacked.

Q.10: Do You Think That Electronic Contracts Have as Much Authenticity as the Ones Made in Person?

The manager discussed that when it comes to trading, many organizations are not always in the same country and they are forced to use electronic contracts and they have to trust a person whom they have never met or never seen due to geographical boundaries. Electronic contracts are built on trust and the quality of services because in the modern era, we cannot even sometimes trust human beings when making contracts in person.

Q. 11: One of the Major Legal Problems Faced by the Government is the Taxation of e-Commerce Businesses. How Can This Be Solved?

The taxation of e-Commerce business is very easy because all the e-Commerce websites have to be licensed and registered at the Ministry of commerce in Bahrain. Once an individual obtains a CR, he is asked for the financial statements of the business from time to time, so taxation is possible. But it is difficult to tax the businesses which are being run on social media, Instagram or other personal websites and the government should monitor and inspect such websites whenever there is a complaint from the customers' side. These businesses should be shut down or controlled by the government to ensure legality.

Q.12: What Should Be Done to Eliminate Scammers and Reduce the Risk of Fraud From Websites Like Expatriates.com and OLX?

The main thing is to educate the consumers so that they are aware of such situations. Whenever any transaction involves western union, they should know that something is fishy and avoid getting into it. The developers should read the ads on a daily basis and delete the posts which do not look authentic. If there are fewer scamming advertisements, the website can be more trustworthy for the consumers.

Q.13: Email Spamming is Also One of the Major Issues Faced by the Consumers. But at the Same Time, It is Also a Marketing Strategy Used By Most of the Businesses. How Can This be Reduced?

The manager said that sometimes the consumers give out their email to some companies to receive important notifications and offers from time to time but at the same time, the email is also passed on to other companies and they start receiving a lot of spam emails but the consumers always have an option in their email to mark these emails as spam or block them so as to get rid of such situations.

Q.14: Majority of the Customers Prefer Cash on Delivery When Buying Products and Services Online. Do You Think This is Right?

When people use a new website, they are not sure if they can trust it so it is important to have cash on delivery for the convenience of the customers, so they can see that the product is authentic and not damaged. In some cases, once the payment is done, it cannot be refunded so the consumer has to see the product and then make the payment.

Q.15: What are Some of the Major Steps Being Taken by the E-Government to Promote e-Commerce in the Country?

The manger discussed that there are many big projects coming up in the future. The main thing which helps the e-Commerce and the e-government is a good infrastructure which ensures high speed internet connections. The telecom companies are developing high speed internet services for the ease of the e-Commerce. Fiber optic networks are being introduced in the country which will boost the power and speed of the internet which will be very beneficial for the e-Commerce users.

Summary of the Findings

The findings of the research report that the majority of the consumers do trust e-Commerce websites and are neutrally satisfied with the channel. The most commonly used platform was found to be Instagram, which proves the rising trend in the country. Since applications like Instagram do not require a commercial registration and it is easy for anyone to start a business and market it, it can be prone to many ethical issues and can be one of the reasons why people confront different problems while purchasing products online. Same is the case with websites like OLX and expatriates.com where any individual can sell anything without any restriction. These factors can be the reason why the individuals are concerned about their privacy and information. They can also contribute to the rise of ethical issues like privacy invasion, fraud, late delivery of products, and so on. False information, advertising and fake products was one of the most common issue and since websites like expatriates and OLX are not monitored or controlled by the government, anyone can be fooled by them. It was also found out that the majority of the users try to contact the customer service in case of an issue so this highlights the importance of a good customer service. Failing to provide a good customer service might result in the user choosing an alternate website which might result in losing the customer. Online payments are considered to be safe by most of the users but some users consider it unsafe as well due to sensitive credit card information.

The findings also reported that e-Commerce tends to increase the employment rate in the country as it is easy to start and can be used as a part time job. Issues like multiple payments and late delivery of products are mostly related to the consumer's lack of knowledge and awareness about using e-Commerce websites. Education and training forms a critical part in solving this issue. The issue of late delivery can also be related to the hesitancy of the consumers to provide private information. Damaged products can be avoided by availing the cash on delivery option, so more and more traders should provide the option of cash on delivery to win the trust of the customers, until and unless it is a well-known and trusted business. But this can be a good start for new e-Commerce businesses to expand and win the customer's trust. Another factor which can help the e-businesses to expand and win the trust of the customers is by registering their businesses at the Ministry of Industry and Commerce. This will also solve the issue of taxation. Educating the people can help them to identify the difference between a secured and an unsecured website, which can reduce the number of issues faced by them.

CONCLUSION AND RECOMMENDATIONS

The research objectives, the main outcomes of the research, a comparison of the findings along with the current literature review on e-Commerce and its implications in the society have been discussed in detail in the preceding sections. There is no doubt that e-Commerce has facilitated the lives of human beings by providing products and services at the distance of a single click. The research has argued that apart from providing many advantages, e-Commerce also gives rise to a number of unethical and illegal behaviors.

The behaviors of the consumers and the sellers of e-Commerce in the Kingdom of Bahrain have been highlighted in Section four. While investigating and collecting the data from the questionnaires and interviews, it has been highlighted that consumers and sellers are aware of the different issues surrounding the e-Commerce and are looking forward to eliminating these problems. But besides this, majority of the consumers do think that e-Commerce is a safe platform and they will continue to use it in the future. The number of consumers who are dissatisfied with the e-Commerce are very less and this shows that the situation is not as fierce as it looks. The findings also highlight the trend of instapreneurs as it shows that the majority of the consumers head over to Instagram every time they want to order a product or service. But at the same time, we cannot deny that websites like expatraites.com are also highly used by the consumers and as stated by the manager such websites increase the risk for the consumers to fall a victim of scam and fraud.

One of the most common reason for using e-Commerce was found to be the ease of placing an order online with a wide variety of choices and cheap prices. Other factors which play a big role for the consumers to decide if they should use the e-Commerce websites are privacy, information security, product authenticity, quality and the delivery time. Whereas the major issues faced by the consumers, as highlighted in the findings were late delivery of products, false advertising and product information, fake products and poor customer service. These issues shape the attitudes and behaviors of consumers while making online purchases, as explained by TBP in Section two. The solutions to these problems were provided by the sellers through different suggestions as mentioned in Section four. On the other hand the major issues faced by the sellers include late delivery, wrong personal information and lack of customers' knowledge which can be solved by training the consumers or winning their trust. Technical issues can also be an important issue but cannot be counted as unethical or illegal. The online payment systems are not perceived to be risky by the majority of the consumers but cash on delivery is preferred when buying products and services from e-Commerce businesses which are not well-known. The consumers and sellers gave various recommendations and suggestions to improve the e-Commerce services which helped to support the research and reach the ultimate conclusions.

While the findings of this research have shown some similarities, contradictions and some difference with the pre-existing theories but at the same time we cannot question the validity of the findings of this research. Although the sample base was restricted to the consumers in Bahrain, the response rate was quite high in a short period of time. The experiences and thoughts of the consumers cannot be dismissed as any business cannot run if the customers are not satisfied. The evaluation of this research has been qualitative as well as quantitative. However, there are a few questions that still remain unanswered and many issues need more investigation. The research proves to be beneficial for a number of reasons. As mentioned above, there are a lot of issues and problems but the increase in the number of internet users and online consumers help to overcome this factor and contribute to the ever growing success of the e-Commerce world.

Recommendations

Based on the findings of the research, and the e-Commerce situation in the Kingdom of Bahrain, it requires concentrated and joint efforts from both the consumers and the manufacturers of e-Commerce to solve the most prominent issues faced by both the parties. This is important because the world of e-Commerce is expanding day by day and the consumers as well as the manufacturers should understand the future consequences and impact of unethical and illegal behaviors on their day to day e-Commerce activities. Therefore, the research recommends the following for the buyers and the sellers who indulge in e-Commerce activities:

Recommendations for the Sellers

According to the Sophos Security Threat Report in 2012, an average of 30,000 websites are hacked every day and it is likely to be increased by now. The security of the consumers greatly lies at the hand of the sellers and the way they conduct the businesses. Therefore, a number of recommendations can be provided to the sellers to save their websites from being hacked and to protect the user information and data as well as to solve the various issues faced by the consumers.

1. **Hacking:** The sellers or manufacturers must choose a secure e-Commerce platform by selecting an existing e-Commerce platform rather than building a new one. This is because there are a lot of security risks associated with building an e-Commerce solution from the scratch and it can be easily hacked. The sellers must not store unnecessary or sensitive customer data which is unessential to their business. An encrypted checkout tunnel should be used for processing credit cards which will ensure that the server does not see the customer's credit card data. The sellers must also update their e-Commerce solutions SSL/TLS to encrypt the browser communications when transmitting confidential information. The websites must be regularly checked for any vulnerabilities and the risky software's which jeopardize online security should be deleted.
2. **Product Authenticity**: In order to ensure the authenticity of the products bought from the supplier, the sellers should introduce a new technology which uses hard to copy symbols which are similar to QR codes and can be scanned and read by a smartphone camera. These codes will help to identify the product authenticity as a part of product labels when any of the sellers request to sell their products. In this way the consumers will also be satisfied that they are actually paying for the product they are receiving. The companies should also register their trademarks with Customs agencies in order to avoid selling

counterfeit products. In case the website sells duplicate or copies of original products, they should clearly mention and inform the consumers beforehand so as to avoid wasting the time and money of the consumer.

3. **False Advertising and Information:** The sellers should stop displaying fake information and advertisements on their websites in order to win the trust of the customers because the customer's satisfaction is the key to success for any business. In order to avoid misleading information in the affiliate marketing, the sellers must monitor the traffic that they are generating. Advertisements which garner a higher click rate should be suspected. The sellers should provide clear guidelines and details of the claims which the advertisements can or cannot make. They should also establish a policy framework and take action against the affiliates who break the policies.
4. **Email Spamming:** The e-Commerce sellers must avoid passing or selling the consumer data like emails and other personal information to the third parties. This will result in the customer doubting the legitimacy of the products sold by the seller and the customers' trust will be deteriorated. At the same time, the e-commerce manufacturers must also avoid sending large number of irrelevant emails to the customers because they do not necessarily interest the consumer and they might block the email which might result in losing the customer's interest in the products or services offered by the seller. The online companies must also use programs which can track things and allow the receiver to opt-in or unsubscribe from receiving the emails whenever they want to.
5. **Cybersquatting:** In order to avoid cybersquatting, the sellers should register their domain names which includes the common misspellings and other typing errors that the users might enter while searching for website. They should also continually ensure that their trademarks are up to date all over the world.
6. **Late Delivery of Products:** In order to avoid problems with the customer regarding the late delivery of products, the sellers must allow them to track their orders. They can also provide the customers with the direct contact of the shipping company so that they are not blamed for the delay. In case the shipping company is causing an unnecessary delay and resulting in losing the customers, then it is better for the sellers to choose a better shipping company with fast delivery.
7. **Damaged Products:** All the products must be checked to ensure that they are in good quality before shipping them to the customers and in case the damage is caused through the shipment then the customers should be refunded for it or the product should be exchanged. In this way, the customer will trust the company and will not hesitate to place orders in the future.

Recommendations for the Buyers

1. **Privacy Invasion:** More policies should be developed to balance the privacy concerns of the consumers with the information needed by the sellers. In this way the consumers will feel secured and safeguarded while purchasing online and the trust issues will be solved. The consumers should also use strong passwords for more protection of their sensitive data and in case they do not trust the online seller, they should directly contact the shipping company to provide information like address and telephone numbers. Another thing to be noted is that the customers should never provide their social security numbers while placing an order as it is not a requirement for purchasing. Moreover, the URL of the e-commerce websites must be checked to ensure that it is safe and secure to use.
2. **Web Tracking:** In order to stop web tracking, the consumers need to delete the third-party cookies from their browser. For deleting the existing cookies, users can install programs like CCleaner which will only target to clean the third-party cookies on the hard drive. Users can also delete all their existing cookies and start over if they do not wish to install such programs. Once the third-party cookies are deleted, the next step is to change the settings of the browsers in order to avoid any third-party cookies in the future. This can be done by changing the internet settings in the browsers and selecting the "block third-party cookies and site data" from the options.
3. **Product Authenticity**: The customers should research about the website before buying products from it and in case they receive counterfeit products from an e-Commerce seller which claims to sell authentic products, they should first report it to the seller because sometimes even the seller is not aware of receiving fake products from the supplier. In case the seller refuses to refund the consumers, then they should report it to the appropriate or responsible entity.
4. **False Advertising and Information:** The consumers should only buy products from a trusted e-Commerce website or source and in case they are buying the products from the seller for the first time, they should insist on paying cash on delivery so that they are satisfied with the product they are receiving and in case of online payments, the unsatisfied customers should ask for a refund. If the consumers see a lot of price difference between the original product and the product being offered by the seller, they should refrain from buying it because it is a sign of false marketing.
5. **Email Spamming:** The consumers can stop receiving emails from a particular e-Commerce website by selecting the unsubscribe option if it is available and in case they do not have this option, they can mark the email as spam, so the emails from that source will always automatically be sent to the junk folder. Anti-spam software can also be used for this purpose. If the users keep receiving

emails even after unsubscribing, then they should report them at the Internet Service Provider's Association who are responsible to regulate spam. It should be noted that there are a large number of identity thieves who send emails to the users and ask them to update their credit card information, online payment information etc. The users should not click any links provided in such emails or respond to any such request for financial information.

6. **Multiple Payments:** In order to avoid multiple payments, the users should make sure that their internet connection is strong. While making online transactions, the users should not refresh the webpage or close it and wait for the webpage to respond. In case of multiple payment, it should be reported to the seller as soon as possible so the money can be refunded. After the payment is made, the consumers should print or save the receipt for future references.
7. **Late Delivery of Products:** Before placing an order online, the users should carefully read and pay attention to the shipping policies and facts. According to the law, the company should deliver the product within the time period stated in the ads. In case of no time frame, the merchant must deliver the products within 30 days or give an "Option Notice" to the user which will allow him to cancel his order and ask for a refund.

REFERENCES

Agag, G. (2019). E-commerce Ethics and Its Impact on Buyer Repurchase Intentions and Loyalty: An Empirical Study of Small and Medium Egyptian Businesses. *Journal of Business Ethics*, *154*(2), 389–410. doi:10.100710551-017-3452-3

Ajzen, I. (1985). From intentions to actions: A theory of planned behavior. In *Action control* (pp. 11–39). Berlin: Springer. doi:10.1007/978-3-642-69746-3_2

Ajzen, I. (1991). The theory of planned behavior. *Organizational Behavior and Human Decision Processes*, *50*(2), 179–211. doi:10.1016/0749-5978(91)90020-T

Ajzen, I., Czasch, C., & Flood, M. G. (2009). From Intentions to Behavior: Implementation Intention, Commitment, and Conscientiousness 1. *Journal of Applied Social Psychology*, *39*(6), 1356–1372. doi:10.1111/j.1559-1816.2009.00485.x

Ajzen, I., & Fishbein, M. (1980). *Understanding attitudes and predicting social behaviour*. Academic Press.

Al-Alawi, A. I. (2014). Cybercrimes, Computer Forensics and their Impact in Business Climate: Bahrain Status. *Research Journal of Business Management*, *8*(3), 139–156. doi:10.3923/rjbm.2014.139.156

Al-Alawi, A. I., & Abdelgadir, M. F. (2006). An Empirical Study of Attitudes and Opinions of Computer Crimes: A Comparative Study between UK and Kingdom of Bahrain. *Journal of Computational Science*, *2*(3), 229–235. doi:10.3844/jcssp.2006.229.235

Al-Alawi, A. I., & Al-Ali, F. (2015). Factors Affecting e-Commerce Adoption in SMEs in the GCC: An Empirical study of Kuwait. *Research Journal of Information Technology*, *7*(1), 1–21. doi:10.3923/rjit.2015.1.21

Al-Alawi, A. I., & Hafedh, E. A. (2006). Auditing of Information Privacy. *Information Technology Journal*, *5*(1), 177–182. doi:10.3923/itj.2006.177.182

Al-Alawi, A. I., & Al-Bassam, S. A. (2019). Evaluation of Telecommunications Regulatory Practice in the Kingdom of Bahrain: Development and Challenges. *International Journal of Business Information Systems*, *31*(2), 282–303.

Alani, F. (2009). *Photos: Top Ten Cybersquatter Cases*. Retrieved from http://www.computerweekly.com/photostory/2240107807/Photos-Top-ten-cybersquatter-cases/1/Cybersquatting-cases-Number-10-Dell

Babu, R. (2011). *e-Commerce Ethical and Legal Issues*. Retrieved from https://blog.qburst.com/2011/03/e-commerce-ethical-and-legal-issues/

Balasoui, A. E. (2015). Unfair competition in online commerce. *Romanian Economic Business Review*, *10*(2), 39–47.

Bart, Y., Shankar, V., Sultan, F., & Urban, G. L. (2005). Are the drivers and role of online trust the same for all web sites and consumers? A large-scale exploratory empirical study. *Journal of Marketing*, *69*(4), 133–152. doi:10.1509/jmkg.2005.69.4.133

Battacherjee, A. (2002). Individual trust in online firms: Scale development and initial trust. *Journal of Management Information Systems*, *19*(1), 211–241. doi:10.1080/07421222.2002.11045715

Boland, R. (2011). *Military Website Spoofing Is No Laughing Matter*. Retrieved from http://www.afcea.org/content/?q=military-website-spoofing-no-laughing-matter

Bouma, G. D., & Atkinson, G. B. J. (1995). A Handbook of Science Social Research. Academic Press.

Bryman, A. (2012). *Social Research Methods* (5th ed.). Oxford, UK: Oxford University Press.

Bryman, A., & Bell, E. (2011). *Business Research Methods* (3rd ed.). Oxford, UK: Oxford University Press.

Byford, K. S. (1998). Privacy in cyberspace: Constructing a model of privacy for the electronic communications environment. *Rutgers Computer & Technology Law Journal*, *24*, 1.

Cabell, D. (2001). *E-Commerce: An Introduction*. Harvard Law School. Retrieved from https://cyber.harvard.edu/ecommerce/

Cohen, S. B. (2000). *Sample Design of the 1997 Medical Expenditure Panel Survey, Household Component (No. 1)*. US Department of Health and Human Services, Public Health Service, Agency for Healthcare Research and Quality.

Cowton, C. J. (1998). The use of secondary data in business ethics research. *Journal of Business Ethics*, *17*(4), 423–434. doi:10.1023/A:1005730825103

Culnan, M. (1993). How did they get my name? An Exploratory Investigation of Consumer Attitudes toward Secondary Information Use. *Management Information Systems Quarterly*, *17*(3), 341–363. doi:10.2307/249775

Curran, J., & Blackburn, R. A. (2001). Older people and the enterprise society: Age and self-employment propensities. *Work, Employment and Society*, *15*(4), 889–902. doi:10.1177/095001701400438279

D'Andrea, A., Ferri, F., & Grifoni, P. (2014). The E-Commerce Business Model Implementation. In *Encyclopedia of Business Analytics and Optimization* (pp. 2509–2520). IGI Global. doi:10.4018/978-1-4666-5202-6.ch224

Donaldson, T. (2003). Adding Corporate Ethics to the Bottom Line, Business Ethics (12th ed.). McGraw Hill.

Dozier, B. (2013). *Ethical issues in Electronic Commerce: Focus on Privacy*. Retrieved from https://barbradozier.wordpress.com/2013/06/20/ethical-issues-in-electronic-commerce-focus-on-privacy/#__RefHeading__1_1773874387

Feilzer, M. Y. (2010). Doing Mixed Methods Research Pragmatically: Implications for the Rediscovery of Pragmatism as a Research Paradigm. *Journal of Mixed Methods Research*, *4*(1), 6–16. doi:10.1177/1558689809349691

Flick, U. (2011). *Introducing Research Methodology: A Beginner's Guide to Doing a Research Project*. London: Sage.

Galant, V. (2005). Blending E-commerce Theory and Application. *IEEE Distributed Systems Online*, *6*(1), 5. doi:10.1109/MDSO.2005.2

George, J. F. (2002). Influences on the Intent to Make Internet Purchases. *Internet Research*, *12*(2), 165–180. doi:10.1108/10662240210422521

George, J. F. (2004). The Theory of Planned Behavior and Internet Purchasing. *Internet Research*, *14*(3), 198–212. doi:10.1108/10662240410542634

Goddard, W., & Melville, S. (2004). *Research Methodology: An Introduction* (2nd ed.). Oxford, UK: Blackwell Publishing.

Goulding, C. (2002). Grounded theory: A practical guide for management, business and market researchers. *Sage (Atlanta, Ga.)*.

Goyal, S., Sergi, B. S., & Esposito, M. (2019). Literature review of emerging trends and future directions of e-commerce in global business landscape. *World Review of Entrepreneurship, Management and Sustainable Development*, *15*(1/2), 226–255. doi:10.1504/WREMSD.2019.098454

Greblikaite, J., & Pervazaite, D. (2014). Ethical Issues related to E-Commerce: Case of Discount E-Shopping Site in Lithuania. *European Integration Studies*, (8), 124-130.

Hakim, C. (2000). *Work-lifestyle choices in the 21st century: Preference theory*. OUP.

Hoffman, D. L., Novak, T. P., & Peralta, M. (1999). Building consumer trust online. *Communications of the ACM*, *42*(4), 80–85. doi:10.1145/299157.299175

Hwang, Y., & Kim, D. J. (2007). Customer self-service systems: The effects of perceived Web quality with service contents on enjoyment, anxiety, and e-trust. *Decision Support Systems*, *43*(3), 746–760. doi:10.1016/j.dss.2006.12.008

Jie, M. W. (2012). *History of E-Business*. Retrieved from http://www.ehow.com/about_5282606_history-ebusiness.html

Jones, J. M., & Vijayasarathy, L. R. (1998). Internet consumer catalog shopping: Findings from an exploratory study and directions for future research. *Internet Research*, *8*(4), 322–330. doi:10.1108/10662249810231069

Kant, P., Kind, O. M., Kintscher, T., Lohse, T., Martini, T., Mölbitz, S., & Uwer, P. (2015). HatHor for single top-quark production: Updated predictions and uncertainty estimates for single top-quark production in hadronic collisions. *Computer Physics Communications*, *191*, 74–89. doi:10.1016/j.cpc.2015.02.001

Kavaiya, R. (2015). *Scope of E-Commerce*. Retrieved from http://www.slideshare.net/rahulkavaiya07/scope-of-ecommerce-rahulkavaiya

Kelly, M., & Williams, C. (2016). *Busn: Introduction to Business*. Boston, MA: Cengage Learning.

Korper, S., & Ellis, J. (2000). *The E-commerce Book: Building the E-empire*. Elsevier.

Kothari, C. R. (2004). *Research Methodology: Methods and Techniques*. New Delhi: New Age International.

Kracher, B., & Corritore, C. L. (2004). Is there a special e-commerce ethics? *Business Ethics Quarterly*, *14*(1), 71–94. doi:10.5840/beq20041417

Kurt, G., & Hacioglu, G. (2010). Ethics as a customer perceived value driver in the context of online retailing. *African Journal of Business Management*, *4*(5), 672–677.

Leitner, M. L., & Strauss, C. (2008, July). Exploratory case study research on web accessibility. In *International Conference on Computers for Handicapped Persons* (pp. 490-497). Springer. 10.1007/978-3-540-70540-6_70

Lightner, N. J., & Eastman, C. M. (2002). User preference for product information in remote purchase environments. *Journal of Electronic Commerce Research*, *3*(3), 174–186.

Lyu, H. S. (2012). Internet policy in Korea: A preliminary framework for assigning moral and legal responsibility to agents in internet activities. *Government Information Quarterly*, *29*(3), 394–402. doi:10.1016/j.giq.2011.12.008

Maury, M. D., & Kleiner, D. S. (2002). E-commerce, ethical commerce? *Journal of Business Ethics*, *36*(1-2), 21–31. doi:10.1023/A:1014274301815

McDonald, B. D. (2001). The uniform computer information transactions act. *Berk. Tech. LJ*, *16*, 461.

McMurrian, R. C., & Matulich, E. (2006). Building customer value and profitability with business ethics. *Journal of Business & Economics Research*, *4*(11), 11–18.

Methmali, S. (2015). *Professional & Ethical Issues in Information Systems*. Retrieved from https://www.academia.edu/13801886/Professional_and_Ethical_Issues_In_Information_Systems?auto=download

Milne, G. R., & Rohm, A. J. (2000). Consumer privacy and name removal across direct marketing channels: Exploring opt-in and opt-out alternatives. *Journal of Public Policy & Marketing*, *19*(2), 238–249. doi:10.1509/jppm.19.2.238.17136

Minoli, D., & Minoli, E. (1997). *Web commerce technology handbook*. McGraw-Hill School Education Group.

Mukherjee, A., & Nath, P. (2003). A Model of Trust in Online Relationship Banking. *International Journal of Bank Marketing*, *21*(1), 5–15. doi:10.1108/02652320310457767

Nanehkaran, Y. A. (2013). An Introduction to Electronic Commerce. *International Journal of Scientific & Technology Research*, *2*(4), 190–193.

Nardal, S., & Sahin, A. (2011). Ethical issues in e-commerce on the basis of online retailing. *Journal of Social Sciences*, *7*(2), 190–198. doi:10.3844/jssp.2011.190.198

Nasir, M. A. (2004). Legal Issues Involved in E-Commerce. *Ubiquity*, *2004*(February), 2–2. doi:10.1145/985610.985607

Nawaz, M., & Alajmi, W. (2014). A Study on Consumer Preferences for E Shopping with reference to Bahraini Consumers. *European Journal of Business and Management*, *6*(29), 187–196. Retrieved from https://www.iiste.org/Journals/index.php/EJBM/article/view/16092/16239

Nemat, R. (2011). Taking a Look at Different Types of E-Commerce. *World Applied Programming*, *1*(2), 100–104.

Neuman, W. L. (2003). *Social Research Methods: Qualitative and Quantitative Approaches*. London: Allyn & Bacon.

Nicholson, S. W., & Bennett, T. B. (2009). Transparent practices: Primary and secondary data in business ethics dissertations. *Journal of Business Ethics*, *84*(3), 417–425. doi:10.100710551-008-9717-0

Niranjanamurthy, M., & Chahar, D. (2013). The study of e-commerce security issues and solutions. *International Journal of Advanced Research in Computer and Communication Engineering*, *2*(7).

Orji, R., Reisinger, M., Busch, A., Dijkstra, A., Stibe, A., & Tscheligi, M. (Eds.). (2016). *Proceedings of the Personalization in Persuasive Technology Workshop, Persuasive Technology 2016*. Retrieved from http://ceur-ws.urg

Paddison, C., & Englefield, P. (2003, November). Applying heuristics to perform a rigorous accessibility inspection in a commercial context. In ACM SIGCAPH Computers and the Physically Handicapped (No. 73-74, pp. 126-133). ACM. doi:10.1145/957205.957228

Paganini, P. (2014). *HSBC Turkey hacked, 2.7 million credit cards exposed*. Retrieved from https://securityaffairs.co/wordpress/30256/cyber-crime/hsbc-turkey-hacked.html

Pavlou, P. A. (2002, August). What drives electronic commerce? A theory of planned behavior perspective. In Academy of management proceedings (Vol. 2002, No. 1, pp. A1-A6). Briarcliff Manor, NY: Academy of Management.

Remenyi, D., Williams, B., Money, A., & Swartz, E. (1998). Doing research in business and management: An introduction to process and method. *Sage (Atlanta, Ga.).*

Riggins, F., & Rhee, H. (1998). Toward a Unified View of Electronic Commerce. *Communications of the ACM, 41*(10), 88–95. doi:10.1145/286238.286252

Saunders, M., Lewis, P., & Thornhill, A. (2007). *Research Methods for Business Students* (6th ed.). London: Pearson.

Saunders, M., Lewis, P., & Thornhill, A. (2009). Understanding research philosophies and approaches. *Research Methods for Business Students, 4*, 106-135.

Saunders, M. N. (2011). *Research Methods for Business Students* (5th ed.). Pearson Education.

Schvaneveldt, J. D., & Adams, G. (1991). *Understanding research methods*. New York: Longman.

Shivani, H. G. (2012). A Study of Ethical and Social Issues in E-Commerce. *International Journal (Toronto, Ont.), 2*(7), 167–174.

Smith, H. J., Milberg, S. J., & Burke, S. J. (1996). Information privacy: Measuring individuals' concerns about organizational practices. *Management Information Systems Quarterly, 20*(2), 167–196. doi:10.2307/249477

Snieder, R., & Larner, K. (2009). *The Art of Being a Scientist: A Guide for Graduate Students and their Mentors*. Cambridge, UK: Cambridge University Press. doi:10.1017/CBO9780511816543

Spencer, K. (2002). In the online world, child porn is explicit and easy to get. *Omaha World Herald, 17*, 1-2.

Srivastava, D. K. (2018). Taxation of E-Commerce: Problems and Possible Solutions. In *Contemporary Issues in International Law* (pp. 447–457). Singapore: Springer. doi:10.1007/978-981-10-6277-3_32

Stead, B. A., & Gilbert, J. (2001). Ethical issues in electronic commerce. *Journal of Business Ethics, 34*(2), 75–85. doi:10.1023/A:1012266020988

Suddaby, R. (2006). From the editors: What grounded theory is not. Academic Press.

Teddlie, C., & Tashakkori, A. (2003). Major issues and controveries inthe use of mixed methods in the social and behvioral sciences. Handbook of mixed methods in social & behavioral research, 3-50.

Teo, T., & Liu, J. (2007). Teo, Thompson SH, and Jing Liu. "Consumer trust in e-commerce in the United States, Singapore and China. *Omega*, *35*(1), 22–38. doi:10.1016/j.omega.2005.02.001

Tiwari, S., & Singh, P. (2011). E-commerce: Prospect or threat for environment. *International Journal of Environmental Sciences and Development*, *2*(3), 211–217. doi:10.7763/IJESD.2011.V2.126

Traver, C. G., & Laudon, K. C. (2008). *E-commerce: business, technology, society*. Pearson Prentice Hall/Pearson Education.

Treese, G. W., & Stewart, L. C. (2003). *Designing systems for Internet commerce*. Addison-Wesley Professional.

Udo, G. J. (2001). Privacy and security concerns as major barriers for e-commerce: A survey study. *Information Management & Computer Security*, *9*(4), 165–174. doi:10.1108/EUM0000000005808

Venkatesh, A. (1998). Cybermarketscapes and consumer freedoms and identities. *European Journal of Marketing*, *32*(7/8), 664–676. doi:10.1108/03090569810224065

Vladimir, Z. (1996). Electronic commerce: Structures and issues. *International Journal of Electronic Commerce*, *1*(1), 3–23. doi:10.1080/10864415.1996.11518273

Wall, J. E. (2014). *Types of E-Commerce*. Retrieved from http://bloomidea.com/en/blog/types-e-commerce

Whysall, P. (2000). Addressing ethical issues in retailing: A stakeholder perspective. *International Review of Retail, Distribution and Consumer Research*, *10*(3), 305–318. doi:10.1080/095939600405992

Williams, J. G., & Premchaiswadi, W. (2016). On-Line Credit Card Transaction Processing and Fraud Prevention for E-Business. In Encyclopedia of E-Commerce Development, Implementation, and Management (pp. 827-846). IGI Global.

Yin, R. K. (2017). *Case study research and applications: Design and methods*. Sage publications.

Related Readings

To continue IGI Global's long-standing tradition of advancing innovation through emerging research, please find below a compiled list of recommended IGI Global book chapters and journal articles in the areas of business culture, business ethics, and corporate social responsibility. These related readings will provide additional information and guidance to further enrich your knowledge and assist you with your own research.

Ang, Y. S. (2015). Ethical Outsourcing and the Act of Acting Together. In R. Wolf, T. Issa, & M. Thiel (Eds.), *Empowering Organizations through Corporate Social Responsibility* (pp. 113–130). Hershey, PA: IGI Global. doi:10.4018/978-1-4666-7294-9.ch006

Avnimelech, G., & Zelekha, Y. (2015). The Impact of Corruption on Entrepreneurship. In R. Wolf & T. Issa (Eds.), *International Business Ethics and Growth Opportunities* (pp. 282–294). Hershey, PA: IGI Global. doi:10.4018/978-1-4666-7419-6.ch013

Ayodele, J. O. (2017). Restorative Justice and Women's Experiences of Violence in Nigeria. In D. Halder & K. Jaishankar (Eds.), *Therapeutic Jurisprudence and Overcoming Violence Against Women* (pp. 44–62). Hershey, PA: IGI Global. doi:10.4018/978-1-5225-2472-4.ch004

Bagdasarov, Z., MacDougall, A. E., Johnson, J. F., & Mumford, M. D. (2015). In Case You Didn't Know: Recommendations for Case-Based Ethics Training. In R. Wolf & T. Issa (Eds.), *International Business Ethics and Growth Opportunities* (pp. 224–249). Hershey, PA: IGI Global. doi:10.4018/978-1-4666-7419-6.ch011

Baraibar-Diez, E., Odriozola, M. D., & Sánchez, J. L. (2017). Storytelling about CSR: Engaging Stakeholders through Storytelling about CSR. In M. Camilleri (Ed.), *CSR 2.0 and the New Era of Corporate Citizenship* (pp. 209–230). Hershey, PA: IGI Global. doi:10.4018/978-1-5225-1842-6.ch011

Begum, R., & Mujtaba, B. G. (2014). Work Ethics Perceptions of Pakistani Employees: Is Work Experience a Factor in Ethical Maturity. *International Journal of Asian Business and Information Management*, *5*(1), 1–14. doi:10.4018/ijabim.2014010101

Ben Rejeb, W. (2017). Empirical Evidence on Corporate Governance Impact on CSR Disclosure in Developing Economies: The Tunisian and Egyptian Contexts. In D. Jamali (Ed.), *Comparative Perspectives on Global Corporate Social Responsibility* (pp. 116–137). Hershey, PA: IGI Global. doi:10.4018/978-1-5225-0720-8.ch006

Berberich, R. (2017). Creating Shared Value and Increasing Project Success by Stakeholder Collaboration: A Case in European Manufacturing. In M. Camilleri (Ed.), *CSR 2.0 and the New Era of Corporate Citizenship* (pp. 101–122). Hershey, PA: IGI Global. doi:10.4018/978-1-5225-1842-6.ch006

Berenstok, G., & Saporta, I. (2015). The Moral Limitations of the Rational-Monistic Model: A Revision of the Concept of Rationality and Rational Action. In R. Wolf & T. Issa (Eds.), *International Business Ethics and Growth Opportunities* (pp. 127–145). Hershey, PA: IGI Global. doi:10.4018/978-1-4666-7419-6.ch006

Boice, W. L. (2017). Non-Profit Leadership Success: A Study of a Small, Non-Profit Organization's Leadership and Culture through the Lens of Its Volunteers. In V. Wang (Ed.), *Encyclopedia of Strategic Leadership and Management* (pp. 485–506). Hershey, PA: IGI Global. doi:10.4018/978-1-5225-1049-9.ch035

Camilleri, M. A. (2017). The Corporate Sustainability and Responsibility Proposition: A Review and Appraisal. In M. Camilleri (Ed.), *CSR 2.0 and the New Era of Corporate Citizenship* (pp. 1–16). Hershey, PA: IGI Global. doi:10.4018/978-1-5225-1842-6.ch001

Chandra, R. R., & Jaishankar, K. (2017). Female Victims of Labor Exploitation Vis-à-Vis Labor Courts in the Southern Tamil Nadu, India: Therapeutic Jurisprudence Solutions for the Prevention of Secondary Victimization. In D. Halder & K. Jaishankar (Eds.), *Therapeutic Jurisprudence and Overcoming Violence Against Women* (pp. 171–181). Hershey, PA: IGI Global. doi:10.4018/978-1-5225-2472-4.ch011

Ciani, A., Diotallevi, F., Rocchi, L., Grigore, A. M., Coduti, C., & Belgrado, E. (2015). Corporate Social Responsibility (CSR): Theory, Regulations, and New Paradigms in the Framework of Sustainable Development Strategy. In R. Wolf, T. Issa, & M. Thiel (Eds.), *Empowering Organizations through Corporate Social Responsibility* (pp. 166–190). Hershey, PA: IGI Global. doi:10.4018/978-1-4666-7294-9.ch009

Ciani, A., Rocchi, L., Paolotti, L., Diotallevi, F., Guerra, J. B., Fernandez, F., ... Grigore, A. (2015). Corporate Social Responsibility (CSR): A Cross-Cultural Comparison of Practices. In R. Wolf, T. Issa, & M. Thiel (Eds.), *Empowering Organizations through Corporate Social Responsibility* (pp. 73–96). Hershey, PA: IGI Global. doi:10.4018/978-1-4666-7294-9.ch004

Clayton, T., & West, N. (2015). In Search of the Good Dam: A Role for Corporate Social Responsibility in Mekong Hydropower Development. In R. Wolf, T. Issa, & M. Thiel (Eds.), *Empowering Organizations through Corporate Social Responsibility* (pp. 288–306). Hershey, PA: IGI Global. doi:10.4018/978-1-4666-7294-9.ch015

Corazza, L. (2017). The Standardization of Down-Streamed Small Business Social Responsibility (SBSR): SMEs and Their Sustainability Reporting Practices. *Information Resources Management Journal, 30*(4), 39–52. doi:10.4018/IRMJ.2017100103

Cramm, D., & Erwee, R. (2015). Business Ethics Competencies: Controversies, Contexts, and Implications for Business Ethics Training. In R. Wolf & T. Issa (Eds.), *International Business Ethics and Growth Opportunities* (pp. 201–223). Hershey, PA: IGI Global. doi:10.4018/978-1-4666-7419-6.ch010

Crewe, H. (2017). Can Therapeutic Jurisprudence Improve the Rights of Female Prisoners? In D. Halder & K. Jaishankar (Eds.), *Therapeutic Jurisprudence and Overcoming Violence Against Women* (pp. 248–263). Hershey, PA: IGI Global. doi:10.4018/978-1-5225-2472-4.ch015

Davidson, D. K., & Yin, J. (2017). Corporate Social Responsibility (CSR) in China: A Contextual Exploration. In D. Jamali (Ed.), *Comparative Perspectives on Global Corporate Social Responsibility* (pp. 28–48). Hershey, PA: IGI Global. doi:10.4018/978-1-5225-0720-8.ch002

de Burgh-Woodman, H., Bressan, A., & Torrisi, A. (2017). An Evaluation of the State of the CSR Field in Australia: Perspectives from the Banking and Mining Sectors. In D. Jamali (Ed.), *Comparative Perspectives on Global Corporate Social Responsibility* (pp. 138–164). Hershey, PA: IGI Global. doi:10.4018/978-1-5225-0720-8.ch007 de Burgh-Woodman, H., Saha, A., Somasundram, K., & Torrisi, A. (2015). Sowing the Seeds for Ethical Business Leadership through Business Education. In R. Wolf & T. Issa (Eds.), *International Business Ethics and Growth Opportunities* (pp. 177–200). Hershey, PA: IGI Global. doi:10.4018/978-1-4666-7419-6.ch009

Del Chiappa, G., Pinna, M., & Atzeni, M. (2017). Barriers to Responsible Tourist Behaviour: A Cluster Analysis in the Context of Italy. In M. Camilleri (Ed.), *CSR 2.0 and the New Era of Corporate Citizenship* (pp. 290–308). Hershey, PA: IGI Global. doi:10.4018/978-1-5225-1842-6.ch015

Del Sherif, S. (2017). Violence Against Women and Therapeutic Jurisprudence in Egypt: An Islamic Approach. In D. Halder, & K. Jaishankar (Eds.), Therapeutic Jurisprudence and Overcoming Violence Against Women (pp. 15-29). Hershey, PA: IGI Global. doi:10.4018/978-1-5225-2472-4.ch002

Devereux, M. T., & Gallarza, M. G. (2017). Social Value Co-Creation: Insights from Consumers, Employees, and Managers. In M. Camilleri (Ed.), *CSR 2.0 and the New Era of Corporate Citizenship* (pp. 76–100). Hershey, PA: IGI Global. doi:10.4018/978-1-5225-1842-6.ch005

Dikeç, A., Kane, V., & Çapar, N. (2017). Cross-Country and Cross-Sector CSR Variations: A Comparative Analysis of CSR Reporting in the U.S., South Korea, and Turkey. In D. Jamali (Ed.), *Comparative Perspectives on Global Corporate Social Responsibility* (pp. 69–95). Hershey, PA: IGI Global. doi:10.4018/978-1-5225-0720-8.ch004

Dörries, A. (2015). A Matter of Justice: Building Trust among Hospital Managers and Physicians. In R. Wolf & T. Issa (Eds.), *International Business Ethics and Growth Opportunities* (pp. 24–41). Hershey, PA: IGI Global. doi:10.4018/978-1-4666-7419-6.ch002

Elicegui-Reyes, J. I., Barrena-Martínez, J., & Romero-Fernández, P. M. (2017). Emotional Capital and Sustainability in Family Businesses: Human Resource Management Perspective and Sustainability. In M. Camilleri (Ed.), *CSR 2.0 and the New Era of Corporate Citizenship* (pp. 231–250). Hershey, PA: IGI Global. doi:10.4018/978-1-5225-1842-6.ch012

García de Leaniz, P. M., & Gómez-López, R. (2017). Responsible Management in the CSR 2.0 Era. In M. Camilleri (Ed.), *CSR 2.0 and the New Era of Corporate Citizenship* (pp. 37–54). Hershey, PA: IGI Global. doi:10.4018/978-1-5225-1842-6.ch003

Gavrielides, T. (2017). Reconciling Restorative Justice with the Law for Violence Against Women in Europe: A Scheme of Structured and Unstructured Models. In D. Halder & K. Jaishankar (Eds.), *Therapeutic Jurisprudence and Overcoming Violence Against Women* (pp. 106–120). Hershey, PA: IGI Global. doi:10.4018/978-1-5225-2472-4.ch007

Grant, C. T., & Grant, K. A. (2016). Improving Moral Behaviour in the Business Use of ICT: The Potential of Positive Psychology. *International Journal of Cyber Ethics in Education*, *4*(2), 1–21. doi:10.4018/IJCEE.2016070101

Griffith, J. A., Zeni, T. A., & Johnson, G. (2015). Utilizing Emotions for Ethical Decision Making in Leadership. In R. Wolf & T. Issa (Eds.), *International Business Ethics and Growth Opportunities* (pp. 158–175). Hershey, PA: IGI Global. doi:10.4018/978-1-4666-7419-6.ch008

Growe, R., & Person, W. A. (2017). Toxic Workplace Environment and Its Impact on Women Professors in the United States: The Imperative Need for Therapeutic Jurisprudence Practices in Higher Education. In D. Halder & K. Jaishankar (Eds.), *Therapeutic Jurisprudence and Overcoming Violence Against Women* (pp. 182–197). Hershey, PA: IGI Global. doi:10.4018/978-1-5225-2472-4.ch012

Gul, M. C., & Kaytaz, M. (2017). CSR and Social Marketing as Enablers of Recovery after the Global Recession: The Turkish Banking Industry. In M. Camilleri (Ed.), *CSR 2.0 and the New Era of Corporate Citizenship* (pp. 274–289). Hershey, PA: IGI Global. doi:10.4018/978-1-5225-1842-6.ch014

Hack-Polay, D., & Qiu, H. (2017). Doing Good Doing Well: Discussion of CSR in the Pulp and Paper Industry in the Asian Context. In D. Jamali (Ed.), *Comparative Perspectives on Global Corporate Social Responsibility* (pp. 226–240). Hershey, PA: IGI Global. doi:10.4018/978-1-5225-0720-8.ch011

Halder, D. (2017). Revenge Porn Against Women and the Applicability of Therapeutic Jurisprudence: A Comparative Analysis of Regulations in India, Pakistan, and Bangladesh. In D. Halder & K. Jaishankar (Eds.), *Therapeutic Jurisprudence and Overcoming Violence Against Women* (pp. 282–292). Hershey, PA: IGI Global. doi:10.4018/978-1-5225-2472-4.ch017

Halder, D., & Jaishankar, K. (2017). Love Marriages, Inter-Caste Violence, and Therapeutic Jurisprudential Approach of the Courts in India. In D. Halder & K. Jaishankar (Eds.), *Therapeutic Jurisprudence and Overcoming Violence Against Women* (pp. 30–42). Hershey, PA: IGI Global. doi:10.4018/978-1-5225-2472-4.ch003

Haro-de-Rosario, A., del Mar Gálvez-Rodríguez, M., & Caba-Pérez, M. D. (2017). Determinants of Corporate Social Responsibility Disclosure in Latin American Companies: An Analysis of the Oil and Gas Sector. In D. Jamali (Ed.), *Comparative Perspectives on Global Corporate Social Responsibility* (pp. 165–184). Hershey, PA: IGI Global. doi:10.4018/978-1-5225-0720-8.ch008

Hassan, A., & Lund-Thomsen, P. (2017). Multi-Stakeholder Initiatives and Corporate Social Responsibility in Global Value Chains: Towards an Analytical Framework and a Methodology. In D. Jamali (Ed.), *Comparative Perspectives on Global Corporate Social Responsibility* (pp. 241–257). Hershey, PA: IGI Global. doi:10.4018/978-1-5225-0720-8.ch012

Holland, P. G., & Alakavuklar, O. N. (2017). Corporate Social Responsibility (CSR) Reporting and Seeking Legitimacy of Māori Communities: A Case from Aotearoa New Zealand Energy Sector. In M. Camilleri (Ed.), *CSR 2.0 and the New Era of Corporate Citizenship* (pp. 123–146). Hershey, PA: IGI Global. doi:10.4018/978-1-5225-1842-6.ch007

Hyatt, K. (2016). Effectiveness and Content of Corporate Codes of Ethics as a Model for University Honor Codes. *International Journal of Technology and Educational Marketing*, *6*(1), 52–69. doi:10.4018/IJTEM.2016010104

Issa, T., & Pick, D. (2017). Teaching Business Ethics Post GFC: A Corporate Social Responsibility of Universities. In D. Jamali (Ed.), *Comparative Perspectives on Global Corporate Social Responsibility* (pp. 290–307). Hershey, PA: IGI Global. doi:10.4018/978-1-5225-0720-8.ch015

Jamali, D., Abdallah, H., & Matar, F. (2016). Opportunities and Challenges for CSR Mainstreaming in Business Schools. *International Journal of Technology and Educational Marketing*, *6*(2), 1–29. doi:10.4018/IJTEM.2016070101

James, H. S. Jr. (2015). Why Do Good People Do Bad Things in Business?: Lessons from Research for Responsible Business Managers. In R. Wolf & T. Issa (Eds.), *International Business Ethics and Growth Opportunities* (pp. 1–23). Hershey, PA: IGI Global. doi:10.4018/978-1-4666-7419-6.ch001

Kaplan, J., & Montiel, I. (2017). East vs. West Approaches to Reporting Corporate Sustainability Strategies to the World: Corporate Sustainability Reporting: East vs. West. In D. Jamali (Ed.), *Comparative Perspectives on Global Corporate Social Responsibility* (pp. 49–68). Hershey, PA: IGI Global. doi:10.4018/978-1-5225-0720-8.ch003

Kaufmann, G. (2015). Analyzing CSR's Expectation Gap through the World System Differential. In R. Wolf, T. Issa, & M. Thiel (Eds.), *Empowering Organizations through Corporate Social Responsibility* (pp. 209–239). Hershey, PA: IGI Global. doi:10.4018/978-1-4666-7294-9.ch011

Kay, M. J. (2015). Corporate Sustainability Programs and Reporting: Responsibility Commitment and Thought Leadership at Starbucks. In R. Wolf, T. Issa, & M. Thiel (Eds.), *Empowering Organizations through Corporate Social Responsibility* (pp. 307–323). Hershey, PA: IGI Global. doi:10.4018/978-1-4666-7294-9.ch016

Koriat, N., & Gelbard, R. (2015). Insourcing of IT Workers: A Win-Win Strategy - Economic Analysis of IT Units in Israeli Governmental Offices. In R. Wolf, T. Issa, & M. Thiel (Eds.), *Empowering Organizations through Corporate Social Responsibility* (pp. 241–254). Hershey, PA: IGI Global. doi:10.4018/978-1-4666-7294-9.ch012

Kousar, H. (2017). Sexual Violence in the University Campuses of Delhi, India, and Therapeutic Jurisprudence for Justice to Victims: A Qualitative Study. In D. Halder & K. Jaishankar (Eds.), *Therapeutic Jurisprudence and Overcoming Violence Against Women* (pp. 198–212). Hershey, PA: IGI Global. doi:10.4018/978-1-5225-2472-4.ch013

Kujala, J. (2015). Branding as a Tool for CSR. In R. Wolf, T. Issa, & M. Thiel (Eds.), *Empowering Organizations through Corporate Social Responsibility* (pp. 266–287). Hershey, PA: IGI Global. doi:10.4018/978-1-4666-7294-9.ch014

Lanzerath, D. (2015). Ethics in Business and Human Flourishing: Integrating Economy in Life. In R. Wolf & T. Issa (Eds.), *International Business Ethics and Growth Opportunities* (pp. 74–96). Hershey, PA: IGI Global. doi:10.4018/978-1-4666-7419-6.ch004

Loverock, D. T., Kool, R., & Kajzer-Mitchell, I. (2015). Workplace Culture as a Driver for Social Change: Influencing Employee Pro-Environmental Behaviors. In R. Wolf, T. Issa, & M. Thiel (Eds.), *Empowering Organizations through Corporate Social Responsibility* (pp. 29–50). Hershey, PA: IGI Global. doi:10.4018/978-1-4666-7294-9.ch002

Makaros, A. (2015). Corporate Social Responsibility: Practice Models for Building Business-Community Collaborations. In R. Wolf, T. Issa, & M. Thiel (Eds.), *Empowering Organizations through Corporate Social Responsibility* (pp. 191–208). Hershey, PA: IGI Global. doi:10.4018/978-1-4666-7294-9.ch010

Manroop, L., & Harrison, J. (2015). The Ethics Portfolio: Building and Promoting Ethical Culture in an Organization. In R. Wolf & T. Issa (Eds.), *International Business Ethics and Growth Opportunities* (pp. 97–126). Hershey, PA: IGI Global. doi:10.4018/978-1-4666-7419-6.ch005

Nedelko, Z., & Potocan, V. (2015). Perception of Corporate Social Responsibility by the Employees: Evidence from Slovenia. In R. Wolf, T. Issa, & M. Thiel (Eds.), *Empowering Organizations through Corporate Social Responsibility* (pp. 51–72). Hershey, PA: IGI Global. doi:10.4018/978-1-4666-7294-9.ch003

Nguyen, L. D., Lee, K., Mujtaba, B. G., & Silanont, S. P. (2014). Business Ethics Perceptions of Working Adults: A Study in Thailand. *International Journal of Asian Business and Information Management*, *5*(2), 23–40. doi:10.4018/ijabim.2014040103

Olukolu, Y. R. (2017). Harmful Traditional Practices, Laws, and Reproductive Rights of Women in Nigeria: A Therapeutic Jurisprudence Approach. In D. Halder & K. Jaishankar (Eds.), *Therapeutic Jurisprudence and Overcoming Violence Against Women* (pp. 1–14). Hershey, PA: IGI Global. doi:10.4018/978-1-5225-2472-4.ch001

Osman, M. N. (2017). Internet-Based Social Reporting in Emerging Economies: Insights from Public Banks in Egypt and the UAE. In D. Jamali (Ed.), *Comparative Perspectives on Global Corporate Social Responsibility* (pp. 96–115). Hershey, PA: IGI Global. doi:10.4018/978-1-5225-0720-8.ch005

Pascal, A. (2015). Business Ethics is Socio-Political, or Not at All: The Case of Roşia Montana. In R. Wolf & T. Issa (Eds.), *International Business Ethics and Growth Opportunities* (pp. 251–281). Hershey, PA: IGI Global. doi:10.4018/978-1-4666-7419-6.ch012

Pittaro, M. (2017). Pornography and Global Sex Trafficking: A Proposal for Therapeutic Jurisprudence as Court Innovation in the United States. In D. Halder & K. Jaishankar (Eds.), *Therapeutic Jurisprudence and Overcoming Violence Against Women* (pp. 121–133). Hershey, PA: IGI Global. doi:10.4018/978-1-5225-2472-4.ch008

Priyadarshini, D. (2017). Women and the Impact of the Shifting Jurisprudence in New Delhi, India: How Therapeutic for Urban Slum-Dwellers? In D. Halder & K. Jaishankar (Eds.), *Therapeutic Jurisprudence and Overcoming Violence Against Women* (pp. 264–281). Hershey, PA: IGI Global. doi:10.4018/978-1-5225-2472-4.ch016

Puaschunder, J. (2017). The Call for Global Responsible Inter-Generational Leadership: The Quest of an Integration of Inter-Generational Equity in Corporate Social Responsibility (CSR) Models. In D. Jamali (Ed.), *Comparative Perspectives on Global Corporate Social Responsibility* (pp. 276–289). Hershey, PA: IGI Global. doi:10.4018/978-1-5225-0720-8.ch014

Radovic, V. M. (2017). Corporate Sustainability and Responsibility and Disaster Risk Reduction: A Serbian Overview. In M. Camilleri (Ed.), *CSR 2.0 and the New Era of Corporate Citizenship* (pp. 147–164). Hershey, PA: IGI Global. doi:10.4018/978-1-5225-1842-6.ch008

Rahdari, A. H. (2017). Fostering Responsible Business: Evidence from Leading Corporate Social Responsibility and Sustainability Networks. In M. Camilleri (Ed.), *CSR 2.0 and the New Era of Corporate Citizenship* (pp. 309–330). Hershey, PA: IGI Global. doi:10.4018/978-1-5225-1842-6.ch016

Raimi, L. (2017). Leveraging CSR as a 'support-aid' for Triple Bottom-Line Development in Nigeria: Evidence from the Telecommunication Industry. In D. Jamali (Ed.), *Comparative Perspectives on Global Corporate Social Responsibility* (pp. 208–225). Hershey, PA: IGI Global. doi:10.4018/978-1-5225-0720-8.ch010

Saade, M. V. (2017). Procedural Remedies as Continuing Violations and Therapeutic Jurisprudence as Best Practice to Prevent Workplace Harassment in the United States. In D. Halder & K. Jaishankar (Eds.), *Therapeutic Jurisprudence and Overcoming Violence Against Women* (pp. 147–170). Hershey, PA: IGI Global. doi:10.4018/978-1-5225-2472-4.ch010

Sánchez-Fernández, M. D., Cardona, J. R., & Martínez-Fernández, V. (2017). Comparative Perspectives on CSR 2.0 in the Contexts of Galicia and North of Portugal. In M. Camilleri (Ed.), *CSR 2.0 and the New Era of Corporate Citizenship* (pp. 165–186). Hershey, PA: IGI Global. doi:10.4018/978-1-5225-1842-6.ch009

Sarter, E. K. (2017). CSR, Public Spending, and the State: The Use of Public Procurement as a Lever to Foster Social Responsibility. In M. Camilleri (Ed.), *CSR 2.0 and the New Era of Corporate Citizenship* (pp. 55–75). Hershey, PA: IGI Global. doi:10.4018/978-1-5225-1842-6.ch004

Schnackenberg, H. L., & Simard, D. A. (2017). *Challenges Facing Female Department Chairs in Contemporary Higher Education: Emerging Research and Opportunities* (pp. 1–90). Hershey, PA: IGI Global. doi:10.4018/978-1-5225-1891-4

Sikulibo, J. D. (2017). International Criminal Justice and the New Promise of Therapeutic Jurisprudence: Prospects and Challenges in Conflict-Related Sexual Violence Cases. In D. Halder & K. Jaishankar (Eds.), *Therapeutic Jurisprudence and Overcoming Violence Against Women* (pp. 214–247). Hershey, PA: IGI Global. doi:10.4018/978-1-5225-2472-4.ch014

Sitnikov, C. S., Bocean, C., & Tudor, S. (2017). Integrating New Visions of Education Models and CSR 2.0 towards University Social Responsibility (USR). In M. Camilleri (Ed.), *CSR 2.0 and the New Era of Corporate Citizenship* (pp. 251–273). Hershey, PA: IGI Global. doi:10.4018/978-1-5225-1842-6.ch013

Tan, B. U. (2017). Responsible Corporate Behaviors: Drivers of Corporate Responsibility. In M. Camilleri (Ed.), *CSR 2.0 and the New Era of Corporate Citizenship* (pp. 17–36). Hershey, PA: IGI Global. doi:10.4018/978-1-5225-1842-6.ch002

Thakre, A. G. (2017). Sexual Harassment of Women in Workplace in India: An Assessment of Implementation of Preventive Laws and Practicing of Therapeutic Jurisprudence in New Delhi. In D. Halder & K. Jaishankar (Eds.), *Therapeutic Jurisprudence and Overcoming Violence Against Women* (pp. 135–146). Hershey, PA: IGI Global. doi:10.4018/978-1-5225-2472-4.ch009

van Tonder, C. L. (2015). Windows on Corporate Ethics: The Organisation and Change. In R. Wolf & T. Issa (Eds.), *International Business Ethics and Growth Opportunities* (pp. 43–73). Hershey, PA: IGI Global. doi:10.4018/978-1-4666-7419-6.ch003

Villegas, M., & McGivern, M. H. (2015). Codes of Ethics, Ethical Behavior, and Organizational Culture from the Managerial Approach: A Case Study in the Colombian Banking Industry. *International Journal of Strategic Information Technology and Applications*, *6*(1), 42–56. doi:10.4018/IJSITA.2015010104

Walker, L., & Tarutani, C. (2017). Restorative Justice and Violence Against Women in the United States: An Effort to Decrease the Victim-Offender Overlap and Increase Healing. In D. Halder & K. Jaishankar (Eds.), *Therapeutic Jurisprudence and Overcoming Violence Against Women* (pp. 63–84). Hershey, PA: IGI Global. doi:10.4018/978-1-5225-2472-4.ch005

Williams, J., Sheridan, L., & McLean, P. (2015). Developing Corporate Social Responsibility Projects: An Explorative Empirical Model of Project Development, Processes, and Actor Involvement in Australia. In R. Wolf, T. Issa, & M. Thiel (Eds.), *Empowering Organizations through Corporate Social Responsibility* (pp. 1–28). Hershey, PA: IGI Global. doi:10.4018/978-1-4666-7294-9.ch001

Windsor, D. (2017). Defining Corporate Social Responsibility for Developing and Developed Countries: Comparing Proposed Approaches. In D. Jamali (Ed.), *Comparative Perspectives on Global Corporate Social Responsibility* (pp. 1–27). Hershey, PA: IGI Global. doi:10.4018/978-1-5225-0720-8.ch001

Wolf, R. (2015). Corporate Social Responsibility in the West (U.S. and West Europe) vs. East (China). In R. Wolf, T. Issa, & M. Thiel (Eds.), *Empowering Organizations through Corporate Social Responsibility* (pp. 97–111). Hershey, PA: IGI Global. doi:10.4018/978-1-4666-7294-9.ch005

Wolf, R. (2015). Corporate Social Responsibility: Contribution to All. In R. Wolf, T. Issa, & M. Thiel (Eds.), *Empowering Organizations through Corporate Social Responsibility* (pp. 255–264). Hershey, PA: IGI Global. doi:10.4018/978-1-4666-7294-9.ch013

Wolf, R. (2015). Self-Awareness: A Way to Promote Ethical Management. In R. Wolf & T. Issa (Eds.), *International Business Ethics and Growth Opportunities* (pp. 147–157). Hershey, PA: IGI Global. doi:10.4018/978-1-4666-7419-6.ch007

Wolf, R., & Thiel, M. (2017). CSR in China: The Road to New Sustainable Business Models. In D. Jamali (Ed.), *Comparative Perspectives on Global Corporate Social Responsibility* (pp. 258–275). Hershey, PA: IGI Global. doi:10.4018/978-1-5225-0720-8.ch013

Yajima, N. (2015). Protecting Traditional Knowledge Associated with Genetic Resources by Corporate Social Responsibility. In R. Wolf, T. Issa, & M. Thiel (Eds.), *Empowering Organizations through Corporate Social Responsibility* (pp. 131–150). Hershey, PA: IGI Global. doi:10.4018/978-1-4666-7294-9.ch007

Yap, N. T., & Ground, K. E. (2017). Socially Responsible Mining Corporations: Before (or in Addition to) Doing Good, Do No Harm. In D. Jamali (Ed.), *Comparative Perspectives on Global Corporate Social Responsibility* (pp. 185–207). Hershey, PA: IGI Global. doi:10.4018/978-1-5225-0720-8.ch009

Young, S. B. (2015). Putting Sustainability and Corporate Responsibility at the Center of Capitalism through Better Valuation of Stakeholder Concerns. In R. Wolf, T. Issa, & M. Thiel (Eds.), *Empowering Organizations through Corporate Social Responsibility* (pp. 151–165). Hershey, PA: IGI Global. doi:10.4018/978-1-4666-7294-9.ch008

Zebregs, A., & Moratis, L. (2017). Serving the Purpose?: Communicating Self-Serving CSR Motives to Increase Credibility. In M. Camilleri (Ed.), *CSR 2.0 and the New Era of Corporate Citizenship* (pp. 187–208). Hershey, PA: IGI Global. doi:10.4018/978-1-5225-1842-6.ch010

Zgheib, P. W. (2015). *Business Ethics and Diversity in the Modern Workplace* (pp. 1–326). Hershey, PA: IGI Global. doi:10.4018/978-1-4666-7254-3

About the Contributors

Ebtihaj Ahmed Al A'ali is an Associate Professor, Department of Management and Marketing, College of Business Administration, University of Bahrain. She holds a PhD degree in industrial psychology and industrial sociology from Lancaster University, United Kingdom. She is a founder of Bahrain management society, working with United Nations Development Programme and UNIDO on project basis.

Meryem Masmoudi is Assistant Professor of Management at the University of Bahrain, College of Business Administration. She holds a PhD in Management from University of Tunis (2013). She has been involved in teaching and research in the areas of management, organizational change and development and management science. Meryem has published research papers in top international refereed journals (ANOR, JORS, ITOR, INFOR). She is member of the International Society on Multiple Criteria Decision Making and the Tunisian Decision Aid Society.

* * *

Yomna Abdulla is an Assistant Professor at the College of Business Administration, Department of Economics and Finance, University of Bahrain, Kingdom of Bahrain. She holds a PhD in Finance from the Manchester Business School, UK. Her research areas of expertise is empirical issues in corporate finance including trade credit, working capital, debt maturity, capital structure and financial policies in public versus private firms

Adel Al-Alawi is an Associate Professor of Management and Information Systems at the University of Bahrain, College of Business, earned his BS and MBA in Business and Information Systems (USA), a Ph.D. in MIS from University of Leeds, UK. Prof. Al-Alawi was the founder of Business Information Systems Dep (BIS) and a Chairperson of BIS department at the College of Business in UOB and also one of the founders of College of Information Technology, and Head of BIS Department, where he served UOB for more than 25 years. His research have been published in several Scopus indexed journals such as Journal of Knowledge Management, Journal of Computer Science, Information Technology Journal, Research Journal of Business Management, Research Journal of Business Management, Journal of International Women's Studies, International Journal of Business Information Systems. His main interest in research is in management and information systems (refer to https://www.researchgate.net/profile/Adel_Al-Alawi). Adel is also one of the founders and the President of ISACA, Bahrain Chapter. Adel is considered as an MIS Authority in the Kingdom of Bahrain.

Sara Abdulrahman Al-Bassam holds a BSc. in Management Information (MIS) from Gulf University for Science and Technology, Kuwait, MSc. in Innovation and Information Systems from Arabian Gulf University in the Kingdom of Bahrain her thesis titled "Investigating the Factors Related to Cybersecurity Awareness in the Bahraini Banking Sector" and Sara is a candidate for a Ph.D. in Innovation and Information Systems. Sara Carries many years of experience in Management Information Systems in Kuwaiti banks and government. Sara is a very active member of many professional associations such as ISACA Bahrain Chapter. Sara's current research area is in Cybersecurity in Banking and Financial Sector and currently published a paper in International Journal of Business Information Systems, Sara is also coauthor of a book entitled Handbook of Research on Implementing Knowledge Management Strategy in the Public Sector (2019) with Dr. Yousif Al-Basstaki and Prof. Adel Al-Alawi.

Ralla Alazali is an Assistant Professor in the Management and Marketing Department in the College of Business Administration at the University of Bahrain. She got her PhD from Curtin University of technology in Australia. Her field of interest knowledge management and ethics.

Gardenia Alsaffar is a Consultant Psychiatrist in Royal Bahrain Hospital. She is member of the Royal College of Psychiatrists in the UK. She did her fellowship in Ireland with a special interest in General Adult Psychiatry and Rehabilitation Psychiatry.

Asma Ayari is an Assistant Professor-Management, University of Bahrain, Department of Management & Marketing, College of Business Administration, Kingdom of Bahrain.

Amal Nagah Elbeshbishi is an International Professional Staff Member holding a Continuing Contract at the United Nations Secretariat, and working as an Economist for the United Nations Economic Commission for Africa (UNECA) - office for North

Africa, Rabat- Morocco. She is also a tenured Professor of Economics at Faculty of Commerce- Mansoura University, Egypt [on sabbatical leave (national assignment) to work for UNECA]. Prior to joining UNECA in 2005, Prof. Dr. Elbeshbishi lectured at universities in Bahrain, Egypt and the United States of America. She has also worked with the United Nations Economic and Social Commission for Western Asia (UNESCWA) and the Egyptian Cabinet's Information and Decision Support Center (IDSC). Prof. Dr. Elbeshbishi is the author/co-author of many research papers and books on several economic and social development issues. She holds a Master's and a Ph.D. degree in Economics from Fordham University- New York, United States of America; and a Master's degree in Economics from Mansoura University, Egypt.

Hala Elias is the Dean and Associate Professor, College of Business & Financial Sciences; Royal University for Women, Riffa, Bahrain, 09/2010 – present. Hala Led the College in 2014 through the program review process whereby the three programs of the College received "Confidence" rating by the Kingdom of Bahrain's National Authority for Qualifications and Quality Assurance of Education and Training and Managed two of the college's programs; Banking and Finance and International Business qualifications; through the mapping process to be placed on the Bahrain National Qualifications Framework. She has the following experiences and qualifications: Over fifteen years of solid teaching experience of accounting and financial management courses in the University. Five years of academic management experience, including the development of academic programs, academic quality assurance and mapping of academic qualifications to the national qualification framework. Over three years of accounting and financial & general administration experience, which included supervising administrative and accounting staff, as well as managing accounts payable, financial reporting and budgeting. Publications in refereed journals and participation in reputable conferences in the area of accounting and finance. Ph.D. Accounting, University of Southampton, United Kingdom (2001). M.Sc. Financial Managerial Controls, University of Southampton, Southampton, United Kingdom (1993). B.Sc. Organizational Management, Ahfad University for Women, Omdurman, Sudan (1991). Certified Nonprofit Accounting Professional (CNAP), Fiscal Management Association (FMA), NY, USA (2007).

Arpita Anshu Mehrotra earned her Bachelor and Master degrees in Commerce (India) and holds a Ph.D. in Commerce from Lucknow University, India. She is an Assistant Professor of Accounting, Finance and Management at the Royal University For Women (RUW), Kingdom of Bahrain. Dr. Arpita is the Head of Banking & Finance Department at the College of Business & Financial Sciences, RUW. She is also the chairperson of the RUW Alumnae Committee and the co-chairperson of the Teaching and Learning committee at RUW. In her 15 years of experience she has also served as the Director of Marketing and Academics in Mumbai School of Business, India. Dr. Arpita has been a leading academician with in depth teaching experience in Financial Management, Accounting and Marketing both at the undergraduate and postgraduate levels. Further, she led a team that organized a national level seminar on "The Emerging Economies and their rising Global Influence" in India. The seminar witnessed the participation of professors, corporate dignitaries and university level students. Dr. Arpita has also presented several research papers in Banking & Finance in International Conferences, wherein two of them she received the "best paper" award.

Hanan Naser holds a PhD in Economics from University of Sheffield, UK and works as an Assistant Professor in Business Studies and Economics at the American University of Bahrain (AUBH), Bahrain. Before joining to AUBH, Hanan was an Assistant Professor in Business Studies and the Head of Research Council at Arab Open University (AOU), Bahrain, for three years. She honors the Fellow and Senior Fellow Awards from the Higher Educational Academy (HEA), UK. Her research expertise area is in energy economics, stock market and environmental issues. She is a co-founder of Bahrain Research Consortium (BRC), Bahrain, which is a non-profit organization that aims at promoting and supporting research activities in the region for academics, entrepreneurs, and SMEs (http://www.bahrainrc.org).

Hina Safdar holds a Bachelors in Business Management and Administration from the University of Bahrain (Class of 2016) and is working as an Executive Manager at AlQoud Group. She has gained professional activities during her study at UOB and after, by participating in managing workshops and conferences such as Bahrain International CSR and Sustainability Conference & Award, International Fire Operations Conference for the U.S Association for Fire Chiefs and during the career day exhibitions. Hina is a creative young professional who is proactive and keen to learn, with strong analytical skills.

Index

A

B

C

D

E

www.ingramcontent.com/pod-product-compliance
Ingram Content Group UK Ltd.
Pitfield, Milton Keynes, MK11 3LW, UK
UKHW051452290926
15471UKWH00008B/1156

9 781799 802730